CHASING CHURCHILL

By the same author

From Winston with Love and Kisses: The Young Churchill
Churchill Wanted Dead or Alive

CHASING CHURCHILL

The Travels of Winston Churchill

by his Granddaughter

CELIA SANDYS

CARROLL & GRAF PUBLISHERS
NEW YORK

CHASING CHURCHILL

Carroll & Graf Publishers
An Imprint of Avalon Publishing Group Inc.
245 West 17th Street, 11th Floor
New York, NY 10011-5300

Library of Congress Cataloging-in-Publication Data is available.

ISBN: 0-7867-1214-7

Printed in the United States of America
Distributed by Publishers Group West

To Edwina

Contents

Illustrations

Black and white

Second Lieutenant Winston Churchill, 4th Hussars, Bangalore, India, 1897. *(© Popperfoto)*

Preparing for polo, India, 1897. *(© Hulton Archive)*

Lieutenant Churchill, South African Light Horse, 1900. *(Private collection)*

Member of Parliament for Oldham, 1900. *(Private collection)*

Under-Secretary of State for the Colonies, in East Africa, 1907. *(Private collection)*

Having shot a white rhinoceros, 1907. *(Private collection)*

Golfing at Cannes with Maxine Elliot, 1913. *(© Hulton Archive)*

Visit to the Western Front as Minister of Munitions, 1917. *(Private collection)*

Secretary of State for War and Air, 1919. *(Private collection)*

On the way to the Palace to receive the seals of office as Chancellor of the Exchequer, 1924. *(Private collection)*

Bathing at Deauville, 1927. *(© Popperfoto)*

Churchill hooks a 188-pound marlin off California, 1929. *(© Popperfoto)*

With Charlie Chaplin, Hollywood, 1929. *(Private collection)*

Setting off for the United States with Clementine and Diana, 1931. *(Private collection)*

Painting in the South of France, 1920s. *(© Topham Picturepoint)*

With President Roosevelt aboard HMS *Prince of Wales*, August 1941. *(Private collection)*

Travelling in Canada, December 1941. *(Private collection)*

Addressing the US Congress, December 1941. *(Private collection)*

Christ Church, Alexandria, Virginia, 1 January 1942. *(Private collection)*

With General Sir Claude Auchinleck, Western Desert, 1942. *(© Imperial War Museum)*

Shooting match with American Generals Eisenhower and Bradley, 1942. *(© Hulton Archive)*

With Roosevelt at Casablanca, January 1943. *(© Hulton Archive)*

At Casablanca, January 1943. *(Private collection)*

With Roosevelt in the tower of Villa Taylor, Marrakech, January 1943. *(Private collection)*

At Allied Headquarters North Africa, Algiers, June 1943. *(© Hulton Archive)*

With Mary, Niagara Falls, August 1943. *(Private collection)*

Returning from the United States with Mary aboard HMS *Renown*, September 1943. *(Private collection)*

Aboard *Renown* with Clementine and Mary, September 1943. *(© Imperial War Museum)*

Malta, November 1943. *(© Imperial War Museum)*

With Roosevelt and Stalin, Tehran, November 1943. *(Private collection)*

Visiting recently recaptured Cherbourg, July 1944. *(© Hulton Archive)*

Crossing the Rhine, March 1945. *(Private collection)*

With Clementine, Hendaye, France, July 1945. *(© Topham Picturepoint)*

Painting in Miami, February 1946. *(© Hulton Archive)*

Painting in the garden of Madame Balsan, Florida, 1946. *(Private collection)*

Churchill on the way to deliver his 'iron curtain' speech at Fulton, Missouri, with President Truman, March 1946. *(Reproduced courtesy of The Winston Churchill Memorial and Library at Westminster College in Fulton, Missouri)*

Donkey ride at La Fontaine-de-Vaucluse, August 1948. *(Private collection)*

Painting at San Vigilio, Lake Garda, August 1949. *(© Camera Press)*

With Clementine at Reid's Hotel, Madeira, January 1950. *(Private collection)*

Painting at Camara de Lobos, Madeira, January 1950. *(Private collection)*

Bathing at Venice, August 1951. *(Private collection)*

Aboard the *Christina* with Aristotle Onassis, 1956. *(Private collection)*

Golden wedding anniversary at Lord Beaverbrook's villa at Cap d'Ail, September 1958. *(© Popperfoto)*

Boarding the *Christina*, 1958. *(© Popperfoto)*

At La Pausa with Emery Reves and Sarah, 1958. *(Private collection)*

Reviewing a guard of honour, Marrakech, 1959. *(Private collection)*

With Wendy Reves at La Pausa. *(Private collection)*

Ashore at Rhodes, 1959. *(Private collection)*

Dining on the *Christina*, 1959. *(© Topham Picturepoint)*

Aboard the *Christina*, 1959. *(© Topham Picturepoint)*

At Tangier with Bryce Nairn and Hadj Mohamed Erzini, 1959. *(Private collection)*

With Celia at the Hôtel de Paris, Monte Carlo, 1960. *(Private collection)*

With Aristotle Onassis, 1960. *(© Hulton Archive)*

With Celia in the hills above Monte Carlo, 1962. *(Private collection)*

Churchill returns from Monte Carlo after breaking his hip, 1962. *(Private collection)*

In the South of France, 1963. *(© Popperfoto)*

State funeral, St Paul's Cathedral, 30 January 1965. *(Private collection)*

Colour

*(Reproduced with permission of Curtis Brown Ltd, London on behalf of
The Churchill Heritage Ltd. Copyright © The Churchill Heritage)*

Ploegsteert (1916).

Jerusalem (1921).

Clementine and Diana in a gondola in Venice (1927).

Lake Louise, Canada (1929).

Château St Georges-Môtel (c.1930).

Sunset at Cannes (c.1933).

The pyramids (1934).

La Montagne St Victoire (c.1935).

Sunset over the Atlas Mountains (1935–36).

Tower of Katoubia Mosque, Marrakech (1943).

The Surf Club, Miami (1946).

La Fontaine-de-Vaucluse (1948).

San Vigilio, Lake Garda (1949).

Lake Carezza (1949).

Cap d'Ail, Alpes Maritimes (1950s).

The fishing port of Camara de Lobos (1950).

Winston Churchill: A Chronology of Milestones and Travels

1874   30 November: WSC born at Blenheim Palace.

1880   Brother Jack born.

1883   First trip abroad, to Paris with his father Lord Randolph.

1888   Enters Harrow School.

1891   Spends Christmas holidays at Versailles to improve French.

1892   Leaves Harrow.

1893   To Switzerland for walking tour. Enters Royal Military College, Sandhurst.

1895   Lord Randolph dies. WSC commissioned into 4th Hussars at Aldershot. Takes leave to observe guerrilla war in Cuba, travelling via New York and Tampa, Florida.

1896   India: to Bangalore with 4th Hussars.

1897   India: to North-West Frontier, attached to Malakand Field Force during tribal war. Returns to Bangalore.

1898   India: North-West Frontier, attached to Tirah Expedition. Sudan: attached to 21st Lancers. Takes part in cavalry charge at Omdurman. Returns to India. First book, *The Malakand Field Force*, published.

1899   Resigns from army. Fails at first attempt to be elected to Parliament. Goes to South Africa as war correspondent for Anglo–Boer War. Captured and escapes. Rejoins army. *The River*

War, account of the Sudan Campaign, published. *Savrola*, a novel, published.

1900   Resigns from army. Elected to Parliament as a Conservative. *London to Ladysmith* and *Ian Hamilton's March*, accounts of the Anglo–Boer War, published. Visits America and Canada for two-month lecture tour.

1904   Breaks with Conservative Party, joins Liberals. To Switzerland for holiday.

1905   Becomes Under-Secretary of State for the Colonies. *Lord Randolph Churchill*, biography of his father, published.

1906   Germany: attends German army manoeuvres. France.

1907   To France, for holiday and to attend French army manoeuvres. Official tour of East Africa, travelling via France, Moravia (now Czechoslovakia), Vienna, Syracuse, Malta, Cyprus and Aden to Mombasa. Thence to Nairobi, Kampala, Khartoum, Aswan and Cairo.

1908   Becomes President of the Board of Trade. Marries Clementine Hozier. Honeymoon at Baveno on Lake Maggiore and Venice. *My African Journey*, an account of his African travels as Under-Secretary, published.

1909   Daughter Diana born. Germany: attends German army manoeuvres.

1910   Becomes Home Secretary.

1911   Becomes First Lord of the Admiralty. Son Randolph born.

1911–14 Frequent cruises in Admiralty yacht, *Enchantress*.

1912   Northern Ireland: to Belfast to speak on Home Rule for Ireland.

1914   4 August: Great Britain declares war on Germany. To Belgium, taking personal charge of defences in Antwerp. Daughter Sarah born.

1915   Resigns as First Lord following failure of Dardanelles campaign. Rejoins army. France, with Grenadier Guards.

1916   Appointed to command 6th Battalion Royal Scots Fusiliers in France. Returns to London, resigns from army and resumes political career.

1917   Becomes Minister of Munitions. Travels frequently to the front in France. Establishes office at Château Verchocq.

1918 11 November: war ends. Daughter Marigold born.

1919 Becomes Secretary of State for War and Air. Travels to Germany and France.

1920 Travels to France and Italy.

1921 Becomes Colonial Secretary. To Cairo and Jerusalem to chair Middle East conference. Mother, Lady Randolph, dies. Daughter Marigold dies.

1922 Loses seat in general election. Six-month stay in South of France. Daughter Mary born.

1923 Returns to London. To France aboard Duke of Westminster's yacht *Flying Cloud*. First volume of *The World Crisis,* WSC's six-volume history of the First World War, published.

1924 Breaks with Liberal Party. Travels to France. Re-elected to Parliament, winning Epping for the Conservatives. Becomes Chancellor of the Exchequer.

1925 To Paris for official negotiations over war debts.

1927 To France, Italy, Malta and Greece. Returns to Italy to meet Mussolini before holiday in the South of France. Five days on Lord Beaverbrook's yacht at Amsterdam. To Venice.

1929 Conservatives defeated in general election. WSC out of office, but retains own parliamentary seat. To Canada and America for three-month tour.

1930 *My Early Life*, an autobiography of his first thirty-four years, and *Thoughts and Adventures*, a collection of essays, published.

1931 Breaks with Conservative leadership over India. Sounds warning of German threat. To France. To America for lecture tour. Knocked down by car and seriously injured in New York.

1932 Returns to America and speaks in nineteen cities. *Thoughts and Adventures*, a collection of essays, published. To France, the Low Countries and Germany for a battlefield tour of Flanders and Marlborough's campaigns. Contracts paratyphoid; taken to Salzburg sanatorium.

1933 Adolf Hitler becomes Chancellor of Germany. WSC gives further warnings about Germany. To France. Further disagreement with party over India. First volume of his four-volume *Marlborough* published.

1934   To France. Holiday in eastern Mediterranean as guest of Lord
Moyne on board his yacht *Rosaura*. Visits Cyprus, Turkey,
Beirut, Palmyra, Damascus, Palestine, Trans-Jordan, Petra,
Akaba and Cairo, Naples. Gives radio broadcast on World War I
in which he warns of further German threat.

1935   Further exhortations for Britain to rearm. To France. To
Marrakech via Paris, Barcelona, Majorca and Tangier.

1936   Further warnings on defence. Visits French army in France.

1937   *Great Contemporaries*, a collection of biographical essays, published.

1938   To France. Fourth and final volume of *Marlborough* published.

1939   Invited by France to annual military review and to visit the
Maginot Line. 3 September: Britain declares war on Germany.
WSC becomes First Lord of the Admiralty again.

1940   To France. 10 May: becomes Prime Minister. Five further visits
to France in May and June. France capitulates. Britain faces
Germany alone.

1941   22 June: Germany invades Russia. WSC to Newfoundland
aboard *Prince of Wales*. Meeting aboard with President Roosevelt.
Returns to Britain via Iceland. 7 December: Japanese attack on
Pearl Harbor. America enters the war. WSC to America aboard
Duke of York. Arrives in Washington by air from Hampton
Roads. Visits Ottawa.

1942   To Palm Beach and back to Washington. By air via Bermuda to
England. To America and back by air. To Cairo by air via
Gibraltar. Visits forward troops at Alamein. To Moscow by air
from Cairo for meeting with Stalin. To Egypt by air from
Moscow. To desert front and via Gibraltar to England.

1943   To Casablanca by air for conference with Roosevelt. Visits
Marrakech with Roosevelt. To Cairo, Turkey, Cyprus, Cairo,
Tripoli, Algiers and back to England. To America aboard *Queen
Mary*. To Algiers by air and back to England. To Canada aboard
Queen Mary for Quebec conference. Returns to England on
Renown. To Algiers, Malta and Egypt aboard *Renown*. Meets
Roosevelt in Cairo. To Tehran by air with Roosevelt to meet
Stalin. Returns to Cairo and on to Tunis. Ill with pneumonia.
Flies to Marrakech to convalesce.

1944 Flies to Gibraltar. Sails home on *King George V.* 6 June: Allied invasion of Europe. 12 June: WSC ashore in Normandy. Visits Montgomery's HQ. Returns to France to visit Montgomery's new HQ. To Italy by air via Algiers. To Corsica to observe landings in South of France. To Naples and the front at Cassino. To Rome and Alexander's HQ at Sienna. To Naples, Rabat and home by air. To Canada aboard *Queen Mary* for second Quebec conference. To New York and back on *Queen Mary*. To Moscow by air; back via Naples and Cairo. To France. Walks down Champs Élysées with de Gaulle. Visits French troops and on to Eisenhower's HQ at Rheims. 24 December: flies to Athens.

1945 Flies to Malta to confer with Roosevelt before both fly on to Crimea for Yalta conference. Returns via Athens, Cairo and Alexandria (for his last meeting with Roosevelt). To Brussels. Observes Allied crossing of the Rhine. 12 April: Roosevelt dies. 8 May: victory in Europe. To France for a week's relaxation south of Bordeaux. To Berlin. Meets President Truman prior to Potsdam conference. General election: defeat of Conservative Party. WSC stands down as Prime Minister. To La Rosa on shores of Lake Como for painting holiday. Then to Italian and French Rivieras.

1946 To Brussels. To America aboard *Queen Elizabeth*. To Florida. Revisits Cuba. Iron Curtain speech at Fulton, Missouri. To Switzerland.

1947 To Marrakech.

1948 To France. First volume of six-volume *The Second World War* published.

1949 To Brussels – European Movement. To Monte Carlo. To America aboard *Queen Elizabeth* to address Massachusetts Institute of Technology. To Lake Garda and Lake Carezza, then Council of Europe, Strasbourg. To Lord Beaverbrook's villa, La Capponcina, at Cap d'Ail near Monte Carlo. To Madeira aboard *Durban Castle*.

1950 To Strasbourg. To Marrakech.

1951 To France and Venice. 26 October: Conservatives re-elected;

WSC Prime Minister again. To America aboard *Queen Mary* to see President Truman.

1952 To Washington and Ottawa. To Cap d'Ail.

1953 To America aboard *Queen Mary* to see President Eisenhower. To Jamaica. To Cap d'Ail for a fortnight to convalesce after stroke. To Bermuda to confer with Eisenhower. Sixth volume of *The Second World War* published.

1954 To America aboard *Queen Elizabeth*.

1955 Resigns as Prime Minister. To Villa Politi, Syracuse. To Cap d'Ail.

1956 First visit to La Pausa, Cap Martin. To Aachen to receive Charlemagne Prize. To La Pausa. First volume of four-volume *A History of the English Speaking Peoples* published.

1957 To La Pausa and Cap d'Ail.

1958 To La Pausa and Cap d'Ail. First cruise on *Christina* in eastern Mediterranean as guest of Aristotle Onassis. Fourth volume of *A History of the English Speaking Peoples* published.

1959 To Marrakech. Cruise on *Christina* to Canary Islands. Cruise on *Christina* in eastern Mediterranean. To La Pausa. To Washington to stay with President Eisenhower. To Hôtel de Paris, Monte Carlo.

1960 To West Indies aboard *Christina*. To Cap d'Ail. Cruise on *Christina* in eastern Mediterranean. To Hôtel de Paris.

1961 To West Indies aboard *Christina*. To South of France and Monte Carlo.

1962 Cruise on *Christina* in eastern Mediterranean. To Monte Carlo: breaks hip.

1963 To Monte Carlo. Last cruise on *Christina*: to Sardinia, Corfu and Athens. Daughter Diana dies.

1965 24 January: WSC dies in London. 30 January: State funeral.

Foreword

The tapestry of Winston Churchill's life is so vast that close magnification of selected areas is very rewarding, as the reader will find in this book by Celia Sandys about my father's – her grandfather's – travels throughout his long life.

In his early cavalry officer days Winston Churchill's restless 'Seeking the bubble reputation/Even in the cannon's mouth' sent him to Cuba, Afghanistan, the Sudan and South Africa, and each campaign gave birth to despatches and books – sword and pen! In the 1920s and thirties his late-discovered passion and talent for painting made him seek out sunshine scenes in the South of France, Italy and Morocco. But painting holidays also saw a steady output of chapters for whichever literary project he was currently engaged upon.

In World War II, Churchill's urgent need to be in eye-to-eye contact with President Roosevelt, Stalin and service chiefs propelled him to undertake air and sea travels, often in Spartan conditions, and always accompanied by dangers.

After the war, painting and writing (in and out of again becoming Prime Minister) once again held sway, and in the family we remember happy holiday times.

My niece, Celia, has followed her grandfather's travels in

detail, and describes them here with the verve which is the hallmark of her writing.

Mary Soames

Prologue

THE GIFTS OF TRAVEL

For the formation of opinion, for the stirring enlivenment of thought, and for the discernment of colour and proportion, the gifts of travel, especially travel on foot, are priceless.
Winston Churchill, *My African Journey* (1908)

Well before his recommendation in the preface to *My African Journey*, published in 1908, Winston Churchill was already widely travelled on four continents – an uncommon achievement a century ago, when most young aristocrats were content with a tour of Europe. In the five years after leaving the Royal Military Academy, Sandhurst, in 1895, he had campaigned in Cuba, India, the Sudan and South Africa. In 1907, as Under-Secretary of State for the Colonies, he had tramped through Uganda. Over the next half-century his frequent excursions abroad would continue. In middle age painting became a 'spur to travel', and wherever practicable his paints went with him.

Churchill's journeys entailed pleasure and work, and sometimes, at least until the end of the Second World War, danger and hardship. Discomfort was occasionally inevitable, but it was the exception rather than the rule. He always travelled in style – it would never have occurred to him to economise by travelling third class or catching a bus. I doubt if he ever packed his own suitcase even as a young officer, for then he had a soldier servant, and later a valet was always to hand to carry out irksome chores that would have distracted Churchill from the purpose of his journey.

His father, Lord Randolph, was an intercontinental traveller, and it was with him that young Winston first went abroad, to Paris at the age of nine in 1883. Lord Randolph had been the most popular Conservative politician of his day, but in 1886 he resigned as Chancellor of the Exchequer when neither the First Lord of the Admiralty nor the Secretary of State for War would agree to reduce his department's expenditure, and he never recovered politically. The young Winston adored his father, but never achieved a satisfactory relationship with him. At first politics kept Lord Randolph too busy to spare much attention to his son, then through ill health his attitude to Winston became increasingly capricious until his death in 1895. Nevertheless, much of his father's political philosophy was passed on, and thirty-five years later Churchill would write, recollecting Lord Randolph's death: 'all my dreams of comradeship with him, of entering Parliament at his side and in his support, were ended. There remained for me only to pursue his aims and vindicate his memory.'

However, on that first journey abroad father and son enjoyed each other's company. In 1946, in a speech at Metz, Churchill recalled driving with his father through the Place de la Concorde and noticing that two of the monuments were covered with wreaths and crêpe. When the nine-year-old Winston enquired why this was so, Lord Randolph explained that these were the monuments to the provinces of France, and that the

French were very unhappy that two, Alsace and Lorraine, had been taken by the Germans in the Franco–Prussian War. Churchill told his audience, 'I remember quite distinctly thinking to myself I hope they will get them back.'

While Churchill's affection for France developed slowly, his lifelong love affair with America began on the day he first set foot in the New World. His admiration for and faith in the United States is reflected in a declaration he made during a card game on a train journey in 1946 with President Harry S. Truman and his staff. It was as they were returning to Washington in a relaxed mood after Churchill's 'Iron Curtain' speech at Fulton, Missouri, that his fellow poker players were astonished to hear him say that if he were born again, he would wish to be an American: 'There is only one country where a young man knows he has an unbounded future.'

Churchill's early introduction to the United States was greatly assisted by his talented American mother, Jennie Jerome, an exceptionally beautiful woman in an age of famous beauties. The daughter of a well-known New York financier, Leonard Jerome, founder of the American Jockey Club, she opened many doors for her son; but the factor which captivated him was undoubtedly the American way of life, to which he was initially exposed on arrival in New York in 1895, his first foreign port of call as a young man. Through his extensive travels in America during the 1920s and thirties he got to know the country and many of its leading citizens. He made and lost large sums of money through American investments. During the Second World War he made six perilous Atlantic crossings to confer with President Roosevelt. It was Churchill, more than anyone, who turned what had been an uneasy alliance between Britain and America into the special relationship which endures to this day.

Although politics and national characteristics played a large part in Churchill's attraction to France and America, there were other places which caught and retained his affection solely because of their visual impact on him as painter. One such was Marrakech, in Morocco, to which he took President Roosevelt in 1943 simply to see the splendour of the sunset on the Atlas Mountains.

'I never take holidays,' he once wrote to the newspaper proprietor Lord Rothermere. For Churchill, change rather than rest was 'the master key' to a satisfactory life: 'Many remedies are suggested for the avoidance of worry and mental overstrain by persons who, over long periods, have to bear exceptional responsibilities. But the element which is constant and common in all of them is change.' For him travel provided that change without interrupting his work, which, in whatever form, writing or politics, travelled with him. Nothing was left to chance. His office and, once he had begun to paint, his studio also, travelled with him. How else could he achieve his many ambitions?

His entourage of secretaries, valet, researchers and advisers would grow, until later in life a whole convoy of vehicles would be required to accompany him. But he set a lifelong pattern as far back as 1907, when he made his first journey abroad as a Minister, to East Africa. The Permanent Under-Secretary, the senior civil servant at the Colonial Office, who looked upon the trip as not much more than a jaunt and thought he could await Churchill's return before being further involved, found himself bombarded by memoranda even before his itinerant minister had arrived. Even in the days before airmail, letters travelled quickly enough for the Under-Secretary to complain of Churchill's 'restless energy', and to note that the Minister's Private Secretary had given 'a vivid description of 14 hours work in one day on these memoranda in the heat and discomfort of the Red Sea'.

His life 'a natural harmony', Churchill obviously counted himself one of 'Fortune's favoured children', one of those 'whose work and pleasure are one'. However, he also recognised that 'those whose work is their pleasure are those who most need the means of banishing it from their mind', and his paints were always to hand, even in the trenches in World War One.

In the light of all this travelling, we should take with some scepticism Churchill's statement that 'A day away from Chartwell is a day wasted.' Much as he loved his home, acquired in 1922, set in the countryside of Kent, its grounds landscaped by him, many of the bricks in the kitchen garden and cottage walls laid with his own hands, he would never have been content to remain there. It was the anchorage waiting to welcome his return from voyages of exploration and regeneration.

CHAPTER I

The *Christina*

My tastes are simple. I am easily satisfied by the best.
Winston Churchill

Although Winston Churchill was the guest of Aristotle Onassis on his magnificent yacht eight times between 1958 and 1963, I met Onassis and saw the *Christina* before my grandfather did. That was in January 1956, when I was with my mother in the south of France, and my uncle Randolph Churchill, who knew Onassis, invited us to join him for a drink on the *Christina*. I was twelve, and had never seen anything so extravagantly luxurious before. It certainly did not cross my mind that three years later I would spend my summer holiday cruising the Mediterranean while witnessing the beginning of one of the most famous love affairs of the twentieth century.

In April 1959 we were at Chartwell when Grandpapa asked my mother if she and I would like to accompany him on the *Christina* in July. He explained that we would sail from Monte Carlo down the Italian coast and cruise around the Greek islands to Istanbul – which he called Constantinople, making it sound even more exotic.

I did not dare say a word, and held my breath until my

mother had accepted what seemed to me the most exciting invitation imaginable. I jumped for joy at the prospect, and can clearly remember the pleasure on Grandpapa's face when he saw how thrilled I was.

I had been brought up in the austerity of post-war Britain, so clothes had never played a great part in my life. Now, this suddenly changed. My mother arranged for me to have a day off from school to go shopping. This was unheard of, and I never did discover how she justified it to the headmistress.

She met me at Waterloo station, and we raced from one shop to another buying bathing suits, sundresses and what my mother rather quaintly described as 'play clothes'. Then we bought evening dresses, my first high-heeled shoes and a string of emerald-green beads, 'costume jewellery', in my mother's vocabulary. I am sure that if I had not looked such an obvious schoolgirl the sales assistants would have imagined that they were supplying a bride with her trousseau. I was certainly never so well equipped for any of my honeymoons.

This was the first time that I had travelled in Churchillian fashion, and the experience was to spoil me for travel in the future. Apart from my grandparents, my mother and myself, our party consisted of my grandfather's Private Secretary Anthony Montague Browne and his wife Nonie; his bodyguard Edmund Murray, a sergeant seconded from Scotland Yard; his nurse Roy Howells (Churchill was now eighty-four); and my grandmother's maid. Churchill could never have been accused of not travelling in style.

We arrived at Heathrow in a cavalcade of cars loaded, apart from the passengers, with quantities of luggage and a cage containing Toby, my grandfather's budgerigar. After stopping briefly at the VIP lounge, where the necessary formalities were observed in a most perfunctory manner, we were driven right

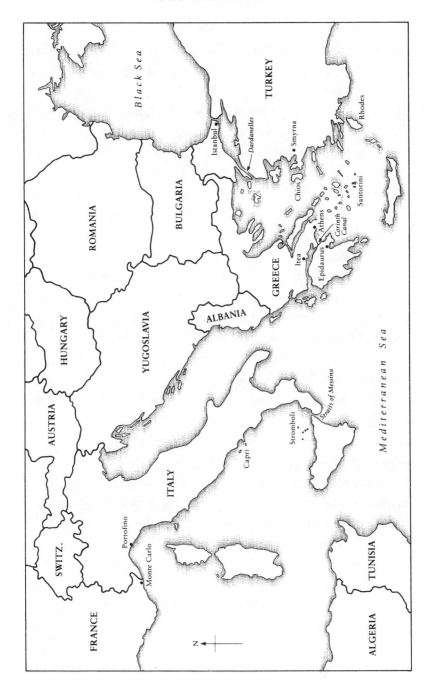

up to the steps of the aircraft. Our party seemed to occupy the whole of the front of the cabin, so it felt as though we had the entire plane to ourselves. The normal announcement that the passengers could smoke once the seatbelt sign was off was amended out of consideration to my grandfather, the usual follow-up request of 'no pipes or cigars' omitting the latter. It was inconceivable that he could be asked to refrain from lighting up his customary cigar.

At Nice there was a fleet of cars waiting to whisk us to Monte Carlo. After a welcome fit for a king, red carpet included, we set off with a large and noisy motorcycle escort of French police. To the wail of sirens we wound our way along the Corniche, with the Mediterranean sparkling on our right and the Alpes Maritimes rising above us on the left. The sirens increased in volume as we approached the border with Monaco, where we watched with fascination as the French escort was replaced by the Monegasque police with a precision normally associated only with the Brigade of Guards.

The harbour came into view, and there was the *Christina*, by far the most magnificent yacht in the harbour, and our home for the next three and a half weeks. Ari and Tina Onassis were waiting at the gangplank, and after greeting everyone, ushered my grandparents on board. Grandpapa immediately installed himself in a large chair on the rear deck with Toby in his cage at his side, and puffed away contentedly at his cigar. Meanwhile around him there was a hum of activity as the luggage was assigned to the various cabins.

I was far too excited to sit still, and raced off to inspect the stateroom that I was to share with my mother. We were shown to a large and incredibly luxurious cabin on the starboard side. My grandparents each had a stateroom opposite, with a sitting room in between. On one side of us were Maria Callas and her husband Battista Meneghini, and on the other Anthony and Nonie Montague Browne.

Everywhere there were maids unpacking suitcases, so, feeling surplus to requirements, I returned to the deck just as Maria Callas appeared at the bottom of the gangplank. We are not a musical family, and I had never been to the opera or, until a few days earlier, even heard of the famous singer who was being guided by our host towards my grandfather. Callas would have been indifferent to my ignorance, but it would not have occurred to her that Winston Churchill had probably shared my lack of knowledge before he had been briefed by his wife or his staff.

Tall, very dark, and striking in a reptilian sort of way was my first impression of Maria Callas. Compared to Tina Onassis she looked large, ungainly and ill at ease. Tina, blonde and petite, was wearing an enchanting summer dress which showed off her tiny waist to perfection, and high-heeled sandals on her small feet. Callas was draped in some sort of beige calico trimmed with heavy embroidery, with flat sandals on her feet, which were in proportion to her height. She looked nervous as Onassis gently propelled her towards his most honoured guest. A local newspaper, *L'Espoir de Nice et du Sud-Est*, whose reporter observed the scene from afar, and certainly out of earshot, gave its account of the meeting between the elder statesman and the great soprano. 'The singer, dressed in beige, approached Churchill. Was the "old lion" weary? Was he annoyed by the tardiness of the diva? In any case, it was without getting up that he took the hand of Maria Callas, who bowed before him. Toby, the budgerigar, on his perch, observed the scene . . . as the singer stood there speechless, he spoke: "Kiss!" Then one saw Churchill and Callas look at each other and laugh . . . The ice was broken.' Since no one ever heard Toby say anything other than 'My name is Toby,' this was a most unlikely tale.

One might have imagined that someone as rich and as exhibitionist as Onassis would have commissioned a new yacht from the finest boatyard in the world. In fact, the *Christina* had seen service during World War II as a Canadian frigate. But it is unlikely that anyone who had served on the *Stormont* would have recognised her after her refit in a German yard. The man in charge of the refurbishment was no stranger to egotistic clients – twenty years earlier he had designed Hitler's Eagle's Nest at Berchtesgaden.

No sooner had we settled into our palatial surroundings than we had to change into full evening dress for dinner at the Hôtel de Paris. Here, sitting on the terrace overlooking the Mediterranean shimmering with the reflection of the stars and the moon, was the first opportunity that the unlikely cast of guests had to look each other over. Tina and Ari sat at either end of the rectangular table. It was quite unremarkable that the host was attentive to Maria Callas on his left, as he shared his time between her and Clementine Churchill on his right. Meanwhile, Tina enchanted my grandfather. It would have been difficult to imagine two more different figures to take part in the drama which was about to unfold. Callas, in marked contrast to her dowdy appearance a few hours earlier, had transformed herself into a model of elegant sophistication in a magnificent black lace evening dress encrusted with beads, while Tina looked like a fairy princess. An added ingredient was the presence of Stavros Niarchos, Ari's rival shipping magnate and the husband of Tina's sister Eugenie. We had all been briefed on the various personalities, and knew that there was a long-standing feud between our host and his brother-in-law. Besides their competition in the shipping world, each considered he had the finer yacht. Undoubtedly the *Christina* was the more spectacular, but Niarchos's beautiful *Creole* was the more elegant. With Winston Churchill and Maria Callas as guests, Onassis clearly felt he had scored a point over Niarchos, and wanted him to witness it in person.

This was perhaps the most convivial meal of the whole cruise. Everyone was determined to please, and as far as one could see everything augured well for the weeks ahead. We did not know it, but the scene was being set for a story that would still be written about more than forty years on.

The *Christina* set sail after we had gone to bed, and the next morning I got up early to be on deck in good time for our arrival in Portofino. The nearer we got to the harbour, the more enchanted I became by the sight of the houses, cheek by jowl, painting the hillsides in various tones of pink, yellow, terracotta and green. After watching the crew go through the arrival drill, a routine which would become familiar in the days ahead, I went to see Grandpapa to tell him that we had arrived. I described the bustling harbour and the coloured houses as Toby flew around the stateroom. My grandfather listened intently, and I felt he was picturing the scene with an artist's eye.

Later that morning, Winston and Clementine sat on deck and waved goodbye as the women in the party set off with Tina for a tour of the town. Tina, quite naturally, always had the perfect outfit for any occasion – after all, this was her everyday life. The rest of us passed muster, not standing out in any way as far as our clothes were concerned. Callas, however, was dressed in a garishly coloured floral jumpsuit, which looked as if it could have been run up from some chintz curtains. Uncomfortably aware of the contrast this presented to Tina's outfit of understated elegance, she soon became ill at ease and bad tempered. It was not a very peaceful expedition as a group of paparazzi followed us from place to place.

That afternoon the Pretender to the Spanish throne, Don Juan, whose father King Alfonso XIII had renounced his claim to the throne in his favour, accompanied by his son, the future King Juan Carlos, came to visit my grandfather.

In the evening, after our first dinner on board, Onassis announced that he would take us to his favourite nightclub. Once again my grandparents waved us off. I was unimpressed by the dark, smoky club, and it was a relief when everyone made a move to go. At that moment a tall young man came up to our table and asked me to dance. I was opening my mouth to refuse when I felt myself being propelled by my mother's hand pushing me in the small of my back. On the dance floor with this stranger, I wondered about my mother's extraordinary behaviour and, more out of shyness than interest, proceeded to ask a series of gauche questions. When he had the chance to reply, my partner smiled and said, 'Don't you remember me? I came with my father to visit your grandfather today.' Red-faced with embarrassment, I realised that I had just had my first dance in a nightclub with the future King of Spain. I also realised that, far from being attracted to a shy sixteen-year-old, he must simply have been told to do his duty by his father.

At Capri, the music-hall singer and actress Gracie Fields and her Yugoslav husband Boris came on board. Our resident diva, who had not been asked to perform by our unmusical family, was definitely not pleased when she realised that she was going to have to suffer this homely woman doing what she did best. Fields serenaded Grandpapa to the tune of 'Volare', then we all stood round the piano and joined in singing the old wartime songs. There was something incongruous about the sight of

Maria Callas pretending to enjoy singing along to 'Daisy, Daisy'. Everyone gave the appearance of great jollity, but things were not all they seemed. I was not feeling very cheerful, as I had just torn the silk Emilio Pucci trousers my mother had bought me that afternoon; Callas was clearly seething, and apparently my grandfather whispered to Anthony Montague Browne, 'God's teeth! How long is this going on for?'

The next evening Ari called us all on deck to see Stromboli. The volcano was smoking, but he wanted a more spectacular fireworks display for his guests. He called out to it to perform, and pressed the boat's siren. To our amazement at that very moment Stromboli erupted, and a glowing red streak of lava started to flow. We knew Ari wanted to please, but this was something even the Onassis fortune could not buy. Ari was clearly shaken by this, and thought it was a bad omen; but in his worst nightmares he could not have imagined how sadly his life would unfold.

By this time we had settled into a routine of life on the *Christina*. My grandfather enjoyed the company of beautiful women, and was clearly enchanted by his hostess. Three generations of his family smiled benignly when Tina flirted with her octogenarian guest, but when Callas tried to feed him ice cream from her spoon our hackles rose. There was something predatory about her approach which left us disgusted and him bemused. We were on board the most luxurious boat imaginable, in the middle of a turquoise-blue sea with any number of crew at our service, but for Callas there was always something wrong. If the air conditioning was on, she wanted it off. If the stabilisers were down, she wanted them up. It was almost as if she felt it was expected of her to complain – and complain she did.

After passing through the Straits of Messina and into the Gulf of Corinth, our first stop in Greece was Itea, a little port at the foot of Mount Parnassus. An open Fiat Cinquecento was low-ered from the deck, Tina and my mother got into the back and Onassis, having helped Grandpapa into the front seat, drove off, with the rest of the party following in rather more prosaic vehicles. It seemed as though the entire population had turned out to cheer, and they were rewarded by a salute from Chur-chill, resplendent in a white suit and naval cap. While we climbed up the steep slope to see the ruins of Delphi, Onassis took Grandpapa to have a drink at the hotel below.

The next day we sailed through the Corinth Canal, the cliffs on either side so close we could practically touch them. That night the Greek Prime Minister, Konstantinos Karamanlis, and the British Ambassador, Sir Roger Alan, and their wives were coming to dinner. In order to avoid the hordes of paparazzi the *Christina* sailed past Athens to pick up the guests at a small town to the south-east of the capital. We then sailed out and anchored in the bay overlooking Cape Sounion.

At first this was not a relaxed occasion. The table was mag-nificent, sparkling with gold, silver, crystal and Sèvres china, but the conversation did not sparkle at all. At times it positively dragged. At one such moment my mother, feeling the need to fill a silence, raised her glass to Sir Roger and said: 'Ambassador, do look at these glasses. They bend.'

Several times in the preceding days Onassis had showed off the flexibility of his new Baccarat glasses. My mother, however, did not quite have the knack, and showered the Ambassador's white dinner jacket with red wine. Onassis, the perfect host, immediately picked up his glass, the one containing water, and squeezed it until it also broke. The Ambassador's dinner jacket was removed to be dry cleaned, and in the meantime he accepted my grandmother's fur wrap to wear around his shoulders.

The broken glass appeared to change the tone of the dinner, and everyone seemed much more at ease. Churchill, who had been somewhat silent, found the perfect way to turn the evening into a resounding success. An emotional man with a prodigious memory, in sight of the Temple of Sounion, on a column of which Lord Byron had carved his name, Grandpapa recited from 'Don Juan':

> *Place me on Sunian's marbled steep,*
> *Where nothing, save the waves and I,*
> *May hear our mutual murmurs sweep:*
> *There, swan-like, let me sing and die.*

Everyone was happy, even the Ambassador, who departed wearing the same dinner jacket in which he had arrived, bearing no evidence of its encounter with a glass of Château Lafite.

It was during these days that it became evident that something was going on between Ari and Callas. My mother, my grandmother and I all liked Tina enormously, and had in no way taken to the singer. It was in this mood that we watched events unfolding, and met each evening in my grandmother's cabin to gossip about the day.

When we arrived at the magnificent amphitheatre at Epidaurus we were overwhelmed by an incredible display of flowers put up by the local people. Callas, who because of her Greek ancestry quite reasonably thought this was her territory, turned innocently to my mother and said, 'What beautiful flowers! How kind! But do tell me, Diana, why are they in the shape of a V?' To which my mother replied with some satisfaction, 'Because, Maria, they are not for you; they are for Papa.' Callas responded with a venomous look, and the subject was rapidly changed.

The seemingly idyllic holiday was beginning to take on a more disquieting air when after visiting the island of Santorini we sat down to dinner and found that two of the party were missing. Tina told us that Callas and Ari had already eaten a special Greek dinner by themselves. She announced this as though it was an everyday event, and despite a somewhat awkward atmosphere we struggled through the evening.

The sea was calm but a storm was definitely brewing on board as the *Christina* sailed towards Rhodes. We spent two happy days there, visiting the various sights. One, which was of particular interest to my grandfather and which I remember best, was the Valley of the Butterflies, an extraordinary place resembling a giant kaleidoscope in which shades of red and gold merged with each other as the millions of tiger moths fluttered around, illuminated by the strong sunlight gleaming through the trees.

A dinner dance was given at the Miramar Hotel, which had opened the year before. Ostensibly the object of the event was to honour my grandfather, but clearly the press coverage would also be very good for public relations.

On our last evening on Rhodes we were relaxing after two days of intensive sightseeing when Ari, who was performing trick dives for the children, misjudged a dive and hit his head on the bottom of the pool. He was pulled out by his brother-in-law Theodore Garoufalides and Anthony Montague Browne. He was unconscious, but soon recovered and allowed Garoufalides, who was a doctor, to examine him. Apparently he passed this perfunctory medical, but Anthony has the theory that this bang on his head had a profound effect on Ari's temperament and behaviour. Whether or not this is true, from that moment on Ari launched himself into his affair with Maria Callas.

After dining with Tina's parents on the island of Chios, their daughter giving not the slightest hint, at any rate in public, that anything was wrong, we set sail for Ari's birthplace, the port of Smyrna on the Turkish coast.

I remember Onassis sitting at my grandfather's feet on the rear deck describing his traumatic childhood, and his escape in his late teens when Turkish troops torched the Greek and Armenian sections of the city, killing civilians with knives while survivors crowded the harbour, hoping in vain for salvation to come from the sea. He told the story in such gory and graphic detail that it was clear that some of those listening would have preferred an expurgated version. However, my abiding memory is that as he was telling us of all the horrors that he had surmounted, Ari was fully aware that it would not have been possible for us, sitting as we were on the deck of his yacht, the most luxurious in the world, not to be impressed by his perseverance, resilience and success against the odds.

From Smyrna we sailed through the Dardanelles at night, in case they stirred up bad memories for the guest of honour of the disastrous campaign there with which he was associated in World War I. 'It will always be incredible to future ages that every man did not rally to an enterprise which carried with it such immense possibilities, and which required such limited resources to carry it into effect,' he had told the House of Commons in 1917. Grandpapa may now have been an old man, but he was quite aware of what was going on. He referred to the Dardanelles at dinner, but did not dwell on the subject, and nor did anyone else.

The Patriarch of the Greek Orthodox Church came on board. It was a wonderful sight, the priest, robed in black with his flowing white beard, and Winston Churchill sitting on the deck as the *Christina* sailed slowly down the Bosphorus. From Istanbul we began the journey back to Monte Carlo. We stopped at Athens, where after visiting the Acropolis we went to a fabulous dinner in the garden of the Garoufalides' villa.

From Athens we sailed non-stop to Monte Carlo. The holiday was over, and everyone – or almost everyone – was ready to return to shore. The sea was rough, and we were quite happy to see the *Christina*'s home port. We all went our separate ways, unaware that within a short while our summer holiday was to become one of the most written-about cruises of all time, that two marriages were over, and that the tragedies of the Onassis family were just beginning.

Apart from the two couples at the centre of all the drama, I was probably the only person on whom the cruise had made a deep impression. Never before or since had I experienced such effortless tourism in such incredible surroundings. I learned for the first time, outside the pages of romantic novels, about affairs of the heart; but more significantly I had the opportunity to be with my grandfather at close quarters over three and a half weeks. I had spent a lot of time with my grandparents before, but this was quite a different experience. Grandpapa had aged considerably in the past few years, but he appeared very happy aboard the yacht. The changing scene every day as we cruised from one magnificent sight to another seemed visibly to stimulate him.

I have never forgotten that amazing holiday, and the experience made me wonder about the other journeys my grandfather had undertaken during his long and extraordinary life. I decided to try to retrace his footsteps in Cuba, India and Africa, where he had had such thrilling adventures in his youth, from which he was lucky to return alive; and in America, the homeland of his mother, where he spent so much time. I was fortunate to be able to relive some of his wartime journeys with those who had accompanied him; and I have my own memories of the painting holidays which were such an important part of the last fifty years of his life.

Of course, some of the places have changed beyond all recognition, and many of his travelling companions are no more; but following the trail of my grandfather's travels through four continents over more than seventy years has made me understand him better, and appreciate all the more his ceaseless energy and incredible zest for life.

CHAPTER 2

A New World

If my father had been American and my mother British, instead
of the other way around, I might have got here on my own.
Winston Churchill in an address to the United States
Congress, 26 November 1941

Churchill's lifelong love affair with America began on Saturday, 9 November 1895 when, three weeks short of his twenty-first birthday, he disembarked in New York from the Cunard steamship *Etruria*. At a little under eight thousand tons she was tiny compared to Cunard's present-day sixty-nine-thousand-ton *QE2*. One of the last of the line to carry sail, the *Etruria* had been tossed about by winter storms, and the young subaltern had not enjoyed the experience. Nor had he enjoyed the company of his fellow passengers. 'There are no nice people on board. I do not contemplate ever taking a sea voyage for pleasure,' he wrote to his mother during the crossing. In this mood he began to look upon his planned three days in New York as little more than an irksome delay in his journey to his ultimate destination, Cuba, and while at sea had decided to cut his stay in New York to a day and a half.

Commissioned nine months earlier into the 4th Hussars and

stationed at Hounslow near London, Churchill had thirsted for action. War service was, he said, 'The swift road to promotion and advancement. It was the glittering gateway to distinction. It cast glamour upon the fortunate possessor alike in the eyes of elderly gentlemen and young ladies.' Unfortunately, in the winter of 1895 there was no prospect of war service with the British Army, as it was almost entirely at peace. There were few junior officers with any active service, and there had been nothing more exciting on Churchill's horizon than ten weeks' uninterrupted leave granted for the purpose of foxhunting. Scanning the world for adventure, he learned that the Captain General of Spain, the renowned Marshal Martinez Campos, had been sent to put down an insurrection in Cuba, which was then a Spanish colony. Some eighty thousand Spanish troops were being shipped to the island to deal with the uprising. Here was a war Churchill might join as an observer. It would be more entertaining and useful to chase Cuban guerrillas through the bush than foxes across the English shires or young ladies through London drawing rooms. A fellow officer, Reginald Barnes, a future general also avid for experience, agreed to accompany him.

Already accustomed by virtue of his family connections to doing business only with those at the top, Churchill had laid his plans with care. The popular press was in sympathy with the Cuban rebels, and the attachment of British officers to the Spanish forces might easily have been taken as an official mission or an endorsement of Spanish policy. Nevertheless, Churchill had personally obtained permission to go to Cuba from the Commander-in-Chief of the British Army, Lord Wolseley. The Director of Intelligence, General Chapman, had provided maps and useful information, and to smooth his path in Cuba Churchill had written to a family friend, Sir Henry Drummond Wolff, the British Ambassador in Madrid, for the necessary

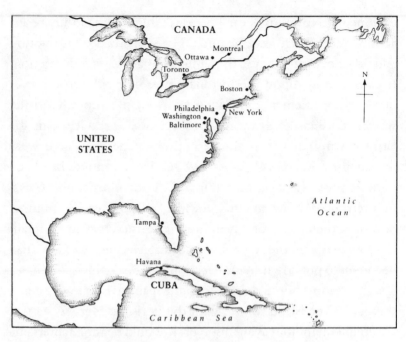

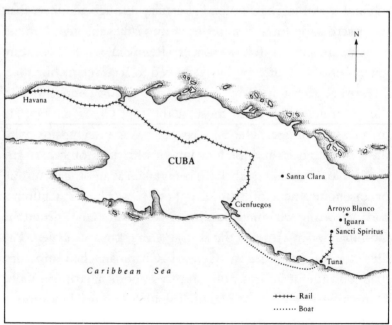

introductions to the Spanish General. To ease his straitened finances he had obtained a contract with the London newspaper the *Daily Graphic* to provide letters from the front for five guineas each.

Churchill's father Lord Randolph had died in January 1895, and Lady Randolph had hoped to see a good deal of her son during his winter leave, but gave grudging approval to his plans and paid his fare across the Atlantic. More importantly, she ensured the best possible welcome in New York for her son. In addition to mobilising her American relations, she arranged that he would be looked after by an admirer whom she had met some months earlier in Paris. He was Bourke Cockran, a prominent New York lawyer and a member of the powerful clique of Tammany Hall Democrats, who had run for his party's presidential nomination in 1882.

From the moment Cockran met Churchill and Barnes on the quayside, the red carpet was rolled out wherever they went. He immediately whisked them off to his apartment on Fifth Avenue, where they were accommodated in comfort and style during their stay. That evening he held a dinner party in their honour, attended by the leading members of the judiciary. The day did not end with the cigars and brandy, for Lady Randolph's cousin Eva Purdy then took the two young men on a tour of New York's nightlife, ending well after midnight at the old Waldorf-Astoria.

By next morning Churchill's views on New York had been completely revised, and all thoughts of an immediate departure for Cuba had been abandoned. 'What an extraordinary people the Americans are!' he wrote to his mother before setting out on Sunday for a day fully occupied with social engagements. 'We are members of all the Clubs and one person seems to vie with another in trying to make our time pleasant.'

During the next few days Cockran gave the young men no time to rest. With their background in mind, he showed them around the establishments of the Atlantic Military District and arranged a tour of the Military Academy at West Point, where Churchill later said he had been treated 'as if I had been a general'. The regime at the Academy was far more rigorous than that which Churchill had recently experienced at Sandhurst, its British equivalent. In describing it to his brother Jack, Churchill expressed horror that the cadets should be denied any leave for their first two years, and be forbidden to smoke or have any money. Young men who resigned their liberty to such an extent, he felt, could never make 'good citizens or fine soldiers.'

Cockran also took Churchill and Barnes aboard the ironclad battleship *New York* after a tugboat tour of the harbour. Churchill's views of the American navy were in stark contrast to his opinion of the army at West Point. He was sufficiently impressed by the ship's company of the *New York* to write to his aunt Leonie Leslie that it was 'the monopoly of the Anglo-Saxon race to breed good seamen'.

Churchill and his companion attended the opening of the New York Horse Show; as cavalry officers, it was an event they much appreciated. They watched fire engines being drawn through the streets by teams of galloping horses when the New York Fire Commissioner arranged a mock alarm specifically for them. A day was spent beside Judge Ingraham, who was presiding over a murder trial. Their time was so filled that six days after arriving, Churchill wrote to his brother, 'We have postponed our departure for three days.'

It is unlikely that Cockran would have taken Churchill around the tenement districts, the sprawling slums along the Manhattan and Brooklyn shorelines, where thousands lived hand to mouth in squalid and overcrowded conditions. Had he done so, his guest would surely have mentioned it in a letter written to his aunt when his mind was full of 'irreconcilable and conflicting facts' about America. As it was he had neither seen nor experienced anything significant to set against the magnificent entrepreneurial achievements he witnessed in New York. Having sampled the city's railways, trams and ferries, he extolled the 'business enterprise' which had secured such benefits for the people while simultaneously providing the promoters with 'colossal fortunes'. The comparison he drew was between such solid achievements and paper money as opposed to English coinage; after paying the toll at Brooklyn Bridge with a dollar bill, he was left wondering how he could 'reconcile their magnificent system of communication with their abominable currency'. He also contrasted the 'hospitality of American Society' with 'the vulgarity of their Press'.

All Churchill had seen impressed him greatly, but he felt he needed to digest it before forming an opinion. New York, just finding its feet, had provided a stark contrast with solid Victorian London. In spite of his doubts, it is clear that in one hectic week Churchill had identified strongly with the America he had seen in New York, and by the time he and Barnes left for Cuba, a favourable opinion had begun to form. 'Picture yourself the American people as a great lusty youth,' he wrote to his brother Jack, 'who moves about his affairs with a good hearted freshness which may well be the envy of older nations of the earth.'

On Sunday, 17 November Churchill and Barnes caught the train south for Tampa, Florida. Bourke Cockran had arranged a private stateroom which enabled the pair to enjoy the thirty-six-hour journey in the comfort and style to which they had become accustomed since their landing in America. Arriving in Tampa in the evening of the eighteenth, they boarded the *Olivette* the following morning for the crossing to Cuba.

They disembarked at Havana the next day, and checked into the Gran Hotel Inglaterra, in Churchill's estimation a 'fairly good hotel'. Havana 'presented a spectacle which was in every respect magnificent'. From here Churchill wrote to Bourke Cockran reiterating his thanks for his 'kindness and courtesy', and adding: 'We had many delightful conversations – and I learned much from you in a pleasant and interesting way.' He had established a lasting friendship with his world-wise host. Years later Churchill was to say of Cockran's political oratory: 'He was my model – I learned from him how to hold thousands in thrall.'

In September 2000, 105 years after my grandfather first set foot in Cuba, I arrived in Havana to see what I could discover of his time there. As Winston Churchill's granddaughter I had been invited by the Hotel Nacional to celebrate its seventieth anniversary. Armed with *My Early Life*, Churchill's account of his first thirty-four years, and copies of his 1895 articles and sketches in the *Daily Graphic*, I was full of optimism. This feeling remained with me as I sipped a *mojito* in the pavement café outside the Gran Hotel Inglaterra.

I compared the scene before me with a pen-and-ink drawing that Churchill had entitled 'Volunteers returning from the front, Havana'. Making allowance for a little artistic licence, and taking away the trappings of modern city life, I felt that I was very likely sitting at the exact spot from which my grandfather had sketched as he enjoyed his first Havana cigar in its country of origin; cigars had become a habit by the time he got to Sandhurst.

As a guest in one of the few countries which still enthusiasti-

cally embraced Communism, I wondered what the Cuban hier-
archy, including President Fidel Castro, thought of Winston
Churchill, whose antipathy towards Communism was legend-
ary. But everyone, including the staff at the British Embassy in
Havana, said that meeting Castro would be impossible, although
I had been treated royally from the moment I stepped off the
plane. I had been provided with a car and a guide and companion, Yamilla, to help me retrace my grandfather's steps
through Cuba. Ever helpful, the director general of the Hotel
Nacional rashly asked if there was anything else he could do
for me. I thanked him for all he had arranged, and said there was
just one more thing: I wanted above all to meet the President. 'I
will do my best,' he replied. 'But it is not easy.' Yamilla thought
it most unlikely.

Our first stop was to pay a visit to the 103-year-old Gregorio
Fuentes, on whom Ernest Hemingway had based the fisherman
in *The Old Man and the Sea*. Weathered by more than a century
of life in the open air, he greeted me with pleasure, grace and
emotion, hugging and kissing me – Cubans kiss a great deal.
He patted the chair next to him, then told me that he
remembered my grandfather having dinner with Hemingway
on his visit to Cuba in 1946. He said that he himself had cooked
the meal, and that afterwards Hemingway and Churchill had
had a cigar-smoking competition. He could not elaborate on
his memories, which were clearly somewhat obscured by the
mists of time, but as he spoke and tried to answer my questions,
tears trickled down the deeply etched lines on his gnarled face.*

In Havana, Churchill turned his mind to the mission on which
he had originally embarked. Presenting his credentials to the

---

* Gregorio Fuentes died in January 2002, at the age of 104.

Spanish authorities, he found that Marshal Martinez Campos had departed on a tour of inspection and was at Santa Clara, some 150 miles east of Havana. The journey by rail would take twelve hours, as the rebels frequently caused delays by attacking the train and damaging the line. It was arranged that on arrival at Santa Clara Churchill and Barnes would be attached to a column commanded by General Valdez which would be setting out in search of rebel forces. 'Tomorrow we start for the front,' wrote Churchill to Lady Randolph on 20 November.

The train the following day was subjected to more delays than usual. By the time it arrived at Santa Clara Valdez and his column had already left for the small town of Sancti Spiritus, forty miles away. To pursue them on horseback through rebel-infested country was judged too dangerous, so the Spanish staff decided it would be necessary to undertake a further journey of 150 miles by rail to the small port of Cienfuegos, thence by sea to Tuna, and then by rail again to Sancti Spiritus. Rebel action on the railway line out of Tuna necessitated an over-night stay in the local hotel. This, Churchill told the readers of the *Daily Graphic*, was 'more homely than pretentious'. But it was considerably more congenial than the 'filthy, crowded, noisy tavern' in which Churchill and Barnes spent the next night in Sancti Spiritus awaiting the arrival of General Valdez.

I was not surprised to fail in my search for the Spanish fortified post near Santa Clara, but was full of hope that I would be able to identify the little church which the advance guard of General Valdez's column passed as they entered Sancti Spiritus. I showed Churchill's sketch of it to several people, who sent me in differ-ent directions, certain that they knew exactly where it was. Eventually, hot and weary, I saw an antiquarian bookstore, and decided that if the owner was there I might perhaps interest him in my quest. He was fascinated by the drawing, and immediately closed up his shop and led me through the hot, dusty streets. We finally arrived at the main square of the town. Here my new friend pointed to a building which bore no resemblance to the church I was seeking, and with some regret explained that at the beginning of the twentieth century the old buildings in the vicinity had been destroyed to make way for the grand piazza built to mark Cuban independence, which followed the defeat of the Spanish forces after American intervention in 1898. I left Sancti Spiritus disappointed, but at least knowing that I had found the place, although it was greatly changed.

General Valdez and his column of three thousand men arrived in Sancti Spiritus the evening after Churchill and Barnes. He was delighted to receive the two young British officers, assuming their attachment to his column was a gesture of their country's moral support at a time when world opinion was on the side of the rebels. The attachment implied nothing of the sort, but Churchill managed a diplomatic response to Valdez's welcome which, elaborated upon by the interpreter, greatly pleased his host. The General did not intend to dally in the smallpox- and fever-ridden Sancti Spiritus a moment longer than necessary, and announced that his men would move out at dawn. The following morning, as the sky began to pale, Churchill rode among the long files of troops heading for the village of Iguara, some twenty miles distant, which was said to be surrounded by rebels. His pistol was loaded, although as a British observer he could use it only in self-defence. But, having travelled across the world at a cost he could ill afford, he had at least got himself to a war. Thirty years later, in *My Early Life*, he painted an enchanting picture of the ride to Iguara: 'The long Spanish column insinuated itself like a snake into the endless forests and undulations of a vast, lustrous landscape dripping with moisture and sparkling with sunshine.'

One of Cuba's great attractions is its lush and glistening landscape. Although there are now more plantations of mangoes, bananas and avocados, the countryside is on the whole much the same as it was a century ago. As I travelled in my grandfather's footsteps past waving palm trees and crops of sugar cane and maize, I could easily visualise the long lines of heavily laden Spanish troops plodding along the twisting tracks as they threaded their way through the luxuriant bush. It was easy to imagine the apprehension the soldiers must have felt as they approached yet another possible ambush among the endless clumps of marabu trees, whose thick and bushy foliage provided perfect concealment for guerrilla forces. They would have been watching out for the appearance of circling *aura tinosa*, the small variety of carrion-eating birds native to Cuba, to give them some warning as they pushed through the dense undergrowth.

Churchill's readers in the *Daily Graphic* learned little about Cuba's landscape but a good deal about the island's politics and military operations, the latter illustrated in each letter by a pen-and-ink sketch. His five letters from the front, a total of some six thousand words written while living rough, were an early indication of his formidable journalistic talents. Privately Churchill sympathised with the rebels' aim of achieving independence for Cuba, if not with their methods, and his first contribution to the *Daily Graphic* acknowledged that they had 'the sympathy of the entire population'. But being attached to a Spanish military force he inevitably developed a comradeship with his hosts which undermined objective reporting.

For several days the column moved through the wonderful scenery without sight or sound of the enemy. Each day the routine was the same. By daybreak they would be on the march.

At around nine o'clock they would stop for breakfast, sling their hammocks between the trees and enjoy a four-hour siesta in the shade. After an afternoon march until dusk the column would have covered upwards of twenty miles since dawn. By the night of 29 November they were bivouacked in the fortified village of Arroyo Blanco.

At Arroyo Blanco I searched again for the subject of a drawing by Churchill, but again I was unsuccessful. Here, however, unlike Sancti Spiritus, this was not as a result of more recent development, but because of the presence of so many little shacks with verandas similar to the one depicted by Churchill in his sketch of General Valdez dining with his staff on the eve of battle. My grandfather's professional attitude is demonstrated by the very fact that he dragged himself away from this scene of warmth and conviviality to sit in the mosquito-ridden undergrowth and record the event. The inevitable cigar would probably have deterred the insects from attacking him.

The troops moved on the following morning, Churchill's twenty-first birthday. On such a day a subaltern in a smart British cavalry regiment would have expected to hear the popping of champagne corks and to have a sumptuous feast. For Churchill there was only the popping of musketry and the thud of a bullet which, missing his head by a foot, killed the horse behind him. In *My Early Life* he would devote ten lines to the fate of the horse, but of his own escape he simply commented: 'So at any rate I had been under fire. That was something. Nevertheless, I began to take a more thoughtful view of the enterprise than I had hitherto.' His birthday feast was a 'skinny chicken' on which he was munching when the column was attacked.

From then on, the column was intermittently in contact with the rebels. The advance culminated in a prolonged skirmish which became known as the Battle of La Reforma. During this

General Valdez rode to within five hundred yards of the enemy, where he surveyed the fighting until his infantry prevailed. Churchill described the experience to his mother: 'The General – a very brave man – in a white and gold uniform on a grey horse – drew a great deal of fire on us and I heard enough bullets whistle and hum past to satisfy me for some time to come.' Not all whistled harmlessly past: a soldier standing beside Churchill was hit and killed.

The column was now running out of rations, and withdrew from the field. General Valdez returned by horseback and rail to Tuna, and Churchill and Barnes accompanied him before taking the train for Havana. Also travelling by rail was the Captain General, Marshal Martinez Campos, who informed Churchill and Barnes that they had been awarded a Spanish decoration, the Red Cross, for bravery at La Reforma.

It was a cross which would be hard to bear in the immediate future, for having undergone his baptism of fire from bullets in Cuba, Churchill was about to receive an equally fierce attack from the press back home in England. 'Mr Churchill was supposed to have gone to the West Indies for a holiday,' wrote the *Newcastle Leader* on 7 December. 'Spending a holiday fighting other people's battles is a rather extraordinary process even for a Churchill.' On the same day the *Eastern Morning News*, obviously unaware that Churchill had obtained permission from the Commander-in-Chief himself, commented: 'Lord Wolseley will probably order him to return at once and report himself.'

As I came to the end of Churchill's Cuban trail I was resigned to the fact that I was not going to meet President Castro and hear what he thought of my grandfather. On my last morning in Havana I called on the British Ambassador, who somewhat smugly indicated that I had been pursuing a lost cause.

Returning to my car, I found an extremely excited Yamilla. 'You have been invited to lunch with the Comandante!' I could not believe that the invitation had come. Perhaps it was the fact that, as I was later told, Castro's first love was called Celia, and was a redhead like me.

An hour later Yamilla, the director general of the Hotel Nacional and I drew up outside the presidential palace, a very plain rectangular building in a style very unlike the elegant architecture of old Havana. As we walked up a huge flight of steps I was clutching a magnum of Pol Roger Cuvée Sir Winston Churchill, which I had brought with me to Cuba just in case the impossible happened.

We were ushered inside, and found that our surroundings were in complete contrast to the stark exterior of the building. We entered an enchanted forest, the trees, a cross between palms and ferns, chosen because they were of the type that had given shelter to the Cuban forces during the War of Independence in 1898. We walked through lush vegetation towards a dark, shimmering lake, lit by strong sunlight. The lake turned out to be a vast floor of black marble; the sun was a huge stained-glass window, in front of which we were told to wait.

With no pomp, ceremony or pretension the Comandante arrived, dressed in what appeared to be brand-new khaki fatigues, and apologised profusely for keeping us waiting. Although he was thinner than I had imagined, his presence filled the room. He led us to the dining room, where a long table was laid with a startling quantity of china, glass and cutlery. We were clearly in for a feast.

Castro placed me opposite him, with an overwhelmed Yamilla on his right and his interpreter on his left. The hotel director and three palace officials completed the table. I had expected Castro to be a compelling and charismatic personality, but I was quite unprepared for his charm, magnetism and twinkly humour. He fired question after question at me about my grandfather's involvement in Cuba in 1895 and in the Boer War, but most of all he wanted to tell me about his educational programme in Cuba. He spoke as though he was thinking out loud, giving everyone time to follow his train of thought as it moved along a carefully conceived path which he knew like the back of his hand.

Castro has beautiful hands, which he uses to great effect to emphasise what he is saying, or to give a touch on the arm or around the shoulder, bringing one even more under his spell. He is a man of instant impulse. No sooner had I told him that I was very disappointed to have missed seeing the Vice President Ramon Jose Fernandez, who had been an aide to my grandfather during his second visit to Cuba in 1946, than a mobile phone was called for to get Fernandez on the line from Sydney, where he was attending the Olympic Games.

After two and a half hours, during which the conversation gave little opportunity to eat much of the sumptuous lunch, the subject somehow turned to the little Cuban boy Elian Gonzalez. In November 1999 he, his mother and stepfather had been among a party attempting to emigrate illegally. They had run into rough weather, and their vessel had sunk. Elian was found floating off the coast of Florida, and had eventually been returned to Cuba after considerable controversy. I said that in Britain we too had followed the story with fascination. 'Would you like to come with me to visit him?' Of course I would.

Then he asked what time my plane was due to fly, and said: 'Don't worry, we can always put a truck in front of it until you get there.'

I gave him my present, explaining that I had brought my

grandfather's favourite champagne to the home of his favourite cigars. Castro took great pleasure in telling me that he had made sure that my grandfather was supplied with cigars right up until his death. Then, the others having departed, Castro, his interpreter and I descended to the basement and squeezed into the back of a car for our afternoon's visit to Elian. Thigh against thigh, with Castro's forage cap and gun sliding about in front of him, we talked about fishing and the beautiful sea. He invited me to bring my family to stay in his beach house.

On arrival at the government guest house we were welcomed on the porch by at least twenty members of Elian's family. There were kisses all round for both the President and his guest. They listened politely as Castro introduced me, then led us out to meet the star of the show. Elian jumped out of the pool where he was having a swimming lesson, and greeted us with a total lack of self-consciousness.

When it was time for me to leave I received a bearlike hug and a kiss, and the pariah of the democratic world repeated his invitation to stay. As I waved goodbye, the interpreter, who was accompanying me back to the hotel, said, 'The Comandante was very sincere in his invitation. I hope you will accept.'

In my short visit I had met the three most famous living Cubans. I was enchanted by Gregorio Fuentes, and thrilled to have succeeded against all the odds in meeting Fidel Castro. Elian was the icing on the cake.

I could not resist making one last call to the Embassy. By this time it was seven o'clock, and the Ambassador, who had been so dismissive of my request for help, had gone home. I left him a message: 'As a matter of courtesy in case he hears it from another source, please inform His Excellency that I have just returned from lunch with President Castro, after which he took me to visit Elian Gonzalez.' I later sent him a report of my meeting with Castro, but received no acknowledgement.

The British Embassy in Havana has since discovered the Cuban interest in Churchill, and the current Ambassador, Paul Hare, has invited me to give a talk on Churchill and Cuba as part of a British cultural event.

While I was in Havana the Cuban sculptor Janio Nunez presented me with a miniature of his life-size sculpture of Churchill which is displayed in the Hotel Nacional. Both versions are moulded from tobacco leaves. I left Havana understanding that the well-known hostility of my grandfather to Communism is not an issue in Cuba, where he is simply regarded as a very great man who was and still is the best advertisement for their national product.

Having crossed from Havana to Tampa, Churchill wrote his fifth and final letter to the *Daily Graphic*. In it he described the bribery and peculation which pervaded the Spanish administration on the island, and concluded that 'a national and justifiable revolt is the only possible result of such a system'. Having laid bare the corrupt nature of the Cuban government, Churchill turned his pen upon the rebels. The towns and villages were full of 'patriotic braggarts' who 'would not hazard a brass farthing – far less life or limb – to promote the cause they profess to hold so high'. The rebels in the field were hardly any better, refusing to submit to military discipline. Churchill rhetorically posed the question, 'Is this the stuff out of which nations are made?' He doubted that the insurgents could provide a better alternative than the Spanish colonial administration, or that a military solution could be achieved, advising that 'a compromise alone is possible' and hoping for better times, when commerce would enable Cuba to exchange 'the cigars of Havana for the cottons of Lancashire'.

On his return to America Churchill was assailed by the press for his involvement in Cuba. He denied that he had actually fought against the insurgents, saying the Red Cross was a courtesy decoration only. When he reached New York his views were earnestly canvassed and fully reported in the *New York World* and *New York Herald*. His final interview was on the dockside on 14 December. He arrived 'within five minutes of the *Etruria*'s sailing time but the pleasant faced young officer submitted as gracefully to the requests of the waiting group of interviewers as though there were hours of leisure on his hands'. There was a deal of amusing banter between him and the reporters. Of the Cuban rebels he said, 'They are not good soldiers but as runners would be hard to beat.' He was credited with a merry laugh when he noted: 'One conspicuous feature of this war is that so few men are killed.' When he prophesied, 'I think the upshot of it will be that the United States will intervene as a peacemaker,' he was closer to the mark than perhaps he thought. In three years' time Cuba would achieve independence following the Spanish–American War.

Writing to his mother from India a year later, Churchill was evidently uneasy about his less than objective reporting during his Cuban adventure:

. . . I read in the papers of the death of Antonio Maceo one of the greatest leaders of the revolt in Cuba. This may smash the insurrection. On the other hand the movement has already supported the loss of many leaders & the president of the embryo republic have lost their lives without the rebels being discouraged. I am inclined to think that Spain must lose the island. I reproach myself for having written uncandidly and for having perhaps done injustice to the insurgents. I rather tried and in some measure succeeded in making out a case for Spain. It was politic and did not expose me to the charge of being ungrateful to my hosts, but I am not quite clear whether it was right.

> *This above all – to thine own self be true,*
> *And it must follow as the night the day*
> *Thou canst not then be false to any man.**

I am aware that what I wrote did not shake thrones or upheave empires but the importance of principles does not depend on the importance of what involves them.

It would be five years before Churchill returned to America. He spent those five years as a soldier and war correspondent, returning home from the Anglo–Boer War in 1900 and being elected to Parliament. To augment his finances he undertook a lecture tour around England based on his experiences in South Africa. Encouraged by the fact that his lectures had been well received and financially successful, he set off for America, where his programme had been arranged by Major James B. Pond of the well-known Lyceum Lecture Bureau. To Bourke Cockran Churchill wrote: 'I pursue profit not pleasure in the States this time.' He anticipated that American hostility to British policy in South Africa might result in a rough ride, and ended his letter by admitting 'no small trepidation at embarking upon the stormy sea of American thought & discussion'.

The *New York Evening Journal* announced Churchill's arrival in its edition of 8 December 1900: 'Winston Churchill, member of Parliament, war correspondent, soldier and author, arrived here on the steamer *Lucania*.' Anxious to avoid a political argument on the quayside, he disarmed his interviewers by referring

---

* Polonius in *Hamlet*, Act I, Scene iii.

to the trend in recent years of marriages between British aristocracy and American wealth. Among others, his uncle and cousin, the eighth and ninth Dukes of Marlborough, had both married wealthy American heiresses. Churchill emphatically stated: 'I am not here to marry anybody. I am not going to get married. I would like to have that stated positively.'

Sunday, 9 December was spent with Cockran, and on Monday Churchill went to Albany in New York State to meet Governor Theodore Roosevelt, who a few weeks previously had been elected Vice President, but who would be President within a year, following the assassination of President William McKinley.

Churchill's first lecture was on Tuesday, 11 December in Philadelphia, where his magnanimity towards the virtually defeated Boers – the war was still continuing – won over a critical audience. When they clapped at the sight of a lantern slide of a Boer, Churchill responded: 'You are quite right to applaud him. He is the most formidable fighting man in the world.' Churchill 'spoke readily, without notes and produced a decidedly favourable impression'. It was a good start to the tour.

New York followed the next day, when after a large dinner party given by Bourke Cockran, Churchill spoke in the Grand Ballroom of the Waldorf-Astoria. He was introduced by Mark Twain, who said that because Britain had sinned against the Boers in South Africa and America had sinned against the Spanish in Cuba, the two countries were 'kin in sin': 'The harmony is perfect – like Mr Churchill himself.' The witty introduction was not an easy act to follow, but Churchill again succeeded in winning 'the entire sympathy of a very brilliant and critical audience'.

Churchill and Twain discussed the causes of the Anglo–Boer

War, and Churchill admitted that the older man had the better of the argument. Churchill was thrilled to have made friends with this literary icon, who signed copies of every one of his twenty-five works for him, inscribing each of them: 'To be good is noble; to teach others how to be good is nobler & no trouble.'

A number of officers who had fought with Churchill in South Africa had petitioned him to confront an American war correspondent, Richard Harding Davis, whose dispatches from the war had been hostile to Britain. Churchill, however, had taken a liking to Davis, and was using some of his photographs to illustrate his lectures. In a good mood after his successful evening at the Waldorf, Churchill decided to call on Davis even though it was well after midnight. It was therefore not surprising that Churchill's scheduled arrival in New Haven late the following morning, for a lecture that evening, was delayed until late afternoon. Nevertheless, by the time he boarded the midnight sleeper to Washington, his visit to Yale University and his lecture at the Hyperion Theater had been judged 'a success in every detail' by the local press.

But lack of sleep and the pace he had been setting himself were taking their toll. He arrived in Washington, where he was to be shown around the Capitol by Senator Chauncey Depew and introduced to President McKinley, feeling unwell. Gritting his teeth, he carried on and gave an afternoon lecture. By now he was running a temperature, and he admitted in a letter to his mother that this talk had not been up to his usual standard. Undaunted, he moved on to Baltimore, where he found Major Pond had attracted a mere five hundred people to a hall which could take five thousand. In spite of this he 'made a pleasant impression', according to the *Baltimore Sun*, before returning to Washington where he collapsed in Senator

Depew's house. After medical attention and a day of rest Churchill had recovered sufficiently by 16 December to take the night train to Boston.

In the spring of 1899 Churchill had become aware that there was an American author also named Winston Churchill. When the British Churchill began receiving congratulations on his skill as a writer of fiction, he thought at first that they arose from the serialisation of his novel *Savrola* in *Macmillan's Magazine* prior to its publication in New York and London. After he realised that there was another Churchill in the field, he wrote to his American namesake proposing that he would always sign himself Winston Spencer Churchill. He hoped that this would avoid confusion, and 'commend itself to Mr Winston Churchill'. It did, and when Churchill arrived in Boston on the morning of 17 December, Mr Winston Churchill came to the Hotel Touraine to greet him

Churchill's lecture that evening at Tremont Hall was perhaps the most successful of the entire tour. The *Boston Herald* thought the audience was one of the largest ever seen there, while the *Globe* spoke of the enthusiastic pro-British reception. The *Herald* gave a detailed appreciation of the lecture, noting that it provoked 'a running fire of laughter and applause'. The talk was followed by a dinner at the Somerset Club, where a group of young men, hosted by the American Winston Churchill, welcomed the British Churchill as their guest of honour. It was 'a merry party', according to the *Globe*. Confusion, however, persisted, and a packet of mail and the bill for dinner were cross-posted to the two Churchills, matters which were speedily rectified.

Considering the impact New York had made on Churchill five years earlier, it seems surprising that his letters say nothing of the changes which had since taken place there. During that interval New York had overtaken Paris to become second only to London as the most populous city on earth. It now teemed with immigrants, and although the outlying districts were still largely rural, the centre was already building upwards to relieve the pressure on land: the thirty-storey Park Row building was the world's tallest. Churchill may have been too concerned with his lecture tour to remark on such physical changes, but it was out of character for him not to comment on political developments. Municipal corruption, inevitably involving the Tammany Society, was under investigation. Mark Twain had written that the United States should have sent the Marines to occupy Tammany Hall rather than Cuba. Perhaps, as he had done in Cuba, Churchill reserved any critical opinions out of consideration for his hosts, many of whom would have belonged to the Tammany Society.

After Boston, lectures followed at New Bedford, Hartford, Springfield – where Churchill toured the famous small-arms factory – and Fall River, before he set out for his first visit to Canada. He was spending Christmas in Ottawa with the Governor General, Lord Minto, from whom he hoped to discover something about Canadian politics

In a letter to his mother, Churchill reported magnificent audiences for his lectures in Montreal, Ottawa and Toronto, but 'a most unpleasant squabble' with Major Pond over the meagre financial rewards. He had become increasingly irritated with Pond, whose management of the tour had left much to be desired. On arrival in Canada Churchill found that Pond had sold venues though local agents for less than a quarter of the amount that, in the event, was taken at the door. Pond's commission was 30 per cent, which, in the circumstances, Churchill thought unduly grasping.

Churchill's visit to Canada brought an exhausting and a

Second Lieutenant Winston
Churchill, 4th Hussars,
Bangalore, India, 1897.

Preparing for polo, India, 1897.

Lieutenant Churchill, South
African Light Horse, 1900.

Member of Parliament for Oldham, 1900.

Under-Secretary of State for the Colonies, in East Africa, 1907.

Having shot a white rhinoceros, 1907.

Golfing at Cannes with Maxine Elliot, 1913.

Visit to the Western Front as Minister of Munitions, 1917.

To General Pershing
with sincere regards. 1919

On his way to the Palace to receive the seals of
office as Chancellor of the Exchequer, 1924.

Secretary of State for War and Air, 1919.

Bathing at Deauville, 1927.

WSC hooks a 188-pound marlin off California, 1929.

With Charlie Chaplin, Hollywood, 1929.

Setting off for the United States with Clementine
and Diana, 1931.

Painting in the South of France, 1920s.

With President Roosevelt aboard HMS *Prince of Wales*, August 1941.

Travelling in Canada, December 1941.

Addressing the United States Congress, December 1941.

Christ Church, Alexandria, Virginia, 1 January 1942. Left to right: Rev. E.R. Welles II, Katrina Welles, Lord Halifax, WSC, Eleanor Roosevelt, Commander Thompson, President Roosevelt, naval aide, General Edwin Watson, Rev. Stewart Matthews.

With General Sir Claude Auchinleck, Western Desert, 1942.

Shooting match with American Generals Eisenhower (left) and Bradley, 1942.

financially disappointing tour to an end. The American tour brought him a profit of only £1600, whereas in England he had raised £3782. Nevertheless, it had been a broadening experience.

On 2 February 1901 Churchill sailed from New York on the *Etruria* for England. It was the day of the funeral of Queen Victoria, the first of the six monarchs that Churchill would serve in Parliament.

CHAPTER 3

Warrior and Writer

Youth seeks adventure. Journalism requires advertisement.
Certainly I had found both. I became for the time quite famous.
Winston Churchill, *My Early Life* (1930)

In January 1896 Churchill returned from Cuba to rejoin the
4th Hussars at Hounslow, just outside London. His fellow
officers were keenly anticipating the pleasures of India – polo,
pigsticking and many servants – which was where the regiment
was destined to sail for an eight-year posting later in the year.
Churchill, however, saw India as a political backwater which
he must avoid, and once again prevailed upon his mother to
use her influence with those who might divert him to more
interesting places. He wished to be posted, as he put it, 'to
scenes of adventure and excitement', and no doubt equally
important in his mind, 'to places where I could gain experience
and derive advantage'.

Having failed to obtain a more exciting posting, he sailed
for India on 11 September 1896. There, in the garrison of
Bangalore, he settled down to peacetime soldiering, alleviated
by a good deal of polo, much reading, for 'the desire for learning
came upon me', and Miss Pamela Plowden, the daughter of

the Resident of Hyderabad, the city's senior British official. Churchill met her at a polo tournament and wrote the following day to his mother, 'She is the most beautiful girl I have ever known . . . we are going to try to do the city of Hyderabad together on an elephant.' The love affair would continue for several years at the desultory pace dictated by Churchill's plans to win the fame and fortune he felt he needed to launch his political career. (Pamela would marry the Earl of Lytton in 1902, remain a lifelong friend of Churchill, and outlive him.)

In the summer of 1897 Churchill came home on leave. While he was enjoying the racing at Goodwood, news arrived of a tribal uprising on the North West Frontier of India, now Pakistan. An expedition, named the Malakand Field Force, had been formed to quell the rebellion, and the General appointed to command it was Sir Bindon Blood, who a year before had promised Churchill a place on his staff should such a situation arise. Abandoning his leave, Churchill took the next boat back to India, cabling the General to remind him of his promise. There was no immediate vacancy on the staff, but Blood suggested Churchill accompany the expedition as a press correspondent, in the hope that a vacancy might arise later. Having persuaded his Colonel to grant him leave, Churchill set off on the two-thousand-mile train journey from Bangalore to the area of operations. He was going as the war correspondent of the *Allahabad Pioneer*, and had an arrangement with the London *Daily Telegraph* to pay him £5* a column for his letters from the front.

During the next month he was involved in heavy fighting, having taken the place of an infantry officer who had been killed, but still he sent a total of fifteen dispatches to the *Daily*

---

* Roughly £250 in modern money.

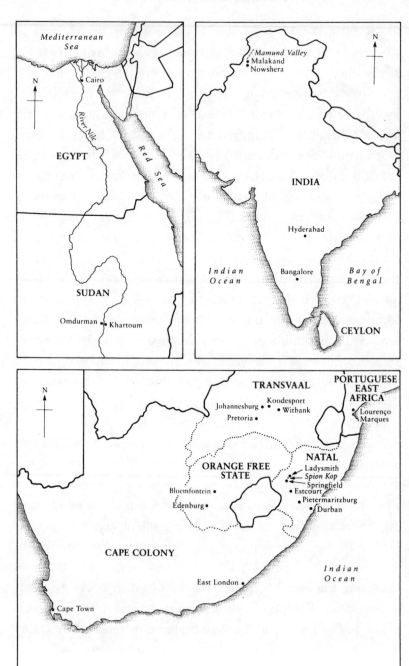

42

Telegraph. His letters home spared his mother none of the details which soldiers usually conceal from their loved ones:

> When the retirement began I remained until the last and here
> I was perhaps very near my end . . . I was close to both officers
> when they were hit and fired my revolver at a man at 30 yards
> who tried to cut up poor Hughes's body. Later on I used a rifle
> which a wounded man had dropped and fired 40 rounds at
> close quarters. I cannot be certain but I think I hit four men.
> At any rate they dropped.

There seems little doubt that he enjoyed the danger, writing to Lady Randolph on another occasion, 'Bullets are not worth considering. Besides I am so conceited I do not think the Gods would create so potent a being for so prosaic an ending.' By now he had enlisted his mother's help in negotiating better terms from the *Daily Telegraph*: 'When I think of the circumstances under wh those letters were written . . . I think they are cheap at the price.'

I followed my grandfather's footsteps from Nowshera, where his train ride from Bangalore ended, to Malakand and on into the Mamund Valley where he had engaged the tribesmen at close quarters. As my battered taxi rattled along the rough roads it seemed that not much had changed there since those days. The country is wild in the extreme, with valley walls rising steeply to four or five thousand feet all around. The rivers are fast-flowing, and the locals still often rely on rope bridges to link the tracks on either side. When my driver learned of my mission he took me to the only visible evidence of my grandfather's presence on the Frontier, and pointed to the word 'Churchill' picked out in white stones beside a hill-top fort known locally as Churchill Picket. I scrambled up to the derelict mud and stone building imagining my grandfather writing, by the light of a candle, his dispatches to the *Allahabad Pioneer* after a long day skirmishing with tribesmen.

Churchill was making the most of his opportunities. In a letter to his commander back in Bangalore, General Blood wrote: 'Young Winston Churchill will have told you I have been putting him in the way of seeing some really tough fighting . . . he is working away equal to two ordinary subalterns. He has been mentioned in dispatches already, and if he gets the chance will have a VC or DSO.' The citation for his mention in dispatches praised his 'courage and resolution'. The campaign over, Churchill returned to Bangalore, where in only five weeks he wrote his first book, *The Malakand Field Force*. Published in March 1898, it was widely recognised as a military classic, and earned its author some £30,000 in today's values.

A second expedition to the Frontier in early 1898 came to nothing, as negotiations brought peace, and Churchill returned to Bangalore. He began to lobby furiously, through his mother, for a place in Lord Kitchener's expedition to reconquer the Sudan, which had been overrun by the Mahdi, a Moslem fanatic whose Dervish forces had seized control of that vast territory, previously administered from British-occupied Egypt. The main stumbling block was Kitchener himself, who took exception to Churchill's attempts to manipulate the system to his own advantage. In later life, when young men asked to take part in active operations, Churchill brushed all objections aside, saying, 'After all they are only asking to stop a bullet. Let them have their way.' Kitchener took no such view, and Churchill only outflanked him by invoking the support of the Prime Minister, Lord Salisbury, when presenting him with a copy of *The Mala-kand Field Force* while on home leave. The military were not amused, and Churchill set off for Egypt having been officially warned that should he be killed or wounded, 'no charge of any kind will fall on British Army funds'. He had also been forbidden to write for the press, but had arranged to send dispatches to the *Morning Post* in the guise of letters ostensibly written to a friend.

Churchill joined the 21st Lancers in Cairo and travelled with them up the Nile to unite with Kitchener's forces a few miles short of Khartoum. We can imagine Kitchener's annoyance when, of all the young officers who might have been sent to reconnoitre the enemy positions, it was Churchill who cantered up to report. 'I saw the Union Jack beside the Egyptian flag,' he was to write many years later. 'Kitchener was riding two or three horses' lengths in front of his Headquarters Staff.' The report given, Churchill reined in his horse to let Kitchener's retinue pass, and heard a friendly voice inviting him to lunch. A row of biscuit boxes appeared. They were covered by white oilcloth, on which were placed 'many bottles of inviting appearance and large dishes of bully beef and pickles. Like a race luncheon before the Derby.'

The following day, 2 September 1898, saw the Battle of Omdurman, and the last ever British regimental cavalry charge. In a clash with thousands of massed Dervishes, 'ten or twelve deep at the thickest, a great grey mass gleaming with steel', Churchill survived unscathed, although in two minutes the regiment lost a quarter of its strength. Due to an injured shoulder he was wielding a pistol instead of the traditional cavalry sword. 'I saw the gleam of [a Dervish's] sword as he drew it back . . . I fired two shots into him at about two yards. I saw before me another figure with uplifted sword. I raised my pistol and fired. So close were we that the pistol actually struck him.' Churchill's book of the campaign, *The River War*, published a year later, was described in the *Daily Mail*'s review as 'an astonishing triumph', and would become the standard history.

By now Churchill had demonstrated that he could earn more by the pen than the sword. He returned to India for the specific purpose of playing in the all-India regimental polo tournament. Having helped the 4th Hussars to victory he resigned his commission in the army to pursue what had, from his days at Sandhurst, been his ultimate ambition: politics. In July 1899 he failed at his first attempt to become a Member of Parliament, being narrowly beaten in a by-election at Oldham. He would try again, but meanwhile the tussle in South Africa between British imperialism and Afrikaner nationalism had brought war over the horizon.

Now an established journalist and an experienced campaigner, Churchill was an obvious choice as a war correspondent. The *Morning Post* was the highest bidder for his services, offering £250 a month, all expenses paid, with the copyright of anything he wrote to remain with Churchill. Thus Churchill became by far the highest-paid war correspondent of the day.

In setting off in my grandfather's footsteps through South Africa, I expected my research to be mostly geographical, as it had been on the North West Frontier. How different South Africa was to prove. Like the North West Frontier, the countryside, at least in the battle areas, was still recognisable from Churchill's own descriptions. But this time the telephone began to ring within minutes of my television appeal for anyone to come forward whose parents or grandparents had been in any way involved with Churchill during his time in South Africa. As I travelled the country I was welcomed with open arms by the descendants of Churchill's friends and foes alike. They all enthusiastically recounted the stories they had heard at their grandparents' and, occasionally, their parents' knees. The result was my second book, *Churchill Wanted Dead or Alive* (1999).

My grandfather, having pulled every available string to ensure he would arrive in South Africa with access to both the most important people and the widest sources of information, sailed from Southampton Docks on the *Dunottar Castle* on 14 October. After calling at Madeira, the ship docked in Cape Town on 30 October. Within a few minutes Churchill learned that the main British forces in Natal had, that very day, been encircled in the town of Ladysmith. It seemed that there was an imminent danger of the Boers breaking though to Durban.

The *Dunottar Castle* was ultimately bound for Durban, but Churchill was too impatient to await its leisurely progress, and within a few hours had set off by rail towards the sound of gunfire. He skirted the Boer frontiers aboard the last train to get through to East London, where he caught an overnight coastal steamer to Durban. During the journey he wrote to his mother with an amazingly accurate forecast of the conflict ahead. It was quite at odds with the complacent opinion in London: 'A fierce and bloody struggle is before us in which at least ten or twelve thousand lives will be sacrificed.' In the event some twelve thousand British and Boers would die in action, and at least as many would succumb to disease.

From Durban Churchill pressed on by rail to Pietermaritzburg, where he hired a special train with the intention of getting to Ladysmith. However, the line had been cut by the Boers, and his journey ended forty miles short, at Estcourt, a small town of three hundred tin-roofed houses and the railhead of the British Army in Natal. Centre stage, in the station yard, he took over an empty bell tent in the middle of the engines' reversing triangle. Here he was joined by a school friend from his Harrow days, Leo Amery of *The Times*. Forty years on, Amery would join Churchill's wartime government.

A seasoned campaigner, Churchill was well aware of the soldier's maxim that any fool can be uncomfortable, and was accompanied by his valet Thomas Walden, who, having previously served Lord Randolph, was an experienced traveller. Churchill had also brought provisions to ease his life in the field. His contract with the *Morning Post* covered expenses, and we may assume that the newspaper paid for the supplies which Randolph Payne & Sons dispatched to accompany Churchill on the *Dunottar Castle:* a dozen and a half bottles of whisky, two dozen bottles of wine, half a dozen each of port, vermouth and eau de vie, and a dozen of lime juice. It was indicative of the traveller's rickety finances that the account for £28.18*s.*, dated 6 October 1899, included £10.18*s.* outstanding since 1895, and was not settled until 1 March 1901.

A century on, Estcourt has spilled much further into the surrounding hills than the small town of 1899, but a good deal of its former colonial character remains. There are still plenty of tin roofs. The Plough, still the local pub, is where the town's horse dealer discovered that he knew less about horses than his young customer. Another regular port of call for Churchill was Dr Brewett's Pharmacy, where he picked up the local gossip from the manager, Mr Tuffy Brickall. The building is still recognisable.

The stationmaster, Robert Clegg, writing in the *Estcourt Gazette* forty years after Churchill's stay, described the young man's daily excursions in a pony and trap to spy out the Boer positions: 'He wanted to know all about everything.' Clegg's grandson, Derek Clegg, told me a story well known in their family. Each evening, at the bar of the Plough or beside a campfire, Churchill would regale the company with stories of India, the North West Frontier and the Sudan. Clegg, the stationmaster, thought these very far-fetched, as each episode contained more excitement than most of the listeners would experience in a life-time. He roared with laughter when the bumptious young raconteur declared, 'Mark my words. I shall be Prime Minister of England one day.' Forty years later Clegg looked up from his newspaper and exclaimed to his daughter, 'By Jove, he's done it!'

One evening Churchill ran into an old friend from his days on the North West Frontier, Captain Aylmer Haldane. Haldane had been wounded in one of the early battles of the war, and was attached to the Dublin Fusiliers while waiting to rejoin his battalion, which was then cooped up in Ladysmith. He had just received orders from the officer commanding the Estcourt garrison, Colonel Charles Long, to take an armoured train on a reconnaissance, and knowing that Churchill had already been out on the train, Haldane invited his young friend to accompany him. Describing to his readers his previous sally on the train, Churchill had called it a 'locomotive disguised as a knight errant'; confined to a track, noisily announcing its approach, it was by no means as impressive as it looked. It invited ambush.

It was drizzling with rain when the train left Estcourt early on the morning of 15 November. At the front was a truck on which was mounted a small naval gun. Next came two steel-plated trucks carrying troops, then the locomotive and tender, followed by two more trucks full of troops and a breakdown wagon. Churchill was well aware that a more fatuous show of supposed strength by three officers, 115 men and five sailors could hardly have been devised. But he was out for news and adventure.

Reporting by telephone from the small stations along the route, Haldane was meant to await permission before crossing the ravine of the Blaaw Kranz river. But at this point Churchill obviously intervened, and the train steamed on at the very moment when Colonel Long would have ordered it to wait. Later Haldane recounted, 'Had I not had my impetuous young friend Churchill with me I might have thought twice before throwing myself into the lion's jaws.'

In company with the reconnaissance train driver's grandson Charles Wagner, who shares his grandfather's name, I visited the scene. The rails have been repositioned to lessen a curve in the line and allow the Johannesburg–Durban express to thunder through without hindrance, but the original line of the railway is still visible as a dirt track running along a low embankment and into a shallow cutting. Standing on this track, Wagner and I needed little imagination to visualise his grandfather putting on more steam when the Boers opened fire from the surround-ing hills, and the armoured train crashing into the boulders which had been placed on the line by the Boer commando Louis Botha, the future Prime Minister of South Africa.

We looked at old sepia photographs taken after the event, and imagined the scene early that morning in 1899. Iron trucks thrown at crazy angles. The troops taking cover in the wreck-age. The locomotive still on the rails but with the driver shelter-ing beneath. The young Winston Churchill, oblivious of the shrapnel shells bursting overhead and the bullets ricocheting from the trucks and whining into the distance, taking charge in order to clear the wreckage. 'No man is hit twice in the same day,' said Churchill to Wagner, who, heartened by this improbable assertion and the promise of a medal, wiped the blood from his head wound and climbed back into his cab. (More than ten years later, Churchill, then Home Secretary, was able to make good his promise by advising the King to award Wagner the Albert Medal, now displayed in a Durban museum.)

With the wreckage sufficiently cleared, the engine could head for home. Churchill ordered the wounded to be loaded aboard and, stationing himself in the cab, directed the driver back towards the Blaaw Kranz bridge and safety. Unwounded troops ran alongside, taking shelter from the rifle and shell fire which increased as the Boers saw their quarry escaping.

I was led by Charles Wagner to the spot, just short of the bridge, where our grandfathers had parted company. 'I can't leave those poor beggars to their fate,' Churchill had said before jumping down from the cab and running back along the line with the intention of shepherding the stragglers to safety. I could picture my grandfather running along the line looking for the men who, unbeknown to him, had already surrendered.

As I walked into the cutting, now somewhat shallower than in his day, and shaded by gum trees which in 1899 were alien to South Africa, I recalled Churchill's account in *My Early Life*. In my mind's eye I could see the platelayer's hut at the end of the cutting, and the two Boers who appeared from behind it came to life: 'tall figures, full of energy, clad in dark flapping clothes, with slouch, storm driven hats, poising on their levelled rifles'. The cutting must have seemed a death trap, and surrender inevitable to anyone but the young Churchill. Bullets sucked the air either side of him as he scrambled up the bank and headed towards Blaaw Kranz ravine.

I also scrambled breathless up the bank. Within sprinting distance I could see the ravine and the iron latticework of the bridge. I imagined the Boer field cornet galloping towards me, pulling up sharply a few yards away and levelling his rifle. In this situation surrender was the only sensible course, but Churchill reached for his pistol. He found he had left it on the locomotive.

This was to prove a blessing in disguise, for with only a pistol facing three rifles, Churchill would certainly have been gunned down. Surrender was now unavoidable.

In November 1999 I returned on the centenary of the ambush to take part in its re-enactment, this time accompanied by my thirteen-year-old son Alexander. He played the part of his great-grandfather, and was captured by a number of well-armed Boers. On this occasion I met the descendants of Sarel Oosthuisen, the field cornet who could have pulled the trigger while Churchill was discovering that his holster was empty. Both my grandfather and I were wounded at the scene of the ambush. He in the hand in 1899, while I have a constant reminder of the centenary in the shape of the scars from hot gunpowder and metal shards when a small cannon, which I had been invited to fire as part of the proceedings, backfired in my face.

After a two-day march and twenty-four hours on a train the captured Churchill and other British prisoners reached Pretoria, where Churchill was incarcerated in the States Model School. Having been opened as a boys' school two years earlier, it had been requisitioned on the outbreak of war to accommodate officer prisoners. Today it looks much the same as it did on the day when Churchill trudged along Skinner Street and turned left into Van der Walt Street before halting in front of the tall, arched entrance. A large, single-storeyed brick building with a high, steep, corrugated tin roof and a wide veranda, it was declared a national monument in 1963 and a new road diverted around it. The interior has been modified to accommodate the library it now contains, but the long central corridor remains, as do most of the dozen rooms which served as dormitories on either side.

The surroundings, however, are now quite different. A

bustling modern city crowds in on all sides. Today's busy dual carriageways and the intersection of Van der Walt and Skinner Streets can be seen from photographs to have been no more than dusty thoroughfares for pedestrians, riders, carriages and carts in 1899. Then the neighbourhood was more gracious, with scattered houses, bungalows, spacious gardens and willow trees.

The Churchill connection is well preserved within the school. On the wall of the room he shared with Haldane, who had also been captured, and others are maps, now under glass, which were drawn by a young officer, Lieutenant Frankland, to enable the occupants to keep track of the war.

Life for the prisoners was undoubtedly monotonous, but not excessively restricted, as I learned from Dr Jonathan de Souza, the grandson of the Transvaal Secretary for War within whose domain the prison fell. He befriended Churchill, who described him as 'a far seeing little man who had a clear conception of the relative strengths of Britain and the Transvaal'. De Souza brought important people to visit Churchill who, having handed round cigars, chaired political discussions. His wife Marie kept a diary written in English. I noticed one entry in which she described an occasion when her husband had taken Churchill a basket of fruit. This was followed by three exclamation marks. I was told these denoted that beneath the fruit was concealed a bottle of whisky, a beverage forbidden to the prisoners.

Churchill's breakout from the school on 12 December 1899 caused controversy which continues to this day. He planned to escape in the company of Haldane and a South African irregular, Lieutenant Brockie, but only he succeeded in climbing the fence unobserved. (In the course of my South African travels I was able to thank the son of one of the guards on duty for his father's short-sightedness!) Those seeking to denigrate Churchill have claimed that he deserted his comrades, but had Haldane and Brockie persevered in waiting for an opportunity to evade the sentries, they too might have got away.* As it was they broke for supper and the moment passed. Having waited in vain in the neighbouring garden for an hour, risking discovery, Churchill put on a slouch hat, adorned at the last moment with the colours of the Transvaal, and mingled with the evening crowds on Skinner Street.

He walked to the railway, resting briefly at a bridge over the Apies River, a dry watercourse awaiting the rains when I followed his footsteps past the adjacent electricity sub-station named 'Winston'. He waited in the bushes at the small station of Koodoesport, then leapt aboard a freight train travelling towards Portuguese East Africa (now Mozambique). After sleeping among coal sacks until just before daybreak, he jumped off for fear of discovery in a grassy valley, and laid up until sunset with the intention of boarding the next train. But no trains were running that night, and he walked along the line, making detours to avoid sentries at the numerous bridges, until, exhausted and soaked from fording streams and rivers, he saw what he thought were the fires of a Bantu *kraal*, where he might be given shelter. I followed the same route, and even from the comfort of the observation car of Rovos Rail I could appreciate why my grandfather had been exhausted enough to take such a risk.

The flames turned out to be the furnace of a coalmine at Witbank. Taking a chance, Churchill knocked on the door of the nearest house. His luck held. The door was opened by an Englishman, John Howard, the mine manager, who provided

---

* See *Churchill Wanted Dead or Alive*.

54

food and whisky while he decided what to do with the fugitive. As day broke Churchill was led to the mine shaft, down which he was to be hidden until his onward movement could be arranged. Under the winding wheel stood Daniel Dewsnap, the mine engineer, whose home town was Oldham, where Churchill had so narrowly failed at the by-election earlier that year. The three men hurtled into the depths where, in his own words reported to me by the mine engineer's grandson, Errol Dewsnap, Churchill's companions for the next few days were 'rats as big as cats'.

Unfortunately nothing remains of the Transvaal and Delagoa Bay Colliery, and my pilgrimage to Witbank was disappointing. Gum trees and long grass now wave over the spot where the winding wheel last turned in the early 1950s. A concrete slab covers the mine shaft down which my grandfather had 'shot into the bowels of the earth'. It seems very short-sighted that such a potential tourist attraction on the route to the Kruger National Park has been razed to the ground.

In his lodge on the edge of the National Park I stayed with Anthony Berlein, the grandson of the mine owner Julius Berlein. Over breakfast it was brought home to me just how lucky my grandfather had been in arriving at that particular colliery. Not only did he find himself among friends, but Julius Berlein, although a German, was staunchly pro-British. Had he been pro-Boer, like most Continental Europeans, Churchill would have found himself back in captivity.

A week after his escape from Pretoria, Churchill was put aboard a railway wagon, concealed in a consignment of wool which a local trader, Charles Burnham, was sending to Lourenço Marques (now Maputo). Provided with a revolver and two roast chickens, meat, bread, a melon and three bottles of cold tea, he settled into a cavity among the bales. As I travelled along the same route I imagined my grandfather peering through the chinks of his wagon at each of the many small stops, not to admire the scenic beauty as the line threads its way through the hills, but to gauge his chances of discovery as Boer soldiers loitered around the wagons. The wool trader's nephew, John Burnham, told me how his uncle also travelled on the train, telling the railway officials that the price of wool was falling and bribing them to keep his consignment moving.

Even so, the journey took forty-eight hours, and it was a very dishevelled Churchill who knocked on the door of the British Consulate in Lourenço Marques late in the afternoon on 23 December. The official who opened the door took the caller to be a seaman and told him to return in the morning. Churchill's reply is not known, but the tenor of it brought the Consul to an upstairs window, after which, Churchill reported, 'every resource of hospitality and welcome were placed at my disposal'.

He sailed that evening on a small coaster, the *Induna*, and arrived in Durban the following afternoon to a hero's welcome in a harbour decked with flags. Overnight, he had become a household name around the world. A speech was demanded and willingly provided. He was then hauled in a rickshaw to the town hall where he again addressed the crowds. At the Boer War centenary celebrations I was asked to read his speech from the same place. His message, 'We shall carry our policy to a successful conclusion,' sounded more like a declaration by the Commander-in-Chief than an impromptu remark by a young correspondent with absolutely no official status.

Wasting no time, Churchill caught the train from Durban that evening, spent the night with the Governor of Natal, Sir Walter Hely-Hutchinson, and on Christmas Eve was back with the army, his tent a few yards from where he had been captured less than six weeks before. General Sir Redvers Buller,

Commander-in-Chief of the British Army in South Africa, commissioned him as a lieutenant into the South African Light Horse, an irregular unit of colonials, gentlemen-rankers and regular British officers where, in his own words, Churchill 'lived from day to day in perfect happiness'. He continued to fulfil his lucrative contract with the *Morning Post*, taking no army pay in order to circumvent the new War Office edict that officers were not to write for newspapers, a regulation prompted by Churchill's columns from India and the Sudan.

The South African Light Horse, having no baggage train and living largely off the country, were able to range widely across Natal. How widely can be seen from the spread of the beautiful pink cosmos flower, a native of Argentina which was imported into South Africa in the British Army's horse fodder. Just as cairns on the battlefields mark where soldiers fell, so their route is marked by the pink swathes of cosmos. As my children picked bunches of these lovely flowers for me I wondered if the seeds from which they originated had germinated in the belly of my grandfather's horse as he had ridden that way.

Following him through the beautiful rolling country along the Tugela River, I learned that no one was more adept at living off the land than Lieutenant Churchill of the Cockyolibirds, as his regiment were known from the plumes of the sakabulu bird which adorned their slouch hats. My favourite tale of his foraging comes from a little town called Winterton, then named Springfield. I went there with Churchill's dispatch of 13 January 1900 fresh in mind: 'three houses, half a dozen farms with their tin roofs and tree clumps'. There are now more than three houses but, like the countryside around, the rural atmosphere is unchanged. At the end of a dusty lane I found the stone ruins of what a century ago was a tin-roofed farm shop with its backyard fenced off from the open country. Its shelves would

have supplied the neighbourhood with their everyday requirements, served across a wooden counter by the owner's young
daughter, Anna Beyers.

Lette Bennet told the story exactly as she had heard it. 'My
mother, Anna Beyers, was in my grandfather's shop at Springfield and remembered the day when she served Winston Churchill. He came trotting up the lane and tethered his horse outside
the shop. He bought candles and sardines. My mother could
not forget the way he lisped when he asked for sardines. He
then spotted the chickens in the yard and asked if he could buy
one. My mother replied, "Yes, if you can catch it."' Churchill
was not to be defeated by a bird, and a few minutes later he
rode off with 'candles, sardines and chicken'. To this day the
local inhabitants still proudly tell the story of the great British
bulldog chasing the chicken around the yard.

I stayed at the Spion Kop Lodge, a comfortable hotel built
astride what was the old Boer wagon trail during the Great
Trek. It is as near as one can judge to where Churchill bivouacked before the Battle of Spion Kop, the day during which,
in the words of the historian Thomas Pakenham, he became a
'self-appointed messenger . . . instinctively taking over the role
of general'. In places over-grazing has encouraged bush and
aloe trees to obscure the view, particularly on Mount Alice,
a few hundred yards from the Lodge, where General Buller
established his headquarters for the battle. And the Tugela Dam
has flooded what in Churchill's time were the fords across the
river. Otherwise, the country has not changed much since then,
and the Lodge has a magnificent view across the Tugela to the
massive feature of Spion Kop – Spy Hill – six miles away, and
the adjacent features which played a part in the battle. The
tourist can perfectly appreciate the events of 24 January 1900
which etched Spion Kop into British regimental histories.

This is not the place to re-enact the battle, which was intended to open the way to the beleaguered British garrison in Ladysmith, and in which Churchill involved himself late in the afternoon. From Mount Alice, where he had positioned himself close to Buller's headquarters, he could see the British were faring badly. Like Buller and his staff he wondered what was happening. Standing on the spot from which Buller had impotently observed the 'acre of massacre six miles away', I could imagine an impatient Churchill swinging himself into the saddle and cantering down the slope towards the sound and sights of gunfire. Crossing the Tugela, he tethered his horse at the foot of Spion Kop and climbed to the summit.

His dispatch to the *Morning Post* described the scene: 'Men were staggering along alone, or supported by comrades, crawling on hands and knees, or carried on stretchers. Corpses lay here and there. Stray bullets struck all over the ground, while the Maxim shells scourged the flanks of the hill and sheltering infantry at regular intervals of a minute.'

I scrambled with my young son up the track which his great-grandfather had climbed a century before. Under a dramatic grey, lowering sky I surveyed the terrain through which Churchill had crawled under shot and shell. The main British trench, which photographs taken immediately after the battle show was piled with dead, is marked by a long, curved mound surrounded by white stones. It is the mass grave of those who died defending it. Monuments to regiments and individuals stand silhouetted against the sky.

In spite of the carnage it was clear to Churchill that the British could and should prevail. He descended the hill to the knoll, still called Three Tree Hill, where General Sir Charles Warren, commanding the troops involved on the summit, had remained with his staff all day. Carrying Warren's instructions,

Churchill climbed again to the top, this time in darkness. By the time he had reached it the Colonel in command at the summit had had enough. A brave man, he had been on the go for twenty-four hours, having assumed command when his superiors were killed, and had been in the thick of close-quarter battle since daybreak. Physically and mentally exhausted, he gave the order to abandon the position. Churchill found his way back to General Warren, and found him asleep. Years later he recounted, 'I put my hand on his shoulder . . . He took it all very calmly. He was a charming old gentleman. I was genuinely sorry for him. I was also sorry for the army.' Had any of the generals, from Buller down, shown a fraction of Churchill's resolution the British would undoubtedly have won the day.

When Ladysmith was eventually relieved on 27 February, Churchill was once more at the centre of events. Following his footsteps I was guided by Pitch Christopher, a local historian and long-established resident of Ladysmith. We traced my grandfather's progress from where he had forded the brown waters of the Klip River to the Christophers' house, Budleigh, where on the night of the relief of Ladysmith the young officer attended a grand dinner for the senior officers. The colonial-style house, with its wide verandas, is virtually unchanged since that day, and sitting in the dining room where my grandfather had sat a century before, I could almost hear the popping of champagne bottles carefully preserved throughout the siege.

In the Ladysmith Siege Museum I came across the diary of Lieutenant Colonel Martin, who had recorded meeting Churchill. 'He wore the slouch hat with the Sakabulu feathers . . . he told me he was Winston Churchill, and that he was a war correspondent attached to the South African Light Horse.' In spite of the dangers which he constantly courted as a lieutenant of cavalry, Churchill evidently considered himself a correspondent first and a soldier second.

With the campaign in Natal virtually over, attention was now focused on the British advance under Field Marshal Lord Roberts through the Orange Free State and the Transvaal, with Pretoria as its ultimate objective. Taking leave from the South African Light Horse, Churchill set off by rail and sea to join this campaign. En route he spent a few days in the newly opened Mount Nelson Hotel in Cape Town, where he found 'more colonels to the acre than in any place outside the United States'. The world and his wife seemed to be staying at the hotel, 'particularly the wife', and there was 'luxury but no comfort'. These days the visitor will find both luxury and comfort in plenty. The surroundings, palm trees and gardens, echo those at the turn of the century, but without the irritations – too many colonels and 'too much shoddy worn' – to which Churchill introduced the readers of the *Morning Post*.

Equipped with wagon and horses, Churchill took the train to Edenburg, fifty miles south of Bloemfontein, and then trekked for a couple of days to join an acquaintance from his days in the Sudan: General Sir Leslie Rundle, whom Churchill called Sir Leisurely Trundle. It was not long before the war correspondent, out for copy, was again in trouble. A party of the locally raised Montmorency's Scouts set out to capture a hill, the commander saying to Churchill, 'Come on, we'll give you a show.'

Writing his dispatch that same evening, Churchill recorded, 'So in the interests of the *Morning Post* we all started.' The Boers beat them to it, and in the ensuing scramble Churchill's horse bolted, and he was dismounted. For the second time he had to flee from Boer riflemen. Fortunately a lone scout, Trooper Clement Roberts, came galloping past, and Churchill clambered into the saddle behind him. 'I had thrown double sixes again,' he wrote in a letter home.

I called on Trooper Roberts' daughter, Doris Maud, in Durban. She showed me a letter my grandfather had sent to her father: 'I have always felt that unless you had taken me up on your saddle I should myself have been certainly killed or captured.' She also showed me her father's Distinguished Service Medal, received as a result of Churchill's recommendation six years later when he learned that the brave action by Roberts had gone unrewarded.

At the beginning of May Churchill joined General Ian Hamilton, another friend from earlier campaigns, for the advance on Johannesburg and Pretoria. He was accompanied by his cousin, the 9th Duke of Marlborough, who had arrived in South Africa with the Imperial Yeomanry. They set off in Churchill's wagon, which had beneath its floorboards 'the best tinned provisions and alcoholic stimulants London could supply'. At Winburg they caught up with Hamilton, and by 1 June were on the outskirts of Johannesburg.

I was unable to follow my grandfather's footsteps through the Transvaal as I had done in Natal; the campaign was too fast-moving for him to have left his mark as it advanced. Disappointingly, I could not trace his one notable exploit, a cycle ride in civilian clothes through the Boer-occupied Johannesburg to carry a dispatch from Hamilton to Lord Roberts. The city has spread and changed beyond any recognition. There was no chance of identifying the road along which he rode, speaking French – no doubt his usual Churchillian version – when a Boer horseman reined in to a walk alongside him. It would have been somewhere between what is now the sprawling township of Soweto and the city centre. The hotel where my grandfather stopped for dinner probably no longer exists.

On 5 June, when Pretoria fell, all the key Boer centres were now in British hands, and Churchill knew that the war would turn into a guerrilla campaign. His exploits had been to the mutual benefit of his country and himself, and with a general election looming at home, he could see little point in staying any longer in South Africa. He remained for one more adventure, just east of Pretoria. General Hamilton, in his memoirs *Listening for the Drums*, explained how 'Winston gave the embattled hosts at Diamond Hill an exhibition of conspicuous gallantry . . . He ensconced himself in a niche not much more than a pistol shot below the Boers . . . Winston had the nerve to signal me . . . with his handkerchief on a stick . . . that we ought to be able to rush the summit.' No doubt Hamilton used the words 'conspicuous gallantry' because it was the language of citations for the Victoria Cross, and after the battle he made persistent efforts to achieve some recognition of Churchill's 'initiative and daring'. But the military establishment were unlikely to give a medal to the bumptious young man who, as a lieutenant, had consistently outperformed them, and who, as a correspondent, had justifiably criticised them.

Churchill now 'resumed his full civilian status' and set off by rail for Cape Town. The train stopped with a jolt a hundred miles south of Johannesburg while he was breakfasting. Running along the track he learned there was an ambush ahead, and not wishing to repeat his experience of the previous November, he again climbed into a locomotive cab in order to direct the driver. The train was reversed to the sanctuary of a fortified camp, but not before some armed Boers appeared. Churchill fitted the wooden stock to his Mauser pistol and sent them scattering, thinking this would be the last occasion on which he would see bullets fired in anger. Thirty years later he would write, 'This expectation, however, proved unfounded.'

The *Dunottar Castle* docked at Southampton with Churchill aboard on 20 July 1900. He would never again visit South Africa, although he never entirely lost touch with it. In 1907, as Minister for the Colonies, he co-operated with Prime Minister Louis Botha, whose commando had captured him in 1899, in the granting of self-government to Transvaal and the Orange Free State. The two men sat together in the Imperial War Cabinet during the First World War. In 1955, on the occasion of Pretoria's centenary, Churchill wrote, 'It is my privilege, as one not unacquainted with Pretoria's hospitality, to offer the city my heartiest congratulations.' He also maintained a lifelong friendship with Jan Christiaan Smuts, who in 1899, as the Transvaal Attorney-General, had glimpsed him at the time of his capture and advised that he should not be released. Field Marshal Smuts followed Botha as Prime Minister of South Africa, and co-operated with Churchill on the world stage during the two World Wars and after.

It is strange that Churchill never returned to the country where he experienced a real-life *Boy's Own* dream – or, as the film director Robert Young put it, played the role of James Bond a hundred years ago. Churchill was almost ninety when, on 10 October 1964, Estcourt awarded him the freedom of the borough. Had they offered it before he was so old and frail he might have taken delight in returning to receive it. Estcourt does however have the distinction of being the only place in the Southern Hemisphere to have honoured Winston Churchill in this way.

CHAPTER 4

Jungle, Bush and Thankless Deserts

I shall enjoy so much showing you around some of the places I know so well.
Letter, Winston Churchill to Clementine,
21 February 1921

By 1904 Churchill found himself increasingly at odds with the instincts of the Conservative Party. In May that year he joined the Liberals, and in December 1905, when they became the governing party, he was appointed Under-Secretary for the Colonies. He was just thirty-one. He had been offered a position in the Treasury, an appointment usually considered a stepping stone to the Cabinet, and had some difficulty in persuading the Prime Minister, Sir Henry Campbell-Bannerman, to send him to the Colonial Office instead, as it involved shuffling people in other jobs.

Churchill was well fitted for the Colonial Office, his service in India, Egypt, the Sudan and South Africa having given him a feel for colonial matters. However, that was not the reason for his choice. At this stage in his political career he was seeking prominence rather than ministerial rank. The Colonial Secretary under whom he would work, Lord Elgin, preferred a leisurely life in Scotland to his department in London, and as he sat in the House of Lords he would necessarily have to leave his junior minister very largely in charge of his important department. It would be Churchill who conducted the important parliamentary business, acting well above the usual level of an Under-Secretary.

For the next eighteen months issues concerned with South Africa occupied a large part of Churchill's ministerial attention. Responsible self-government was established in the Transvaal and the Orange Free State. Then, in April 1907, a conference in London brought together all the colonial prime ministers, after which Churchill decided to tour East Africa. The Prime Minister, with Churchill's recent workload in mind, begged him to 'mind his health' and not 'over do it'. But few expected that the tour would be anything other than a working holiday.

The visiting prime ministers had included Transvaal's General Louis Botha, whose commando had captured Churchill in 1899 and who now became a close friend of his former captive. Botha was accompanied by his nineteen-year-old daughter Helen. Vivacious, pretty and well educated, she was already the toast of several European courts, and while in London would catch the eye of King Edward VII. Churchill saw a good deal of Botha – and, judging by the rumours of the time, at least as much of Helen. However, he was free of romantic entanglement when he left for East Africa in October 1907.

Living more by his pen than his ministerial salary, Churchill contracted to write a series of articles for the *Strand Magazine*. These were expanded into a book, *My African Journey*, published in 1908. In it Churchill describes his first view of the capital of British East Africa: 'The aspect of Mombasa as she rises from the sea and clothes herself with form and colour at the swift approach of the ship is alluring and even delicious.' The reader

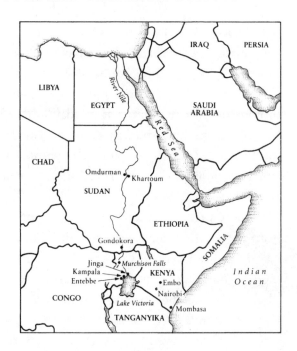

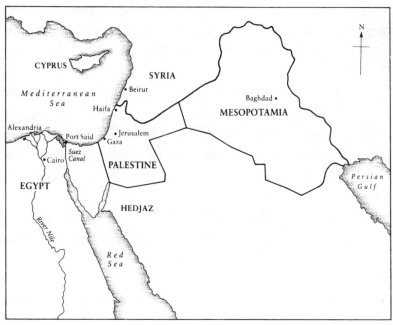

is then led over the route by which the author arrived. 'To appreciate these charms the traveller should come from the North . . . see the hot stones of Malta . . . visit the Island of Cyprus before the autumn rains have revived the soil . . . He should walk for two hours at midday in the streets of Port Said . . . thread the long red furrow of the Suez Canal, and swelter through the Red Sea . . . pass a day among the cinders of Aden and a week among the scorched rocks and stones of Northern Somaliland.'

By now streams of memoranda on action to be taken resulting from the journey so far were reaching London. The senior civil servant at the Colonial Office, Sir Francis Hopwood, resented these precursors of Churchill's wartime 'ACTION THIS DAY' labels which kept essential business moving briskly along. Hopwood suggested to Lord Elgin that the Under-Secretary should have 'reserved his points until he returned home – anybody else would have done so both out of caution or at the dictation of personal convenience'. With a touch of malice he passed on the fact that Eddie Marsh, Churchill's Private Secretary, had given 'a vivid description of 14 hours work in one day upon these memoranda in the heat & discomfort of the Red Sea'. (Marsh would have been applauding rather than complaining about what had been achieved; he became Churchill's lifelong companion and remained his Private Secretary for twenty-four years, except for two breaks each of two years when Churchill was out of office.)

From Mombasa Churchill set off up country through what is now Kenya. *My African Journey* gives a vivid and sometimes exciting picture of Africa and the author's progress. It is also instructive, as befits Churchill's instincts as an itinerant politician. Thus, when describing the high standards of the Uganda Railway, the train which 'rolls along as evenly as upon a

European line', he reassures the public at home of its commercial value. They read that although built solely to 'secure British predominance on the Upper Nile . . . there is already a substantial profit of nearly eighty thousand pounds a year'.*

His letters, written as he travelled, provide a more spontaneous and lively account. Writing to his mother he regrets that there is no time to give her 'full accounts of all this most interesting journey. But my days are occupied literally from sunrise till bed either in shooting and travelling or else on official work wh presses upon me from every side.' The commercial value of the Uganda railway is passed over in favour of its comfort: 'dining & sleeping cars at my disposal all the way, whenever I wished it to stop – it stopped . . . We sat on the front of the engine with our rifles & as soon as we saw anything to shoot at – a wave of the hand brought the train to a standstill . . . From the railway one can see literally every kind of animal in the Zoo.'

A rhinoceros is seen grazing a quarter of a mile away, 'a grim black silhouette of this mighty beast – a survival of prehistoric times – roaming the plain as he & his forerunners had done since the dawn of the world . . . We started to sally out against Behemoth.' Two more were seen close at hand. Churchill fired at the biggest, 'with a heavy 450 rifle & hit her plumb in the chest. She swerved round & came straight for us at that curious brisk trot which is nearly as fast a horse's gallop, & full of surprising activity. Everyone fired & both the rhino turned off – much to our relief, and then in a few more seconds down came the big one . . . You cannot resist a feeling that they are invulnerable & will trample you under foot however well you shoot. However all's well that ends well.'

The letter is continued four days later. Churchill had now

---

* £4 million in present-day money.

left the train: 'All the time I have been moving about so fast, hunting lions, visiting stations, receiving native chiefs & riding through the country, and have been jolly glad to sleep in my clothes at the end of the day. The lion hunting was nervous work especially beforehand – until one had familiarised oneself with the idea.' Three days before there had been a 'great Durbar of natives: 4000 – with all the chiefs stark naked in all essentials, – and in their full war toggery – they & women all dancing together & chanting incurious rhythms from daybreak on'. Among the presents Churchill received were 108 sheep and seven bulls, which he explained would be sold by the government, and in return the chiefs would receive presents of greater value. He 'also made a speech wh comforted their anxious hearts'. Why 'anxious', he did not say.

Churchill was so taken with the country that he changed his plans. 'So we chucked much kit and other petty arrangements to the winds . . . Embo is a new station opened only last year in hitherto unpenetrated country. The two white officers there were properly astonished to see us swoop down upon them for the night. But they gave us a most excellent dinner & we all slept on floors & chairs & blankets utterly but naturally tired. What a difference to the fag of London day.' Churchill thought the country richer than any he had seen in India or South Africa, and on arrival in Nairobi he told 'the Governor he may now advance further into the country and establish a new station . . . beyond Embo. This will bring 15,000 natives under our direct control & add several English counties to our administration area. We do not propose to consult the Colonial Office till it is an accomplished fact. Thus the Empire grows.'

In the Highlands of East Africa Churchill pondered the question of racial tensions in the region many years before they actually arose. A whole chapter of *My African Journey* is devoted to the subject. In the first paragraph he concludes that the strident tones of the Colonists' Association are misplaced. He judges their cry, 'We mean to make East Africa a white man's country,' to be no more than a futile wish, for the white man had not left Europe in order to undertake the harsh toil of the land himself. Rather the Europeans saw themselves as the commanders of an army of indigenous private soldiers. 'Yet hear the other side,' writes Churchill. What of the Indians who were there long before any British official? They may count as many generations of useful industry in East Africa as the white settler has years, and their industry and thrift enable them to out-perform economically the white professional classes – bankers, engineers, contractors, overseers, accountants and clerks. It is not easy to measure the degree of 'political instability that will be introduced'. And what of the African, asks Churchill, 'Rich in that he lacks everything and wants nothing?'

Churchill's solutions may betray his Victorian origins, but he gave deeper thought to these problems than was usual in those times: 'I am clearly of opinion that no man has a right to be idle. He is bound to go forward and take an honest share in the general work of the world. And I do not except the African native.' He eulogises the 'disciplined soldiers of the King's African Rifles' and 'the smart sailors of the Uganda Marine', who he contrasts with 'the population from which they have emerged. Just and honourable discipline, careful education, sympathetic comprehension, are all that are needed to bring a very large proportion [of the indigenous population] to a far higher social level than that at which they now stand. And why should men only be taught to be soldiers? Cannot peaceful industry be made as attractive?'

After a dozen pages Churchill acknowledges that the reader 'will have had as much of East African politics as I had, when after three days of deputations and disputations, the train steamed out of Nairobi to take us to the Great Lake and beyond'. Winding his way by the Ugandan Railway he observed the ceaseless activity needed to keep back the jungle. If the track had been neglected for a year 'it would take an expedition to discover where it had run'. In order for Churchill to be able to appreciate virgin tropical forest, the railway's English contractor arranged for a leafy tunnel, a mile and a half long, to be cut across a loop in the line. The abundance of manual labour required led Churchill to ruminate on the economics of the logging industry. He told his readers that the engine was fuelled by wood cut from the forest by a 'floating population of workers' with 'choppers more like a toy hoe than an axe', and carried a quarter-mile on their heads to the wood stack. He suggested a mechanical alternative which in a single day would accomplish the equivalent of a week's work by sixty-five men. It was 'no good trying to lay hold of Tropical Africa with naked fingers'.

Arriving at Lake Victoria, Churchill embarked on a steamer for Entebbe. It is not surprising that Churchill was more impressed by Uganda – subsequently described by many as the Jewel of Africa – than by any other colony. He wrote to King Edward VII describing both its delights and dangers, the beauty and the sleeping sickness which between 1901 and 1906 killed at least two hundred thousand people. Half a dozen pages of *My African Journey* are devoted to the scourge of this disease, the tsetse fly which transmits it, and other ailments: 'Uganda is defended by its insects.' Churchill had no doubt that 'order and science would conquer', and that John Bull would be 'master in his curious garden of sunshine and deadly nightshade'.

The twenty-four-mile journey from the ancient capital of Entebbe, on the shores of Lake Victoria, to the administrative capital at Kampala was by a procession of rickshaws carrying Churchill, the Governor of Uganda Sir H. Hesketh Bell, and their respective entourages. Each rickshaw was pulled by one man between the shafts and pushed from behind by three more, the whole team being relieved every eight miles. The journey took four hours, and three miles from their destination people lined the road to welcome the procession, which eventually halted before a hillock on which stood a pavilion of elephant grass. From this the Kabaka, the King of Uganda, at that time a boy of eleven, descended to welcome Churchill. Around him were various officials, including the Prime Minister, Sir Apolo Kagwar, dressed in a crimson robe displaying the Order of St Michael and St George, British campaign medals and many other decorations.

Churchill, a paternalistic Victorian, was charmed by the Kabaka and the Buganda people. In *My African Journey* he described with obvious approval the 'three separate influences, each of them powerful and benevolent', which exercised control of the nation. First was the Imperial authority, 'secular, scientific, disinterested, irresistible'. Second came 'a native Government and feudal aristocracy, corrected of their abuses, yet preserving their vitality'. Thirdly, there was a 'missionary enterprise on an almost unequalled scale'. In the heart of Africa, Uganda seemed an 'island of gentle manners and peaceful civilisation' amid barbarism, violence and squalor. On his return to Britain Churchill would receive a beautifully written letter from the young Kabaka:

Dear Mr Winston Churchill,

I have sent the pictures which you asked me to send them to you. I have sent two pictures of me; and the others ones are the men which you saw the day when you came to see me. I am quite well, and I hope you are quite well too. Our football are going on very nicely, and the other day the Budu boys came to play football with my boys, and we beat them, but they are learning more. The words on the fortographs mean I am your friend.

I am your friend
DAUDI CHWA

At Jinja the Ripon Falls impressed Churchill not only as an impressive spectacle but also as a potential source of hydro-electric power. Almost half a century later Queen Elizabeth II, on inaugurating the Owen Falls Scheme, as it became known, telegraphed Churchill, then Prime Minister, 'Your vision has become a reality.'

From Kampala there followed twenty days' travelling on safari, partly on foot and partly by boat, to Gondokoro, on the River Nile eight hundred miles south of Khartoum. The progress on land was limited by the speed and endurance of the porters. Once again the reader of *My African Journey* is treated to the author's ideas on improving communications. Bicycles and a 'system of stone, fumigated, insect-proof rest-houses at stages of thirty miles along the main lines of communication would mean an enormous saving in the health of white officials and a valuable accession to their powers'. Had Churchill known more about the country before going to Uganda he would have sent porters in advance to establish camps, and trebled the area he was able to visit. As it was he covered about twelve miles a day, intoning 'Sofari so goody' at the end of each day's march. The reader, in the comfort of his English house, read of odious worms, painful to the feet, scorpions which lurked in boots abandoned for the night, snakes and 'a perfectly frightful kind of centipede', and the 'admirable prophylactic', quinine.

Plans were changed as Churchill became captivated by diversions en route. When he learned of the wonder of the Murchison Falls, runners were dispatched to the nearest telegraph offices, and messages flashed back to Kampala and relayed to the flotilla waiting further on, instructing it should steam to the foot of the falls. Face to face with them, Churchill prophesied that the day would come when the sparsely inhabited region would 'throb with the machinery of manufacture and electric production'.

After pausing for several days' big-game hunting, the safari and the writ of the Colonial Office ended at Gondokoro, an imposing name on the maps of the day, but in fact no more than half a dozen houses, a telegraph station, courthouse and prison, and the lines of the King's African Rifles. Beyond Gondokoro lay the 'domain of that undefined joint authority which regulates the Soudan, which flies two flags side by side on every public building, and which you can only correspond with through the British Foreign Office'. Although Churchill was now returning home by the quickest route, he still had a long way to go. He had followed the River Nile from its source for almost five hundred miles and still had a similar distance to travel before reaching Khartoum, in the heart of the Sudan, and a further twelve hundred miles to Alexandria, where he would embark for Europe. However, he was travelling in comfort by steamer and rail, and 'could not traverse the Soudan without the keenest interest'. The reader of *My African Journey* learns that 'Uganda is the pearl. We leave the regions of abundant rainfall, of Equatorial luxuriance, of docile peoples, of gorgeous birds and butterflies and flowers. We enter stern realms of sinister and forbidding aspect.'

No doubt Churchill had in mind his previous excursion into these realms when, nine years before, he had charged with the

21st Lancers at Omdurman. However, much had changed for the better since then, as 'nowhere presented in so striking and impressive a form than in the capital'. Yet none of this was to prevent Churchill 'taking away a sombre impression of Khartoum'. His manservant, George Scrivings, was suddenly taken ill with cholera, and died after only fifteen hours. In a letter to his mother, Churchill remarked that he always seemed to follow funerals at Khartoum.

Churchill had been away for five months when he arrived back in London on 17 January 1908. Like most of his travels the journey had been an enjoyable adventure, although, judged by Sir Francis Hopwood's complaints to Lord Elgin, there had been a good deal of work done. But it was work in a minor key, concerning low-level colonial administration. Churchill's next visit, to the Near East, would see major historical achievements on an international stage.

In the meantime he would rise through the Cabinet, first becoming President of the Board of Trade, then Home Secretary, then First Lord of the Admiralty, the political head of the most powerful navy in the world, a position he occupied at the outbreak of World War One. As First Lord he conceived the ill-fated Dardanelles campaign for which he became the scapegoat when, mismanaged by the War Cabinet at home and indifferently led by commanders on the spot, it went wrong. Following this, the greatest political disaster of his public life, he went off to command a battalion in the trenches, returning to end the war as Minister for Munitions.*

At the end of World War I the British Army was occupying large areas of what had been the Turkish empire. These included

---

* For more on this period of Churchill's life, see Chapter 7.

Palestine and Mesopotamia, both of which were to be mandated to Britain by the League of Nations. In January 1919 Churchill became Secretary of State for War and Air, and upon him fell the task of maintaining the armies of occupation, a financial burden the British government was keen to reduce. Withdrawal of troops and reduction in expense was hindered by an Arab revolt in Mesopotamia. Churchill as usual had ideas, but his attempts to influence government policy were frustrated by three other departments of state, the Foreign Office, Colonial Office and India Office, all of which had political and administrative responsibilities in the territories in question.

Thus, by the beginning of 1921 Churchill found himself in charge of a War Office with no war, committed to economies he could not realise, policies with which he disagreed, no outlet for his constructive talents and no challenge to his administrative skills. His demobilisation programme following the end of the war had been a considerable triumph, but it was not enough for him. The revolt in Mesopotamia was involving thirty-five thousand British and Indian troops, and Churchill felt he needed a change from what he called 'these thankless deserts'.

On the last day of 1920, at Churchill's suggestion, the Cabinet decided to set up a Middle East Department within the Colonial Office, to concentrate within a single department the existing divided responsibilities of the War Office, the Foreign Office, the Colonial Office and the India Office. The Colonial Secretary, Lord Milner, wanted no part of these increased and heavy responsibilities, and resigned. Not surprisingly, Churchill was appointed in his place, but before accepting the post he moved to ensure that the job specification was to his liking. Writing to the Prime Minister, Lloyd George, he set out his requirements. 'It is absolutely necessary,' he wrote, 'for me to have effective control of the general policy and all orders sent by the

War Office should be in general accordance with the policy I am pursuing.' The Prime Minister agreed, but it was not until 15 February 1921 that Churchill received the seals of his new office and was formally appointed Colonial Secretary.

He decided to settle the future shape of the Middle East by means of a conference of all interested parties in Cairo, and planned to leave London for Egypt on the evening of 1 March. Travelling by train across France, he was joined by his wife Clementine at Marseilles.* On holiday in France, she had suggested accompanying him to Cairo. Delighted, he had replied: 'The *Sphinx* is a beautiful ship and we have excellent accommodation on board. I am travelling at the Government's expense but I shall of course pay everything which is on account of you. The people in Egypt are getting excited at my coming, as they seem to think it has something to do with them. This is, of course, all wrong.' He then struck a warning note, surely unnecessary to anyone who knew him, that he would be very busy, but added: 'I shall so much enjoy showing you around some of the places I know so well.'

For a couple who were happily married for fifty-seven years, the Churchills would spend a good deal of time apart. Churchill travelled not to rest or to sightsee or for cultural enlightenment, but for a change of environment and to meet important people. Clementine enjoyed cruising and sightseeing. Although she was energetic, her health was by no means robust, and she would also go abroad for health cures. Alternatively, she would benefit from a less exhausting regime at home while her husband was away travelling.

The Cairo Conference opened on 12 March 1921. Not only

---

* In 1908 Churchill had married Clementine Hozier, the daughter of Lady Blanche Hozier and Colonel Sir Henry Montagu Hozier.

would the participants need to be persuaded of the decisions arrived at, but these would still need to be agreed by the British Cabinet and ratified by a vote in Parliament. So there were many opinions for Churchill to take into account. Not the least of the difficulties on the parliamentary horizon was the fact that, on the question of Palestine, nine-tenths of British political and military opinion supported the Arabs rather than the Jewish demand for a homeland. Nevertheless, within a week a great deal was achieved. The foundations of Israel, Jordan and Iraq – though not then with those names – were laid.

While Churchill and his officials were hard at work, life for the wives back at the Semiramis Hotel had been less entertaining. Jessie Crosland, the wife of the War Office Director of Finance Joseph Crosland, recalled: 'When things were boring in the hotel everyone would cheer up when Winston came in, followed by an Arab carrying a pail and a bottle of wine.' She continued: 'He was unpopular with the Egyptians but he didn't care. He took his easel out and sat in the road painting – he also talked quite loudly in the street and the generals got quite nervous.' One day his party, which included Clementine and T.E. Lawrence, rode by camel to the pyramids. When the others left by car for their hotel Churchill stayed behind to paint. Lawrence, his adviser on Arabian affairs, remained with him, and the pair then returned by camel. The painting is very evocative of how the area must then have been – magnificent ancient monuments in a hot, empty space, not swarming with tourists as it is now.

From Cairo the Churchills went by rail to Jerusalem. Arriving at Gaza, the first railway station in Palestine, Churchill was met by the High Commissioner, Sir Herbert Samuel, and a police guard of honour. Also on hand was a howling mob shouting in Arabic 'Cheers for the Minister!' and 'Cheers for Great

Britain!' But even more frenzied were their cries of 'Down with the Jews!' and 'Cut their throats!' Churchill's ADC reported that his master and Sir Herbert were delighted with the reception, being quite unaware of its anti-Zionist nature.

The following day there were demonstrations in Haifa, resulting in the death of a Christian boy and a Muslim woman. These were ill omens for the future. Planting a tree at the still uncompleted Hebrew University in Jerusalem, Churchill declared: 'I believe the establishment of a Jewish National Home will be a blessing to the whole world.' The disturbances, which continued during the following months, were described by Churchill as an attempt to frighten him out of his even-handed policies – which seemed to have got the balance right, as they provoked equal protests from both Arabs and Jews.

Having set the stage, Churchill would spend the rest of his life, more than forty years, playing only an indirect role in the evolution of Israel and the conflict between Arab and Jew. But it was a process which he observed at first hand. In the summer of 1934 he and Clementine cruised in the Near East in Lord Moyne's yacht the *Rosaura*, going ashore in Beirut and driving through Palestine and Transjordan before rejoining the yacht at Alexandria. Lord Moyne was a friend of Churchill, and former Financial Treasurer to the Treasury. During this holiday Churchill steered clear of political involvement in the area, keeping busy with the third volume of his biography of his ancestor the 1st Duke of Marlborough, the early stages of *A History of the English Speaking Peoples*, a projected film script of the life of George V for the film producer Alexander Korda, and painting.

In 1952, addressing the United States Congress, Churchill first paid tribute to the achievements of those who had founded the Israeli state in 1947. He then went on to speak of possible future difficulties: 'if they are to enjoy peace and prosperity they must strive to renew and preserve their friendly relations with the Arab world without which widespread misery might follow for all'. His words were to prove sadly prophetic.

CHAPTER 5

Coast to Coast

I wanted to see the country at close quarters and nibble the grass
and champ the branches.
Winston Churchill, letter to Clementine,
11 August 1929

It may seem odd that having, at the turn of the century, been so enamoured with the American way of life, Churchill did not cross the Atlantic again until 1929. It was not as if he did not travel during those years. Far from it. He took frequent holidays on the Continent. He went to witness German and French army manoeuvres before the First World War. As Minister for the Colonies he had tramped through East Africa and as First Lord of the Admiralty he had taken every advantage of cruising on the Admiralty yacht, the *Enchantress*. Then came the hiatus of the First World War. In the aftermath he was fully involved in the process of returning the world to peace.

The fall of Lloyd George's coalition government in 1922, with the loss of his own seat in Parliament and the need to find another, kept Churchill close to home. The acquisition of a country house, Chartwell, near Westerham in Kent, writing his six-volume account of the First World War, *The World Crisis*, and domestic politics saw him through to 1924 when, having rejoined the Conservative Party, which was now back in power, he became Chancellor of the Exchequer. This was a position he held, delivering five annual budgets, until Stanley Baldwin's government was defeated in a general election on 30 May 1929.

At fifty-five, having been at the centre of power for many years, Churchill was out of office and relegated to the back benches of Parliament. The Canadian Pacific Railways offered him a crossing from east to west, and he decided it time to visit the New World again, to see Canada, go back to the places he had visited in 1900, and visit the West Coast of America for the first time. He would promote the recently published second volume of *The World Crisis*, lecture and gather material for a series of articles to be published in the *Daily Mail*.

He would also take his time. Writing to the American financier Bernard Baruch he explained, 'I want to see the country and to meet the leaders of its fortunes. I have no political mission and no axe to grind.' In a second letter he added, 'I do not want to have too close an itinerary. One must have time to feel a country and nibble some of the grass.' Baruch, four years older than Churchill, had been Chairman of the War Industries Board, and thus Churchill's opposite number in the American administration, at the end of the War. From their close co-operation had come an enduring friendship.

Somewhat similar sentiments were echoed in a letter Churchill wrote to the press baron William Randolph Hearst: 'We must discuss the future of the world, even if we cannot decide it.' To his friend the newspaper proprietor Lord Beaverbrook, Churchill wrote, 'What fun it is to get away from England and feel one has no responsibility for her exceedingly tiresome and

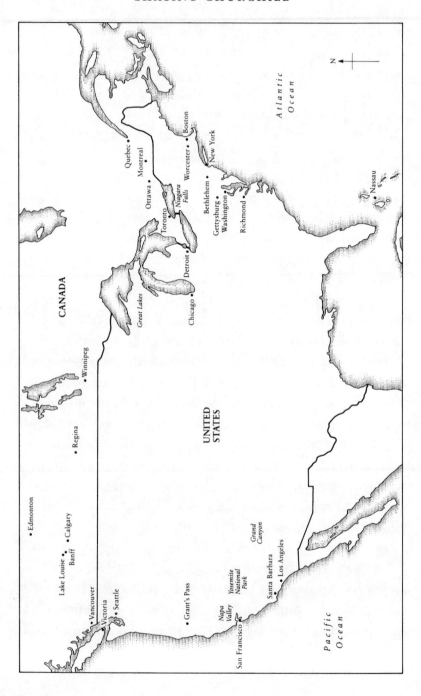

embarrassing affairs.' Over a number of issues he was beginning to feel at odds with his political colleagues.

On 3 August 1929 Churchill, accompanied by his brother Jack and their sons Randolph and Johnny, eighteen and twenty respectively, embarked at Southampton on the *Empress of Australia*. The invitation had been extended to both wives, but as neither had wished to go (Clementine had not fully recovered from an operation to remove her tonsils) the boys had been included instead. Churchill had explained to Hearst that he 'thought it would be a good thing for these two young boys, who are undergraduates at Oxford, to see these mighty lands at a period in their lives when the proportion of things are established in their minds'.

With his political responsibilities much diminished, Churchill's own mind was tuned largely to other work; writing was not only a labour of love, but without a ministerial salary he would need to bolster his finances. While crossing the Atlantic he wrote to Clementine: 'I have been reading a good deal on Marlborough. It is a wonderful thing to have all these contracts satisfactorily settled, and to feel that two or three years agreeable work is mapped out and, if completed, will certainly be rewarded.' To Leo Amery, an old school friend and a political colleague who happened to be on board, he confided that he 'had been all he ever wanted to be short of the highest post, which he saw no prospect of', and that he might even retire from politics and 'devote himself to making money'.

On 10 August, having disembarked at Quebec the previous evening, Churchill and his party were offered a tour of the city. Asked what in particular he would like to see, he replied, 'The Heights of Abrabam.' His hosts were surprised, saying that it was only a golf course. Churchill explained that it was the battlefield where Wolfe had scaled the Heights to defeat the

French forces under General Montcalm in 1759. Maps were sent for, and in a fleet of cars the party arrived at the foot of a grass-covered cliff. 'You two,' said Churchill, pointing his walking stick at Randolph and Johnny, 'are General Wolfe's army. Climb the Heights, and the rest of us will engage you at the top.' When the boys eventually scrambled over the rim, they were faced with the sight of Churchill, playing the part of Montcalm, surrounded by Quebec's top dignitaries representing various enemy regiments.

The Canadian Pacific Railroad Company had provided a shorthand typist to whom, during the morning of Sunday the eleventh, Churchill dictated the speeches he was scheduled to make in Montreal. After lunch his party drove through the surrounding countryside, stopping at a bungalow which turned out to be a small country club providing, as Churchill described in a letter to Clementine, fishing for 'twenty members in modest circumstances – quite Arcadian! Nothing would serve, when I was recognised, but to produce Champagne and the warmest of welcomes.' That night Randolph recorded in his diary: 'Papa said, "Fancy cutting down all those beautiful trees we saw this afternoon to make pulp for those bloody newspapers and calling it civilisation."'

On the twelfth, Churchill's private railway carriage, the Mont Royal, was hitched to a train for Montreal. Churchill, who once said, 'I am a man of simple tastes, easily satisfied by the best,' was impressed with the carriage's luxury. Dictating a letter to Clementine, he described it as 'a wonderful habitation'. There were large beds and private bathrooms, 'a fine parlour with an observation room at the end and a dining room which I use as the office and in which I am now dictating, together with kitchen and quarters for the staff'.

From Montreal the party moved on to Ottawa, where they

were the guests of the Governor General, Lord Willingdon, who had been a colleague of Churchill in the Liberal government before the First World War. During the two days in Ottawa, Churchill lunched with William Mackenzie King, the Prime Minister, and addressed the city's branch of the Canadian Club. In a letter to Clementine he remarked upon the number of men whom he had not seen for many years who came up to shake his hand. A former sergeant in the Royal Engineers, who in 1898 had helped Churchill draw the maps for *The River War*, introduced himself in the street and presented him with a box of cigars. 'He was in quite humble circumstances and I was greatly touched.'

Toronto, Niagara Falls, Winnipeg, Edmonton, Regina and the Calgary oilfields followed over the next few days. At the oilfields Churchill's questions were so searching that a scientist had to be summoned to answer them. That evening over dinner Churchill declared, 'I think I now understand how oil is produced and refined.' He gave the two boys a summary of what he had learned, and concluded by saying, 'Tonight I propose to write a short treatise on the matter.' When Randolph observed that it was a pity that the oil magnates, after spoiling the scenery in pursuit of riches, were not sufficiently cultured to make proper use of their money, his father replied, with some asperity, 'Cultured people are merely the glittering scum which floats upon the deep river of production.'

From the oilfields the party drove to the Prince of Wales's ranch at High River, where they rode all morning among the fertile hills of Alberta before motoring to Calgary for yet one more speech, and then on to Banff in the Rockies. Lake Louise proved irresistible for the artist, and Churchill loaded his painting equipment into a rowing boat and commanded Johnny to row him to a spot from which he could paint the lake and the mountain beyond. Although vicious bears were said to roam the neighbourhood, he insisted on being left alone, and it was with relief that on his return Johnny found him safely engrossed in his painting, shaded from the sun by his ten-gallon stetson.

Leaving Banff on 28 August, Churchill and his party continued their motor tour of the Rockies, arriving in Vancouver on 1 September. Here his activities were fully reported in the local press, as they had been throughout his visit. His speeches were covered in full. As usual he spoke frankly. On 4 September the *Vancouver Sun*'s readers were told, under the banner headline 'CHURCHILL EXPOUNDS EMPIRE POLICIES', that 'Winston Churchill cast the charm of his engaging personality upon a notable audience . . . He championed his views with consummate skill and the audience rejoiced in his candour.'

Randolph had also attracted attention. 'Ex-Chancellor's Son Coming Here' ran a headline over a photograph in the *Vancouver Colonist* of 1 September, while the *Ohio State Lantern*, a daily newspaper published by the students of journalism at Ohio State University, reported that he was speaking at university clubs on topics such as 'Fate of an Empire' and 'Why I am a Conservative'. Churchill, no less impressed than the student reporter, wrote to Clementine that Randolph 'speaks so well, so dexterous [*sic*], cool & finished'.

On 6 September Churchill crossed to Victoria, the capital of British Columbia, where he gave his fourteenth and last speech before leaving for America. It is clear from his letters to Clementine that he had been greatly attracted to Canada. There was the buoyancy of an expanding nation, and politics with 'Eighteenth Century vigour'. 'Darling,' he wrote, 'I am greatly attracted to this country. Immense fortunes are to be made in many directions. The tide is flowing strongly. However, the time to take decisions is not yet.' It is almost inconceivable that Churchill would ever have quit politics or left Chartwell, but his experience of crossing Canada had planted the thought that he might 'clear out of politics & see if I cannot make you & the kittens [their children Diana, Randolph, Sarah and Mary] a little more comfortable before I die. Only one goal still attracts me [that of becoming Prime Minister], & if that were barred I shd quit the dreary field for pastures new.'

From Vancouver the party sailed for America. 'We are now on the ship bound for Seattle, American soil and Prohibition,' wrote Randolph in his diary. 'My big flask is full of whisky and the little one contains brandy. I have reserves of both in medicine bottles.' Knowing that his father had a letter, permitting customs formalities to be waived, from the American Ambassador in London, he added, 'It is almost certain we shall have no trouble.' However, the customs officer insisted on examining every item of luggage, much to Churchill's annoyance.

'What are you looking for,' he demanded. 'I have already told you we have nothing to declare. The point of this letter from the Ambassador is to assure you of our integrity.'

'We are looking for guns and ammunition,' came the reply.

'Monstrous. Absolutely monstrous,' fumed Churchill.

Then, when the examination was over, the officer apologised for the inconvenience and invited the party into his office. When the door had been firmly closed he produced two bottles of champagne, Prohibition notwithstanding. The Churchills had started their American tour.

Randolph was accosted on the quayside by an attractive woman reporter, but loftily declined to give an interview. His father was less pompous, and spent some ten minutes with her. The ex-Chancellor of the Exchequer had the figures at his fingertips when the subject of Prohibition was raised, and was able diplomatically to avoid any criticism of American policy by making the shrewd observation, 'We realise £100 million a year from our liquor taxes, which amount, I understand, you give to your bootleggers.'

Before leaving Seattle Churchill had an unexpected reunion with a man with whom he had shared the hazards of active service in 1897, ex-Sergeant John McGill, who had served under him on the North West Frontier of India. He also met Mrs Ted Lee, the daughter of Joe McKenna, one of the miners who had concealed him underground during his escape from the Boers in 1899.

From Seattle the party went by train to Grant's Pass in south-west Oregon, from where they continued by car to San Francisco. The six-hundred-mile journey took them through the Redwood forests, where they were astonished by the size of these giant, ancient trees, some four or five thousand years old. In a letter to Clementine, Chuchill noted that the biggest was 380 feet high, and that it took fourteen of them to join hands around the trunk. The journey also introduced Churchill to a form of accommodation that is now commonplace world-wide: 'Every dozen miles or so rest camps – motels as they are called – have been built for the motorist population.'

On 9 September the Churchills entered the vineyards of George de Latour, a Frenchman resident in the Napa Valley. As Churchill later reported, his winery was protected from being closed down under Prohibition by the fiction that its large production was destined for sacramental use. 'The Consti-tution of the United States, the God of Israel, and the Pope – an august combination – protect, with the triple sanctions of Washington, Jerusalem and Rome this inspiring scene. Never-theless, there is a fragrance in the air which even the Eighteenth Amendment [Prohibition] cannot deprive us of.'

The party arrived in San Francisco on 10 September and were

comfortably accommodated in Hillsborough, which Churchill described as 'the garden suburb of San Francisco notables', under the auspices of an eminent banker, William H. Crocker. As usual there were dinners and lunches, and a press conference at which Churchill was questioned on the subject of recent fighting between Arabs and Jews in Palestine. He replied, 'The Jews have developed the country . . . The Arabs are much better off now than before the Jews came and it will be only a short time before they realise it.' This turned out to be an unusual failure of political prophecy.

On the twelfth Churchill drove into the mountains where, four thousand feet above sea level, he was shown around the Lick Observatory. True to form, he wished to know everything – which, considering this was virtually his introduction to astronomy, was more than could be explained in a few hours. Having described to Clementine what he had seen through the huge telescope and all he had been told, he concluded by wondering why 'one worries about the Epping Division [his parliamentary constituency]'.

On 13 September the party reached San Simeon, the ranch and mansion of their Californian host William Randolph Hearst. Outriders in the form of private policemen met Churchill's cavalcade several miles from the entrance to the ranch. The gates were set in an entrance resembling a medieval castle, and rose like a portcullis to allow the visitors to pass beneath. No sooner were they inside than they were surrounded by buffalo, giraffe and elephants. What was called a ranch was actually a three-hundred-square-mile game preserve running along thirty-five miles of Pacific coast. The house, filled with a vast accumulation of European art, was on a similar grand scale. Churchill, writing later to Clementine, thought the collection lacked discrimination, but that his host's two establishments were magnificent, and his two wives charming. This was a reference to Mrs Hearst and the film actress Marion Davies, Hearst's mistress.

To begin with, Churchill and Hearst approached one another warily. Hearst felt that Britain was balking at proposed international restrictions on naval shipbuilding in order to retain its naval superiority over America. However, the former First Lord of the Admiralty and his host hit it off from their first meeting, and Hearst invited Churchill to write for his newspapers – contributions which would provide one more political platform, and another source of literary income. Randolph and Johnny meanwhile were more interested in their host's other guests, among whom were a number of attractive young ladies. But rather than the warm welcome they anticipated one night on climbing through the window of a guest bungalow, they received a blast of disapproval. They had chosen the wrong bungalow, and found themselves in Churchill's bedroom.

After four days at San Simeon, a motorcade with Hearst and Churchill in the leading car set off to cover the two hundred miles to Hollywood. Hearst was a powerful figure in the film industry, he and Louis B. Mayer being the effective rulers of the Metro-Goldwyn-Mayer empire. While he provided the perfect introduction to Hollywood society, Marion Davies proved to be the ideal hostess. On the eighteenth, Hearst and Mayer gave a lunch for Churchill at the MGM studios, a lavish affair with a twenty-piece orchestra and entertainment provided by several of Metro's stars and a chorus line of twenty-five girls.

Following a day relaxing at the Biltmore Hotel in Santa Barbara, where the Churchills were accommodated with every expense paid by the banker James R. Page, the social round began again. That evening they dined at Marion Davies' beach house with a galaxy of stars, one of whom was Charlie Chaplin, who entertained everyone with impersonations of Napoleon, Uriah Heep and other characters. Chaplin and Churchill took an immediate liking to one another, and sat up long after midnight, Churchill suggesting that he would write a script in which Chaplin would play Napoleon.

The next day there was a tour of MGM, and the day after deep-sea fishing on the Hearst yacht. Churchill hooked a 188-pound marlin and landed it in twenty minutes, which was said to be a local record. Their final event was lunch and a tour of Chaplin's United Artists studios, where he acted a scene from the film he was making, *City Lights*, an attempt to prove that silent film was superior to the new 'talkies'. Writing to Clementine, Churchill commented that 'if patter & wit still count for anything it ought to win an easy victory'. In the same letter he described Chaplin, who would be a visitor to Chartwell in the following years, as 'bolshy in politics & delightful in conversation'.

After Churchill left Los Angeles he reported to Clementine, 'I met all the leading people & have heard on every side that my speech & talks (to circles of ten or twelve) have given much pleasure. I explained to them all about England & her affairs – showing how splendid & tolerant she was & how we ought to work together.' In the *Daily Telegraph* on 30 December he wrote of Los Angeles that it was 'a gay and happy city' where 'you motor ten miles to luncheon in one direction and ten miles to dinner in another. The streets are ablaze with electric lights and moving signs of every colour. A carnival in fairyland.'

The visit had been an undoubted political success. The British Consul-General in San Francisco wrote to Churchill that it had produced 'wonderful and immediate results among those who, up to recent times, have been antagonistic towards us and our interests'.

The party now continued as the guests of Charles Schwab, the President of Bethlehem Steel, from whom Churchill as First Lord of the Admiralty had ordered six submarines in World War I. (They had been built in the record time of six months, and assembled in Montreal to avoid breaching America's neutrality.) Schwab provided a private railcar which was hitched to normal trains and shunted off whenever Churchill's party wished to stop en route. They first left the train to drive through the magnificent Yosemite Valley, the foliage a splendid colour in the autumn. Rejoining the train they continued through the Mojave Desert to the Grand Canyon. Here Randolph and Johnny stood on their heads, a trick of perspective making it appear to the remainder of the party that they were performing the trick on the very edge of the canyon. Not surprisingly, everyone reacted 'with a loud shout of alarm'.

Churchill arrived in Chicago on 2 October. A tour of the city sights included the renowned Armour meatpacking plant. 'What you are about to see,' announced their guide, 'are the processes by which animals come to the factory alive and in a short space of time leave in the form of sausages or tins of meat.' Johnny was further discomforted when, at the end of the visit, his uncle was presented with a box of soaps and cosmetics made, in the words of the guide, 'from parts of the animal which are not edible'. Johnny recorded that the whole process was so gruesome that 'it was days before I enjoyed eating meat again'. A more important event was the dinner that evening at the Commercial Club, where Churchill spoke of the need for a naval agreement between Britain and America.

Leaving Chicago for New York on the evening of 5 October in a private railcar provided by Bernard Baruch, the Churchills arrived in Manhattan the following morning. Here they took up residence at the Savoy-Plaza, from where Randolph and

Johnny lost no time in heading for Tony's, a well-known and fashionable speakeasy. They left disappointed, finding it did not live up to its reputation. But Tony's was not the epitome of New York social life, as they discovered shortly before they sailed for Britain on 12 October for their next term at Oxford. They saw New York society at its best during a lavish party given by the magazine publisher Condé Nast at which Johnny danced the evening away with Fred Astaire's sister Adele.

Baruch's nephew Perry Belmont Frank, fourteen at the time, recalled Churchill's stays with his uncle: 'Nudity was not a state that concerned Churchill and it would not have bothered him to chat with a press person from the bath, and many a time I was sent down the hall to wash his back.' He also recounted an occasion when Baruch and Churchill were going to a white-tie dinner. Baruch, already dressed, was waiting in the drawing room, where some members of the press were assembled hoping for a few words before his guest departed for dinner. 'Churchill suddenly appeared in the doorway, wet from the tub, with a large white robe clutched around him. His secretary appeared alongside him with four books bound in gold. "Baruch, I want you to have these books for your library," said Churchill, who retreated down the hall, returned ten minutes later fully dressed and immediately went off to dinner with Baruch. Not a word was said to the press, who were completely awed.'

Politics and speeches occupied Churchill in New York for some days, before he and Jack set off for the American Civil War battlefields. Gettysburg, where in Churchill's account of the campaign in *A History of the English Speaking Peoples* 'the South had shot its bolt', was the first stop. Then, after a visit to Schwab's steelworks at Bethlehem, he was off along the byways of Virginia to Chancellorsville, Spottsylvania and Fredericksburg, where, in an area only a hundred miles square, the ferocity and slaughter had been a foretaste of what was to follow fifty years later in World War I. Churchill viewed the ground with a keen military eye, writing, 'No one can understand what happened merely through reading books and studying maps. You must see the ground; you must cover the distances in person.' In addition to the account of his battlefield tour in the *Daily Telegraph*, he wrote a series of articles for *Collier's Magazine*, bringing in some £90,000 in today's values.

Inevitably, it was difficult to find many people who had witnessed my grandfather's visit to America in 1929. I did however have the good fortune to meet Senator Harry Byrd Jr, who remembered with astonishing clarity how he had met Winston Churchill more than seventy years before. Like Perry Belmont Frank, Senator Byrd was fourteen when his father, Governor Harry Byrd, told him that a very distinguished British politician was coming to stay at the governor's mansion in Richmond, Virginia. Young Harry Byrd and his older cousin got their first glimpse of the guest as he descended the staircase before dinner. They were both in their best clothes, and Churchill, thinking that the older boy was a member of the household staff, asked him to go and buy him a newspaper. On his return he was duly rewarded with a quarter, which he kept as a treasured possession all his life. Each day Churchill would return from visiting the battlefields with his guide Douglas Southall Freeman, who having written a biography of Robert E. Lee was ideally suited to the task, and make himself thoroughly at home in the Governor's mansion.

One night there was a state dinner for Churchill and thirty local dignitaries. The main course was baked Virginia ham. The guest of honour asked his hostess for some mustard, and Mrs Byrd sent to the kitchen for it, only to be told that there was none in the house. Apologising to Churchill and trying to make light of the problem, she said that if he really wanted mustard she could send someone to the store. To her astonishment he replied that he would like some, and the whole party had to toy with their rapidly cooling food while they waited for this apparent necessity.

The fact that this visit was made during the time of Prohibition placed the Governor in a difficult position. He knew that his guest would not be happy to abstain from alcohol, but at the same time he did not wish to openly break the law. The problem was solved with the help of a local publisher, John Stephen Brown, who had the best cellar in Richmond. He supplied Churchill with brandy, which he drank in private, presumably in his bedroom before dinner.

Apart from Bernard Baruch in New York, the Canadian industrialist Frank Clarke in Miami, and President Herbert Hoover at the White House, Churchill stayed longer with the Byrds than with anyone else. For ten long days Mrs Byrd entertained her demanding visitor. Her son told me that although his father was delighted by his guest, his mother had considerable reservations. Apart from needing mustard with his ham, Churchill wanted not only to decide at what time meals should be served, but what the menu should be. To add to the consternation of his hostess he would walk around – one assumes upstairs – dressed only in his underwear. As the Governor and Mrs Byrd waved their guest goodbye, Senator Byrd remembers his mother turning to her husband and saying, 'Don't you ever invite that man here again!'

Twenty-two years later, in 1951, when Churchill had become Prime Minister for the second time, Harry Byrd Jr, by then a journalist, was in London. He got an appointment to see Churchill, and told me how for the first twenty minutes the Prime Minister talked to him about the battlefields he had visited while staying in his parents' house. What really impressed Byrd was the extent of the older man's knowledge – Churchill was, he said, 'far more knowledgeable than I about the area where I had lived all my life'.

Returning to New York on 24 October, Churchill stayed with Percy Rockefeller, a member of the New York Stock Exchange, while he completed various literary contracts. His return coincided with the collapse of the stock market and the beginnings of the great Wall Street Crash. That evening when Bernard Baruch gathered some fifty leading financiers to dinner, the toast proposing Churchill's health was, 'Friends and *former* millionaires.' Churchill had invested heavily on the New York Stock Exchange, and his own losses were considerable, almost half a million pounds at present-day prices. Nevertheless, as he sailed home on 30 October 1929 he took the long view: 'this financial disaster, cruel as it is to thousands, is only a passing episode in the march of a valiant and serviceable people'. For him, personally, it meant a frenzy of writing to repair his finances and, for both him and Clementine, some economies.

The 'passing episode' turned into the Great Depression which, casting a blight on the world economy during the early thirties, hastened the demise of free trade, a principle for which Churchill had fought in Parliament for three decades. Nothing he could say or do would convert the Conservative Party to the Anglo–American co-operation which he saw as the best way of combating the economic downturn. Equally important for his relations with his party was his split with them on their policy for India. When the Conservative Party returned to government as a member of the coalition under Ramsay Macdonald in November 1931, no one was surprised, although some were dismayed, that Churchill was not offered a place in the Cabinet. He was busy with his biography of Marlborough and various newspaper commitments, but he could work on these while on the move. He had political ideas to develop, but he also needed to recoup the money he had lost in the New York stock market crash. He looked again to America.

He wrote to Bernard Baruch: 'My lecture tour in the States has been fully booked up and the Agency have had no difficulty in letting the largest halls at the highest prices.' His two principal themes were to be confidence in Britain's future and the need for closer Anglo–American co-operation. He had contracted to give forty lectures for a minimum fee of £30,000 at today's values, while the *Daily Mail* would pay him £24,000 for a series of articles, the publication of which in America he remained free to negotiate. These were considerable sums, but from them he needed to pay his own expenses and those of his entourage.

Travelling with Churchill were Clementine, their daughter Diana, then aged twenty-two, and a bodyguard. This was Detective Sergeant Walter Thompson, who had protected Churchill from the threat of Irish assassins when he had been heavily involved in negotiating Home Rule for Ireland in the early twenties, and who would be recalled to the same role in the late thirties. On this occasion he had been assigned because it had been learned that an Indian terrorist organisation in America planned to assassinate Churchill during his lecture tour, as a result of his having opposed the British government's policy of granting dominion status to India.

The party was originally booked to travel by Cunard, but the arrangements had to be adjusted to allow Churchill to speak in Parliament, resulting in their embarking instead on the German liner *Europa*, the only ship which would get him to New York in time for his first lecture. Churchill 'swore and banged his cane about', furious that, at a time when the *New York Times* was reporting a 'buy British' campaign, he had no alternative to travelling by the German ship which had just taken the Blue Riband for the fastest Atlantic crossing from Cunard.

The *Europa* docked in New York on 11 December 1931. Churchill lectured in Worcester, Massachusetts, on the twelfth, then returned to New York. After dinner that evening he set off by taxi from the Waldorf-Astoria to Baruch's house further up Fifth Avenue to meet a few mutual friends. The driver did not know precisely where the house was, and Churchill did not know the number and could not recognise it. After a fruitless search for close on an hour, during which Churchill grew increasingly impatient, particularly because he was unaccustomed to the frequent stops at traffic lights (they had yet to be introduced in Britain), he told the driver to stop while he crossed the road to see if he could recognise Baruch's house. Being accustomed to the British rule of driving on the left he became disorientated and, pausing in the centre of Fifth Avenue to check that he could continue to cross, looked the wrong way and was knocked down by a car travelling at thirty miles an hour.

Although in great pain, Churchill remained conscious. 'I do not know why I was not broken like an eggshell or squashed like a gooseberry,' he wrote in the *Daily Mail*. He recounted that the policeman who arrived at the scene first asked his age before accepting his statement that the driver was completely blameless. An ambulance appeared, and the crowd which had gathered demanded that the driver take the casualty to the nearest hospital; but he already had a patient on board, so Churchill was instead lifted into a taxi and taken to the Lennox Hill Hospital. When he came round from the anaesthetic he found Clementine, Diana and Baruch by his bedside. He had suffered a severe cut to his scalp, two cracked ribs, multiple contusions and a sprained shoulder. Pleurisy developed as a result of his injuries, and it was not until 21 December that he was discharged from hospital.

Legend has it that the vehicle that struck Churchill was a taxi. It was in fact a private car driven by a young truck driver, Mario Constasino. Anxious about the health of the man he had knocked over, he called daily at the hospital, and was eventually allowed to see the patient. During his conversation with Churchill and Clementine he disclosed that he was out of work and, his mother having died, was supporting his two sisters. A staunchly self-reliant young man, Constasino declined the financial assistance Churchill offered, whereupon he was presented instead with an inscribed copy of the latest volume of *The World Crisis*. Subsequently Constasino attended Churchill's first New York lecture after his recovery.

The *New York Times* of 22 December reported that Churchill 'appeared to be in good spirits' on leaving hospital the previous day. No doubt he was glad to be out, but he would have to remain in bed for a further two weeks. His lecture tour was in ruins, and needed to be completely rearranged. Meanwhile his expenses were mounting, diminishing his potential profits. Still a convalescent, Churchill interviewed a young British-born woman for the position of travelling secretary. Phyllis Moir later recalled the interview: 'Buried in an enormous Queen Anne armchair by a blazing fire, I caught sight of a humpty-dumpty sort of a figure . . . A deep livid gash on his forehead . . . and the droop of his powerful shoulders betrayed a weariness which the jauntiness of his attire could not disguise.' She was told that Churchill was about to leave for Nassau in the Bahamas, and that her job would start in about three weeks. 'Not a timid person', she nonetheless recalled: 'Never in my life have I felt so unimportant beside another human being.'

Like others of Churchill's secretarial staff, she would discover that the demands and impatience of her employer were often alleviated, however briefly, by flashes of understanding and gratitude.

For three weeks Churchill remained in the Bahamas. He was depressed at his slow recovery, and worried that he would not be able to cope with his programme of lectures. He did not open his paintbox, even though he was surrounded by 'the most lovely tints of blue, green and purple'. Clementine, writing to Randolph, doubted if he would recover completely from the three blows to which he had been subjected in the last two years: the loss of his position in the Conservative Party, the loss of money in the Crash and now this serious accident. At home, due to the initiative of his friend and political colleague Brendan Bracken, a group of eight friends decided to make a gift to him of a Daimler car to celebrate his recovery. Churchill was delighted. He was beginning to feel better, writing to Randolph, 'I expect the electric atmosphere of New York will act as a tonic itself after this soothing and somewhat enervating climate.'

And so it proved. Starting in New York on 28 January 1932, he set off to lecture in a different city each day. In Detroit and Chicago, the likely flashpoints for Indian agitators, Thompson's protection was supplemented by police, detectives and secret service. There was no trouble; instead, reported the *Chicago Tribune* on 3 February, 'Round upon round of applause, spontaneous and vehement followed the closing words.' At home the *Daily Telegraph*, following the tour closely, reported on 10 February that the tour had developed into a 'triumphal progress'. Thirteen days later the *Atlanta Constitution* commented on Churchill's 'eloquence and wit', and continued: 'He commands an unrivalled fund of information . . . and his views . . . command respectful attention in the capitals of the world.'

With Roosevelt at Casablanca, January 1943.

At Casablanca, January 1943.

With Roosevelt in the tower of Villa Taylor, Marrakech, January 1943.

At Allied Headquarters North Africa, Algiers, June 1943.

With Mary, Niagara Falls, August 1943.

Returning from the United States with Mary aboard HMS *Renown*, September 1943.

Aboard HMS *Renown* with Clementine and Mary, September 1943.

Malta, November 1943. To WSC's left is Field Marshal Lord Gort.

With Roosevelt and
Stalin, Tehran,
November 1943.

Visiting recently recaptured Cherbourg, July 1944.

Crossing the Rhine, March 1945.

With Clementine, Hendaye, France, July 1945.

Painting in Miami, February 1946.

Painting in Madame Balsan's garden at Casa Alva, Lantana, Florida 1946.

On the way to deliver his 'iron curtain' speech at Fulton, Missouri, with President Harry S. Truman, March 1946.

Donkey ride at La Fontaine-de-Vaucluse, August 1948.

In Washington, Churchill stayed in the British Embassy where each morning the Ambassador, Sir Ronald Lindsay, discussed the day's itinerary with his guest. Miss Moir, by now well accustomed to her employer's unconventional working habits, recalled the bizarre scene: 'the immensely dignified diplomat standing extremely ill at ease at the foot of the old-fashioned four poster-bed and the Peter Pan of British politics sitting up in bed, a cigar in his mouth, his tufts of red hair as yet uncombed, scanning the morning newspapers'.

Churchill had not been able to write the articles he had undertaken for the *Daily Mail*: 'I have not had the margin of life or strength to do them while travelling and speaking so many nights in succession,' he wrote to Esmond Harmsworth of the *Mail*'s owners, Associated Newspapers. 'We must talk about it when I come home, which, I rejoice to say, will be soon.' The American press noted that he was 'patently tired out' when he arrived at Boston's South Station at 8.30 a.m. on 10 March for his final speech in the Symphony Hall that evening. However, a sparkle appeared when the questions turned to Ireland, although his wit may not have endeared him to the large Irish population of Boston. A reporter asked about the recent electoral triumph of Eamon de Valera as Prime Minister of the Irish Republic, to which Churchill quipped, 'I thought it was going to happen because it was the most unreasonable thing that could happen.'

His speech in Boston over, he took the night train to New York. The next day he boarded the *Majestic* for Southampton, where his friends met him on 17 March with his new Daimler.

CHAPTER 6

The Paris of the Sahara

It's the most lovely spot in the whole world.
Winston Churchill to Sir Charles Wilson,
24 January 1943

It was 24 January 1943. The ten-day conference in the Hôtel
d'Anfa at Casablanca involving Prime Minister Winston
Churchill and President Franklin Delano Roosevelt and their
staffs was over. The future strategy of the war had been mapped
out. Fifty journalists had attended the final press conference to
hear both the Prime Minister and the President declare their
commitment to the unconditional surrender of Germany, Italy
and Japan. Churchill now planned to spend a few days in Marrakech before continuing his month-long journey through the
Middle East, while Roosevelt was intent on returning immediately to America. But Churchill wanted his fellow statesman
and friend to accompany him to, as he put it, 'the Paris of the
Sahara, where all the caravans had come from Central Africa
for centuries to be heavily taxed *en route* by the tribes in the
mountains and afterwards swindled in the Marrakech markets,
receiving the return, which they greatly valued, of the gay life
in the city, including fortune tellers, snake-charmers, masses of

food and drink, and on the whole the largest and most elaborately organised brothels on the African continent. All these institutions were of long and ancient repute.' He spoke persuasively to Roosevelt: 'You cannot come all this way to North Africa without seeing Marrakech. Let us spend two days there. I must be with you when you see the sun set on the Atlas Mountains.'

With an armoured car escort on the ground and fighter aircraft circling above, the party set off for Marrakech, where a villa owned by an American, Mrs Taylor, but leased by the American Consul Kenneth Pendar was being prepared for the Prime Minister and the President. American and British secret services descended on the villa to ensure the security of the two leaders. Security was not the only consideration, for ramps and handrails had to be positioned to enable Roosevelt, confined to a wheelchair, to move around. The American and British officials referred to the two visitors as 'Your Number One' and 'Our Number One', or 'A1' and 'B1'. It seems surprising that, with such transparent dissimulations, the locals reported sightings of the King of England wandering through the garden, and of the Pope reading his breviary.

The journey of 150 miles from Casablanca to Marrakech took five hours, including lunch in the desert – surely one of the twentieth century's more extraordinary picnics. The snow-capped mountains came into view on the horizon while the convoy was still a long way from its destination, and the sun was low in the sky by the time they reached Marrakech.

Soon after their arrival Churchill insisted Roosevelt accompany him up the tower of the villa, at the edge of town, to look over Marrakech and see the changing colours of the landscape as the snow-covered peaks of the Atlas were caught by the setting sun. Two of his servants made a chair of their arms, and

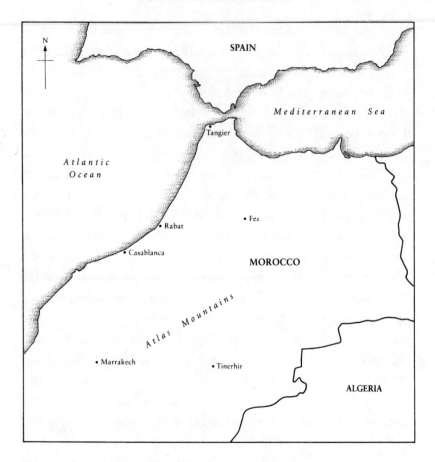

Roosevelt was lifted from his wheelchair and carried up the winding stairs to the rooftop. Reclining on a divan, he was so taken by the scene he said to Churchill, 'I feel like a sultan; you may kiss my hand my dear.' In his diary Churchill's doctor recorded, 'We stood gazing at the purple hills, where the light was changing every minute. "It's the most lovely spot in the world, the PM murmured."'

Marrakech has developed in the years that have since passed, but the lovely spectacle looking over the city towards the mountains remains unchanged, although it is no longer possible to appreciate it from the Villa Taylor. Local legend has it that Mrs Taylor sold the villa after the war because, as a staunch Republican, she had been incensed that Roosevelt, a Democrat, had slept in her bed. After an intermediate owner, the Comte de Breteuil, the villa was bought by the late King Hassan of Morocco, who intended to refurbish it as a residence for the Crown Prince. However, it soon became obvious that it was unsuitable for this purpose, being overlooked by newer buildings, and now it stands empty.

I was denied admittance by two obdurate policemen who were deaf to my family connections and historical interest. At the Hôtel de Ville the Head of General Affairs interrupted his business in an attempt to obtain the permission I required, but an hour's endeavour failed to find anyone willing to provide it. The villa seems destined to deteriorate like the empty shell of the Hôtel d'Anfa at Casablanca, the other building in Morocco which played a significant part in World War II.

Dinner that January night in 1943 at the Villa Taylor had a family air. Churchill and Roosevelt made short, affectionate speeches to each other, and the President proposed the health of the King. Even as these festivities proceeded, the final documents from the Casablanca Conference were brought to the table for the two leaders' approval, but this did not deter Churchill from singing and everyone joining in the choruses.

When Roosevelt left the following morning, Churchill appeared in his embroidered bedroom slippers and a dressing gown covered with red dragons. Thus flamboyantly dressed he climbed into the President's car and accompanied him to the airfield. Churchill lingered in Marrakech for the remainder of that day before taking off for Cairo in the evening. At midday he got out his paints, and from the tower of the villa began the only picture he would paint during the war. It depicts the view across

Marrakech, with the prominent tower of the Katoubia Mosque, over the town walls to the distant mountains with their white peaks and purple shadows. Several years later Mrs Taylor offered to buy it, and was told that Churchill had presented it to the man who had so enraged her by sleeping in her bed.

It was eight years before the Casablanca Conference, at the end of 1935, that Churchill had discovered this 'most lovely spot'. At odds with British government policies over rearmament, and his hopes of further Cabinet office frustrated, he decided to take a long-awaited winter holiday. It was not the sort of holiday to which most people look forward when they book a trip to Marrakech, with its medieval architecture, bustling bazaars and romantic Berber atmosphere. Churchill found all this a very agreeable environment, but one in which to work rather than relax, and told his publisher that he planned to start work on the third volume of *Marlborough*. He would also write several newspaper articles – a ready source of income and political influence. There would be plenty of lively political discussion, as he would be accompanied by his son Randolph, while his friend and scientific adviser Professor Frederick Lindemann and the newspaper proprietor Lord Rothermere would join them en route, and Lloyd George, Prime Minister in World War I and now a backbench Member of Parliament, was already there. Churchill would be exercised in particular by the shameful secret pact between the Foreign Ministers of Britain and France, Sir Samuel Hoare and Pierre Laval, which sought to end the Italian invasion of Abyssinia by appeasing the aggressors. He would also become concerned that his position in the domestic political arena might be undermined by Randolph's acceptance to stand in a by-election as Conservative parliamentary candidate for Ross and Cromarty against Malcolm MacDonald, a Cabinet Minister in the National Government who had lost his Labour seat in the recent general election. Churchill feared that the Prime Minister, Stanley Baldwin, might take this as 'a definite declaration of war by me'. But, with all this to engage him, he would still find time to paint.

On 10 December 1935 Churchill and Clementine flew to Paris, where, after lunch with Pierre Flandin, formerly the French Prime Minister and about to become Foreign Minister, they took the train for Barcelona. Here he worked on *Marlborough* and painted until the twentieth, when Clementine returned home for a family Christmas while Churchill and Randolph, joined by Professor Lindemann, took the boat for Tangier, where his ancestor John Churchill, later the 1st Duke of Marlborough, had served as a lieutenant aged sixteen in 1668. He stayed in the El Minzah, a hotel in the centre which to this day retains a typical Moroccan atmosphere, but his hopes of several days' painting were frustrated by incessant rain. Impatiently he set off with Lord Rothermere on 26 December to join Lloyd George in Marrakech. Passing through Rabat on the same day, he wrote to Clementine deprecating political upheavals in the Cabinet, and ending, 'your wandering, sun seeking, rotten, disconsolate W'.

Ensconced in the Hôtel Mamounia in Marrakech, which would become his headquarters on all future peacetime visits, Churchill fretted about Britain's problems, writing to Clementine, 'We are getting into the most terrible position . . . our government less capable a machine for conducting affairs than I have ever seen.' Of his holiday he wrote, 'I am painting a picture from the balcony, because although the native city is full of attractive spots, the crowds, the smells and the general discomfort of painting have repelled me.' It was a somewhat similar view to the one he would paint in wartime eight years later, but without the weight of the world to worry him, it is a better picture. It demonstrates not only how proficient an artist Churchill had become, but what a considerable innate talent he had.

La Mamounia, one of the world's great hotels, takes its name from the surrounding gardens, Arset Al Mamoun, which were given to Prince Moulay Mamoun by his father, Sultan Ben Abdullah, as a wedding present in the eighteenth century. Created in 1922 by the architects Prost and Marchiso, it combined the latest in art deco design with Moroccan architectural features – and, although it has since more than doubled in size, it retains its original atmosphere. Its grandest set of rooms today is the Winston Churchill Suite, overlooking the extensive gardens.

While at the Mamounia Lord Rothermere offered Churchill two bets. The first was £2000 that he could not remain teetotal for the whole of 1936. Churchill calculated that, free of tax, this would be worth £3500, to which could be added a further £500 he would save on drink. But he reported to Clementine, 'I refused as I think life would not be worth living . . . I have however accepted his second bet of £600 not to drink any brandy or undiluted spirits in 1936.' History does not record the outcome of this wager, but as whisky well diluted with soda was his favourite drink, it is unlikely that my grandfather collected his winnings. In the New Year Randolph left to fight the by-election, but the family atmosphere in Marrakech was maintained by the arrival of my parents. My father, Duncan Sandys, who had married Churchill's daughter Diana the previous September, was a young Member of Parliament with similar views to his father-in-law on rearmament and appeasement. When invalided from the army during the Second World War he would become a member of my grandfather's wartime government. He also painted, and in Marrakech sat side by side with Churchill capturing the same scenes.

'It is vy nice having Diana & Duncan here,' Churchill wrote to Clementine. 'They are so happy. They say it is a second honeymoon . . . The more I see of him, the better I like him. They read political books to each other under the palm trees while I paint.' Since I only remember my parents in later and less happy times of their marriage, it is nice to know that this was not always so.

In 1935 the most influential man in Morocco was Thami El Glaoui, the Pasha of Marrakech. This cosmopolitan head of one of the great Berber families of the High Atlas was four years younger than Churchill, and his highly placed European mistresses could have conducted their affairs only with the connivance of their husbands. His political and military support of the French colonial power was both clever and ambitious, and had brought him the Croix de Guerre avec Palme in 1916 and the Grand Croix de la Légion d'Honneur in 1925. No eminent foreign politician could arrive in Marrakech without receiving an invitation from El Glaoui.

Thus, in mid-January Churchill and Lloyd George were his guests at Meknes and at Fez, some two hundred miles to the north-east. It was said that to be entertained by El Glaoui was like going back hundreds of years in time. One of the entertainments to which Churchill was subjected was a dance by a hundred women. He obviously found this less than enthralling, for writing to Clementine he hoped the feast would be 'my last for a long time', and remarked, 'my taste is more attuned to the Russian ballet, but the natives seem to have been thrilled by this for thousands of years'. Churchill stayed in Meknes for only three days, finding the area pleasant and healthy but far less warm and 'far less paintable' than Marrakech.

No doubt he took his paints with him, but there is no canvas recording his visit.

Churchill and El Glaoui obviously hit it off. No doubt Churchill, who had always lived life to the full, appreciated the style which had brought El Glaoui such unofficial titles as 'Lord of the High Atlas' and 'the Black Panther'. Until his death in 1956 he was always on hand whenever Churchill arrived in Marrakech. An enthusiastic golfer, his plus-fours and golfing shoes often glimpsed incongruously beneath his Arab robes, he and Churchill played together on his private course.

On 20 January 1936 King George V died. Churchill, invited to present the Address of the House to the new King, Edward VIII, broke off his holiday and returned to England. He had completed three draft chapters of *Marlborough*, ruminated a great deal over politics and painted seven canvases. Some of these had been done in the 'native city', indicating that the lure of the 'attractive spots' had overcome his distaste for the crowds and the smells.

He had also written a number of newspaper articles. One for the *Daily Mail*, under the headline 'I was Astonished by Morocco', shows how far he had fallen under the spell of the French colony. It begins: 'Morocco was to me a revelation. Reading about the Moroccan question in the newspapers, or in official documents, affords not the slightest impression of the charm and value of this splendid territory.' Towards the end of some thousand words Churchill confesses himself 'captivated by Marrakech. Here in these spacious palm groves rising from the desert the traveller can be sure of perennial sunshine, of every comfort and diversion, and can contemplate with ceaseless satisfaction the stately snow-clad panorama of the Atlas Mountains. The sun is brilliant and warm but not scorching; the air crisp, bracing but without being chilly; the days bright, the nights cool and fresh.' Of course, Churchill's visits to Marrakech were always in the winter. When I followed his footsteps there it was August, and a good deal warmer, scorching in the desert, but despite the heat I too was captivated.

Churchill twice returned to Morocco during the war: first for the brief visit in January 1943 with Roosevelt, and again at the end of the same year for a longer stay while he convalesced from a lengthy overseas tour. He had been feeling far from well as he left Britain on 12 November aboard the battleship *Renown*. The effects of a heavy cold had been exacerbated by a reaction to inoculations against cholera and typhoid. It was therefore hardly surprising that an exhausting programme of conferences and visits in the Middle East, culminating in the first Big Three conference with Roosevelt and Stalin in Teheran, had left him more tired than he had been at any previous time during the war. On 12 December, at Carthage in Tunisia, he contracted pneumonia. When a heart attack followed two days later, Clementine flew out to join him. However, he worked from his sickbed until Christmas Eve, and by 27 December was fit enough to fly to Marrakech.

Arrangements there were in American hands, and the British Vice-Consul, Bryce Nairn, was left unaware of Churchill's impending arrival. Also unaware that for security reasons the Prime Minister was often referred to as 'Colonel Warden', Nairn was surprised when a wing commander carrying a bulging briefcase of papers enquired about the whereabouts of the Colonel – after all, as Vice-Consul he knew every British officer in Marrakech. All was revealed the following day when Churchill's personal assistant, Commander Tommy Thompson, called to ask that the Pasha of Marrakech, El Glaoui, be in-formed of the Prime Minister's arrival. It transpired that that consummate politician, although he made a show of surprise and pleasure, had been well aware of Churchill's movements.

For the next two and a half weeks Churchill's life at the Villa Taylor entailed work, conferences and picnics while he regained his strength. His visit brought a welcome break from the normal routine for the American garrison of Marrakech, not least because his staff included twenty-four girls, many of whom were under less than usual pressure, and were thus able to enjoy luxuries not available in wartime London. In a letter to her mother, Churchill's secretary Elizabeth Layton remarked, 'We've really had such fun here,' their New Year's Eve at the Mamounia 'certainly making up for the mouldy Christmas'. Touching on her imminent return to London, she included the thought, 'I've been so spoilt, men being in the majority, heaven knows if I'll ever settle down.'

Churchill attracted many visitors, one of whom was the leader of the Free French, General Charles de Gaulle, at that time based in Algeria. Elizabeth Layton describes the large, colourful parade which de Gaulle invited Churchill to review: 'First came Senegalese troops in red tunics, then a contingent of the French Foreign Legion, followed by white-turbaned Spahis in red jackets and blue pantaloons trotting past on lively Arab horses. Later came the rumble of tanks and guns and the roar of fighters and bombers flying low overhead. Churchill took the salute dressed in the uniform of an Air Commodore, and was much moved by the cries *"Vive Churchill!"*, which predominated even over the cries of *"Vive de Gaulle!"*'

His health repaired, Churchill left Marrakech on 14 January 1944, flying to Gibraltar, where he boarded the battleship *King George V* for Britain.

Soon after his return to London he received a letter from Mr Lucien H. Tryng of New York:

Some fifteen years ago I purchased 250 acres of land near Marrakech . . . it is my recollection that a number of years ago Nigel Blackhawkins, who represented my interests in Morocco, reported to me that you . . . were interested in part of this property. Your recent choice of Marrakech as a place for convalescence indicates that such a place, for the more peaceful days to come, may still be in your mind. If so Mrs Tryng and I would be very happy if you would accept such portion of the land as you might wish for your purpose. We should feel – and I am sure our countrymen would share the feeling – that we were uniquely privileged in being able to offer something you would find of use, as a slight token of what we realise you have meant to this country, and to the world.

Before the war Churchill had indeed contemplated building a 'winter dwelling', as Mr Blackhawkins described it in correspondence, in or near Marrakech. However, much had happened since then, and there could be no question of accepting such a generous gift. He replied through his Private Secretary:

Mr Churchill desires me to say in reply that, while he is indebted to you and Mrs Tryng for your exceedingly kind thought, he does not feel able to accept your proposal to present him with some of your land at Marrakech. He wishes me to assure you however that he values none the less the motive which inspired you and Mrs Tryng to make this generous offer.

Four years later, no longer Prime Minister, and his doctors having recommended a spell during winter in warmer climates, Churchill planned to spend the best part of December 1947 and January 1948 in Marrakech, at the Mamounia. The Prime Minister who had steered Britain through six years of war had now to attend to such mundane matters as petty finance. In the austere years following the Second World War, strict currency regulations prohibited foreign exchange, but Churchill's American publishers, Time-Life International, were anxious that he should get on with his wartime memoirs under the most favourable conditions, and overcame the financial problem by inviting him as their guest and depositing the necessary funds in Marrakech.

British Aviation Services called a special meeting of its directors, as a result of which Silver City Airways provided an aircraft for Churchill and his party free of charge. He was accompanied by his daughter Sarah, now thirty-three, and Bill Deakin, who had assisted him during the writing of *Marlborough*, had parachuted into Yugoslavia during the war, and was now helping Churchill with his war memoirs. In addition there was the usual entourage of two secretaries, a valet and a detective. Clementine's health not being good, she decided to remain at Chartwell, entreating Sarah to ensure that her father did not sit out painting when the temperature dropped at sunset.

The party with its mountain of luggage, painting equipment and documents left Northolt on 10 December 1947. They arrived in Marrakech the following afternoon after an eight-hour flight from Paris, where the journey had been broken for Churchill to attend a party at the British Embassy given by Duff Cooper, the departing Ambassador. At Marrakech they were met by El Glaoui and Colonel Hautville, the French military commandant. The Colonel drew Bill Deakin to one side and explained that as Marrakech was a military area, a telephone call to him would be all that was necessary should anyone or anything prove inconvenient or upsetting.

The party in Paris the previous evening and the long flight notwithstanding, Churchill immediately began work in earnest.

In a letter to Clementine a little over twenty-four hours after his arrival he wrote: 'I worked hard all morning on the book and shall begin again after dinner.' That afternoon he had also painted 'for a couple of hours from the roof of the hotel . . . The Atlas are magnificent and as glorious as ever.'

A routine was established, and proofs were sent back each day to the printers in London. Churchill explained to Clementine: 'Wake about 8am, work at Book till 12.30, lunch at one, paint from 2.30 till 5, when it is cold and dusk, sleep from 6pm till 7.30, dine at 8, Oklahoma [an American card game] with Mule [a nickname for Sarah, coined on account of her stubbornness]. At 10 or 11pm again work on the Book.' At this late hour the routine varied: 'Here I have been rather naughty; the hours of going to bed have been one o'clock, two, three, three, three, two, but an immense amount has been done and Book II is practically finished . . . The painting has not gone badly but I have only these two and a half short hours of good daylight. Three daubs are on the way.'

A highlight of the visit was another dinner with El Glaoui. Writing home, Sarah reported, 'I have been commanded by Papa to write to you all, a full description of the dinner . . . It really was a most sumptuous evening . . . we sat around a low table. The juniors on poufs, and Papa and the Glaoui on a low sofa.' Servants 'padded about carrying to and fro great copper and earthenware bowls and plates of food'. Much of the dinner was eaten Arab style with the fingers, but occasionally it was correct to use a spoon. 'Papa committed one social error by plunging his hand into a great bowl . . . only to be handed a spoon . . . Later, somewhere about the tenth course, an ice cream turned up. I am sorry to say that though it was quite clear that this was one of the courses to be eaten with a spoon, Papa was enjoying himself so much that, muttering, "I simply must," he

117

plunged his fingers into the ice cream. The Glaoui and son were luckily highly amused . . . An Arabian night to be sure.'

Colonel Hautville, who on Churchill's arrival had offered to deflect any unwelcome intrusions, had rightly appreciated the difficulty which someone of his visitor's fame might find in avoiding well-intended but inconvenient distractions. The Anglican Bishop in North Africa, G.F.B. Morris, wrote to Churchill on 20 December asking 'if you and your party, together with any British people in Marrakech, would like a Church of England Service on Sunday 28th inst . . . I am spending a few days with the Missionaries here and I think I could arrange with the French Pasteur to borrow their church.' He no doubt felt obliged to offer his services, although if he had read *My Early Life* he might well have anticipated the reply. Churchill did not attend church regularly, and having recounted obligatory attendance at Harrow and during school holidays, noted with satisfaction: 'I accumulated in those years so fine a surplus in the Book of Observance that I have been drawing confidently on it ever since.' He continued to do so while in Marrakech, and replied by telegram to the Bishop: 'Thank you very much for your kind letter. I do not wish to trouble you in this matter.'

Writing to Clementine on 24 December, Churchill reported a picnic at Ourika in the desert, where they had had three picnics together during his convalescence four years before. By now he had 'six pictures on the stocks', which he thought better than those he had painted there in 1935. He went into some detail about his financial outgoings in a paragraph 'for your expert mind. The expense for the first week for seven of us is £300, which is little more than a fiver per day per head. Considering the excellent food, and service of the highest class, and that we have an office and a studio besides our bedrooms, this is not excessive, taking into account the state of the world ... £300 for six weeks = £1800. £2500 in dollars are being supplied and Miss Sturdee [his secretary] has had a message from Mr Graebner [the London representative of Time-Life] that there is plenty more if necessary.'

Churchill obviously felt he needed to justify Time-Life's generosity, and continued: 'When you recollect how much it means to all these publishers to get delivery of Volume I by the end of February, and that they would perhaps lose many thousands of pounds and suffer immense inconvenience if I failed them, I feel fully justified in the course I have taken, which results only from the fact of our own currency regulations which prevent me using my own money.'

Expenditure of his own money was confined to the two cases of whisky which had been dispatched by air by Berry Bros of London, Miss Sturdee sending instructions that the account would be settled in British currency on his return. Whatever Churchill's view of the state of his finances in Marrakech, she ended her note, '. . . the money here aren't arf going'.

Churchill's letter of 24 December to Clementine also re-counted a visit from a 'Crazy French colonel . . . now retired and quite dotty'. He had received the Colonel, who, he thought, was bringing some expected book proofs from Rabat. Mean-while the French police had searched the Colonel's suitcase and discovered a loaded automatic pistol, which they promptly removed. Colonel Hautville ordered the Colonel to return to Rabat, and although Churchill exchanged a friendly farewell with him in the hotel restaurant he turned up again at the Christmas Eve party, carefully watched by the French police.

Christmas Eve was a gala evening. Sarah, in a letter home, described how 'When midnight struck, they lowered the lights, and with one accord the international melee rose as a man to their feet just on the spur of the moment and looked to Papa. They raised their glasses, and clapped and "Vive Churchill" and "Bravo" echoed around the room . . . the Christmas pudding was brought in . . . and received by Papa just as he does a casket on being given the freedom of a city.' During the dancing which followed Churchill noticed a lady sitting alone. He stopped by her and said, 'You are the Christmas fairy. May I have a dance?' Her identity was never discovered, although the detectives thought she might have been a spy. Later a telegram arrived: 'You will never know my name but I am proud to have danced with Winston Churchill.'

The party long since over, Sarah, sound asleep in her room, was woken by a tap on her shoulder. It was a French detective who, in answer to her query if her father was all right, replied that he was her protector. She said, 'So keep protecting us!' The gallant Frenchman removed himself, and was later removed from duty.

In spite of Clementine's warnings, Sarah's vigilance and his own care, Churchill caught a cold. After discussing his condition with a local doctor, he telegraphed his English doctor, Lord Moran: 'I shall be grateful if you feel you can come.' Clementine flew out with the Morans on 2 January, and once his own doctor had reassured him that he had not got pneumonia, Churchill forgot about his illness and life continued as before. However, the press were not reassured, and three journalists flew out from England, where, they told him, 'there has been great public anxiety about your health'. He replied, 'I am much better. I am going painting this afternoon.'

By now there had been many conflicting suggestions on the drafts so far produced of Churchill's book about the war. Most were concerned with the problem of reconciling a dramatic but complicated narrative with the supporting material which needed to be incorporated. Sarah advised him: 'Don't listen to too many critics – Each critic criticises from a personal angle . . . write this book from the heart of yourself . . . and let it stand or fall by that – it will stand – everyone will listen to your story.' Perhaps the most useful suggestion came from Emery Reves, Churchill's foreign rights representative, who proposed the title for Volume I which was eventually chosen: *The Gathering Storm*.

Churchill, Clementine and their party left Marrakech on 18 January 1948 and arrived in London the following day, having stayed overnight in Bordeaux. It had hardly been a holiday. Volume I of *The Second World War* was virtually finished, and upwards of half a dozen canvases completed. But Churchill was undoubtedly refreshed – he had needed a change rather than a rest. He began at once to work on a speech he would make in a parliamentary debate four days later.

In early 1950 a general election returned Clement Attlee's Labour government to power, but with only a slender majority of six seats. With the political situation in the balance Churchill, as leader of the Conservative Party, decided to dispense with holidays abroad for the rest of that year, and to concentrate on politics and his memoirs. By December he needed a change, and thoughts of a warmer climate and the prospect of more painting lured him back to Marrakech. The Mamounia was full, but a message from the hotel manager indicated that by cancelling bookings or 'if necessary turning the people out', accommodation would be available. He would 'do anything to make [Churchill] comfortable and happy'. Therefore, accompanied by his literary advisers, secretaries, detective and a valet, he flew out on 17 December.

Walter Graebner of Time-Life described how hotels 'turned themselves inside out' to make Churchill comfortable:

> Churchill took with him all the equipment for an office other than tables and chairs. Nothing was left to chance . . . The office was always installed near the middle of the Churchill wing, since it functioned as the nerve centre for the entire party. All plans for the day were issued through the office. The management of this vital part of the holiday operation was entrusted to two secretaries who came out from the London staff, one of whom was available whenever Churchill called between 8 am and 2 am . . . Equally important was the installation on arrival of a studio where Churchill could paint when inclement weather kept him indoors . . . One large well lighted room was set aside for this, and the equipment brought from England included about fifteen frames, several dozen canvases, six or eight easels, and three or four powerful lamps.

He began painting at once, on the eighteenth from the hotel balcony and the following day at his usual picnic spot at Ourika. He considered a painting trip to Timbuktu, but had clearly not identified its position on a map, for when he broached the subject with the British Consul he was told it was 1500 miles distant. The Consul suggested a better place, as Churchill explained in a letter to Clementine: 'It is six hours motoring, and the next day six hours more, but there is a good hotel at each place run by the same management as the Mamounia; so it may be that later I shall make a dart in that direction.' This was Tinerhir, which Churchill again mentioned in a letter on Christmas Day: 'We are developing our plan to go to Wowowow, which they are going to call it in future.'

Meanwhile there were many visitors, and another dinner

with El Glaoui. To his wife Churchill described the spectacle which followed the feast: 'I never saw dancing, music, or the human form presented in such an unattractive guise . . . All were dressed up in quilts and blankets – they looked like bundles of cotton waste. However no one could say it was not highly respectable. The music brays and squawks . . . and the singing, which was maintained throughout, was a masterly compendium of discords. I have a great regard for the Glaoui who no doubt has endured all this and many other afflictions in his journey through this vale of sin and even more woe.'

There was also 'painting for a few hours each day', and the book, which, Churchill wrote, was 'the one thing that has gone best of all . . . eight chapters of Volume VI have gone to the printers. I have worked as much as eight hours a day in my bed which is very comfortable . . . I hope the tale will please you. I came here to play but so far it has only been work under physically agreeable conditions.'

Churchill had been occupied by more than the book and painting. A long letter on 8 January 1951 to Anthony Eden, who would succeed him as Prime Minister in four years, showed that international affairs and domestic politics were never far from his mind. He was particularly exercised by events in the Korean War, and what he saw as a flawed American strategy.

The planned visit to Wowowow was made by a chartered aircraft, a four-engined Skymaster, to avoid the long journey by road. From there Churchill telegraphed his wife: 'We have . . . found a sunlight painting paradise at Tinerhir.' On his return to Marrakech a second telegram announced: 'Returned safely over mountains last night after two lovely days. You will have to see that place which is in French military occupation. Officers most attentive and look forward to your visit which I promised them.' The hotel at Tinerhir was little more than a hostel, so Churchill's entourage virtually took it over. He painted furiously while there, and unless he was entertaining the French Commandant, his canvases would be displayed for his contemplation during dinner. His visits to Tinerhir produced a dozen paintings, some of which would be completed at Chartwell.

By the end of the first week of January Churchill had been joined by Clementine and Diana. Painting picnics now became even more highly organised. Walter Graebner, who had joined the party, describes the procedure:

Departure time was usually at 11 sharp. About two minutes earlier the whole party, with the exception of Churchill, had arranged themselves in their automobiles. The moment Churchill appeared the cavalcade set forth. The party normally consisted of some ten cars. Churchill, anxious to arrive at his destination, preferred fast driving. Once when his car struck a sheep, he stopped the car, growled at the driver, sympathised with the shepherd and gave him 500 francs.

At the picnic site Churchill would spend a few minutes selecting the spot for his easel. Then he went to work, a whisky and soda having been poured for him in the meantime. Twenty or thirty yards away from him the tables were set up and covered with white cloths . . . with the exception of Mr Churchill, who painted busily away with sublime disregard for the bustle going on behind him, everyone, from Mrs Churchill and assorted elderly peers and generals down, pitched in to help the detectives and Norman the valet get things in readiness . . . Everyone laughed, everyone was unbraced . . . Gayest and most unbraced of the company was always Churchill . . . who delighted in singing old songs . . . At Marrakech he took delight in a couple of picnic customs which he elevated to the rank of formal

ceremonies. One was the drinking of old Indian army toasts
. . . and at the end of each picnic we would solemnly rise and
drink the toast of the day. On Sundays it was 'To Absent
Friends' . . . [through to Saturday's] 'To Wives and Sweethearts'.
The other was a verse from Thomas Gray's *Ode on the Spring*.

> *Beside some water's rushy brink*
> *With me the muse shall sit and think*
> *(At ease reclined in rustic state)*
> *How vain the ardour of the Crowd,*
> *How low, how little are the Proud,*
> *How indigent the great.*

There was a moment of alarm on the final visit to Tinerhir.
Walter Graebner describes how as their plane took off, Churchill attempted to stub out his cigar in the ashtray in the arm
of his seat. Finding it too small, he removed it, deposited the
cigar in the hole and replaced it. Soon the smell of burning
permeated the cabin and a cloud of smoke enveloped Churchill.
A stewardess was summoned, and water poured down the hole.
Still not satisfied, he sent for one of the aircraft officers and
demanded that the cigar be retrieved. This done, he settled
back and announced, 'Now we can go over the mountain.'

During his last days in Marrakech, Churchill spent some time
in the studio of a French painter, Jacques Majorelle, who had
lived in Morocco for thirty years. Impressed with the vivid
effects Majorelle was achieving using tempera, Churchill invited
him to his studio at the Mamounia for a demonstration. Later
Churchill would write to his Swiss paint supplier for the
necessary ingredients. It was not however a technique with
which he persevered; it suited neither his temperament nor his
style.

On 20 January 1951 Churchill flew to Paris, where he spent two days before taking the train for London. It would be eight years before he returned to Marrakech, in the future lay four more years as Prime Minister and, in spite of his busy political life, the completion of his *History of the English Speaking Peoples*, which he had started in the early 1930s.

On 7 January 1959 Winston and Clementine flew to Marrakech for his sixth and final visit. Arrangements made in advance for their party included three dozen bottles of Pol Roger, his favourite champagne, and seven dozen bottles of other wine and spirits. A further three dozen of Pol Roger would follow. Ten daily broadsheets and tabloids and five Sunday newspapers would also be provided. Accompanying them as their guests in the Olympic airliner provided specially for the journey by Aristotle Onassis were Churchill's former Private Secretary 'Jock' Colville and his wife Meg, and Lady Monckton, whose husband Sir Walter had been Minister of Labour in Churchill's Cabinet.

For their arrival the King of Morocco had arranged a guard of honour, the whole of which Churchill, despite his eighty-four years, inspected without showing any signs of age or infirmity. Among the welcoming party was Sir Charles Beresford-Duke, the British Ambassador, who had motored the two hundred miles from Rabat, and the splendidly uniformed Governor of Marrakech, Omar ben Shemsi, in whose huge Lincoln Churchill drove to the Mamounia. Once again nothing was too much trouble for the local authorities. The Governor's huge car, with a driver and two detectives, was at Churchill's disposal throughout his visit, while the French airbase in Marrakech changed its flying schedules to avoid waking him too early, the first flights being postponed until nine o'clock.

Close on the heels of this party came the Paris correspondent of the *Daily Express*, Robin Stafford, and his photographer, sent by Churchill's friend and their proprietor, Lord Beaverbrook, who was convinced that Churchill had gone to Marrakech to die. Stafford later wrote that he and his photographer 'spent a very pleasant three weeks at the Mamounia proving Beaverbrook wrong'. One item which the cameraman snapped was the case of Pol Roger included among the arriving luggage.

Churchill painted two pictures during this visit, one from the hotel terrace and one in the gardens. Painting in the gardens he chatted over his shoulder to Anthony Montague Browne, his Private Secretary. After relating his opposition to the policy of unconditional German surrender forced on him by the Americans, which he was convinced had prolonged the war in Europe, he suddenly broke his reminiscing and said, 'Go and put on something warm. They say of the breeze off the Atlas that it is too gentle to blow out a candle, but strong enough to snuff out the life of a man.'

Evening entertainment centred around poker, which Clementine learned to play during this visit. Other players included an American lawyer, William Whitney and his English wife, and actress Adrienne Alan. The stakes were small, said Robin Stafford, noting that on one occasion the Churchills relieved the Whitneys of £5.

In 2001 I was introduced to Lahcen Khaoui, whose father had been a cook at the Mamounia. He had only been a boy on Churchill's earlier visits, but had taken note of the attention paid to this apparently important guest. In 1959 he had been a waiter, and told me how everyone stood when Churchill passed by. He collected and still treasures four long matches which my grandfather had used to light his cigars. I also met Henriette Bauchet, who with her husband Jean was staying at the Mamounia. She remembers Churchill 'dressed in a very relaxed manner as he painted in the hotel garden, but at dinner he looked most elegant. My husband and Sir Winston used to exchange cigars while discussing their provenance and the best way to light them.'

Aristotle and Tina Onassis came to Casablanca on the *Christina* and, together with Ari's sister Artemis, her husband Theodore Garoufalides and Margot Fonteyn, flew in their amphibious plane to Marrakech on 17 February. That evening Winston and Clementine gave their last dinner party in Marrakech, for Ari, Tina and their companions. On 18 February the Churchills left the Mamounia for the last time to join the *Christina* at Safi for a cruise to the Canary Islands and along the Moroccan coast.

My grandfather was not to visit Marrakech again, but he would set foot briefly once more in Morocco as the unexpected guest of Bryce Nairn, who had been the Vice-Consul in Marrakech searching for 'Colonel Warden' in January 1944. Flying to Gibraltar on 8 March 1960 to join Onassis on the *Christina*, Churchill and Clementine were diverted to Tangier because of a severe storm over southern Spain. Bryce Nairn was now the Minister at the British Legation. His wife Margaret was an artist who had often painted side by side with Churchill in Morocco and France. The Churchills arrived at the Nairns' house in the middle of a dinner party, Clementine declaring, 'Oh dear, oh dear, the poor darling Nairns. Here we are descending upon them like a lot of wounded ducks.'

Abdelkader Erzini, the Swedish Consul in Tangier, told me how Nairn took his unexpected guests, together with the Onassises, who had arrived from Gibraltar, to the Erzinis' family house at Tetuan. Erzini's father had been responsible during World War II for fulfilling an unusual British request. On a visit to Gibraltar, Churchill had been informed that the colony of apes which roamed the Rock was dwindling alarmingly. No one knew for sure how the apes had arrived there, but everyone knew the superstition that if they left Gibraltar, British rule would come to an end. My grandfather, having a superstitious nature, and also worried that the people of Gibraltar might believe the legend, had ordered the ape colony to be reinforced without delay. The Governor, with more pressing matters on his mind, shelved this task until, out of the blue, came a telegram from Churchill: 'The establishment of apes on Gibraltar should be 24 and every effort should be made to reach this number and maintain it thereafter.' Passed down the line, the problem landed with the British Consul General at Tetuan, Cecil Hope-Gill. The Erzini caged colony of Barbary apes provided the reinforcements.

The *Christina* sailed from Tangier, carrying Churchill from Morocco for the last time. It was a country which for a quarter of a century had provided him with the leisure and environment to achieve a huge amount of work. His time there was ample demonstration of his philosophy that a change of atmosphere is essential for those, like him, whose work is their pleasure.

CHAPTER 7

Wartime Journeys 1914–18
and 1939–43

To hell with that. I'm going, whatever happens. This is too
serious a situation to bother about the weather.
Winston Churchill to Colonel Hollis,
13 June 1940

Winston Churchill is remembered by many as the inspirational leader to whom Britain turned in 1940, but those of us born after the mid-thirties have no direct recollection of his galvanising effect upon events. My own personal memories are of a peacetime Prime Minister and a much-loved and loving grandfather. When I was a child, the adulation he received impressed on me that he was regarded as someone very special; but I, like others of my generation and after, have to rely upon history for an understanding of his leadership.

I have listened to his recorded speeches which rallied Britain and gave hope to a conquered Europe. I have seen many times the pictures of a grim Churchill standing defiantly amid the smoking ruins of London, and a charismatic Churchill with a cherubic smile making a V sign on the steps of Number Ten.

Perhaps my favourite is of my grandfather parodying the American gangster Al Capone: Churchill in Homburg hat, pinstriped suit, a cigar clamped between his teeth and a tommy-gun under his arm. There are also pictures of Churchill abroad: meeting Roosevelt and Stalin; in the desert surrounded by troops; at a religious service beneath the fifteen-inch guns of a battleship; and dozens of others. But these photographs, showing a peripatetic Prime Minister and war leader, are only a part of the legend.

It took an American legend, General Douglas MacArthur, to put these epic journeys into context: 'If disposal of all the Allied decorations were today placed by Providence in my hands, my first act would be to award the Victoria Cross to Winston Churchill. Not one of those who wear it deserves it more than he. A flight of ten thousand miles through hostile and foreign skies may be the duty of young pilots, but for a Statesman burdened with the world's cares it is an act of inspiring gallantry and valour.'

Churchill's wartime travels fulfilled a number of functions. They were mostly prompted in the first instance by the requirement, as he saw it, personally to influence people and make things happen. These were logical reasons which would have prompted any ordinary political leader to quit his desk occasionally. But, as we know, Churchill was no ordinary leader. The adventurer had reasons of his own: 'A man who has to play an effective part in taking, with the highest responsibility, grave and terrible decisions of war may need the refreshment of adventure. He may also need the comfort that when sending so many others to their death he may share in a small way their risks. His fields of personal interest, and consequently his forces of action, are stimulated by direct contact with the event.'

'Travelling seemed to recharge his batteries. He was more

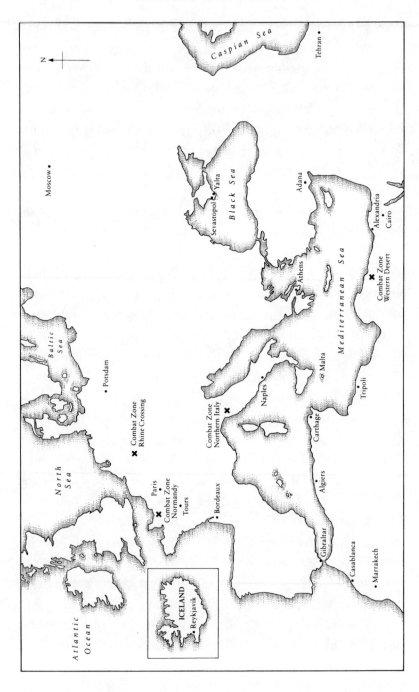

relaxed,' was how one of Churchill's secretaries, Elizabeth Layton, put it. Joining Number Ten in 1941, she accompanied him on all of his overseas wartime visits from 1943 and had an intimate view of him at work at home and abroad. Grace Hamblin, who had been his secretary before the war, then worked for Clementine, described Churchill as 'an adventurous soul who loved going away'.

His enthusiasm for seeing events at the sharp end was nothing new. As First Lord of the Admiralty on the outbreak of the First World War, he took personal charge of the defence of Antwerp in which the Royal Naval Division was playing a prominent part. Then came the ill-fated Dardanelles campaign of 1915, which aimed at eliminating Turkey, bringing Greece, Bulgaria and Romania into the war on the Allied side, and opening up a route to support a hard-pressed Russia. There was no convenient way for Churchill to visit the region and when he tried to arrange to go there the Cabinet vetoed the idea. The campaign failed, leaving him to tell the House of Commons: 'It will always be incredible to future ages that every man in this country did not rally to an enterprise which carried with it such immense possibilities, and which required such limited resources to carry it into effect.' That it failed was largely due to a lack of strategic co-ordination in the War Cabinet. The Prime Minister, Herbert Asquith, was in the hands of various Ministers, each of whom was fighting his own corner. Lord Kitchener, the Secretary of State for War, changed his mind several times over the army's contribution, while Churchill, as First Lord of the Admiralty, had insufficient authority to match the responsibilities he had undertaken. A campaign designed to avoid the slaughter of the Western Front did no more, in the end, than replicate it at Gallipoli. Churchill learned the lesson well, and the moment he became Prime Minister in World

War II he created an organisation which would not repeat such a mistake.

Churchill was made the political scapegoat for the Darda-nelles campaign, the failure of which cost him his office. Within six months, only a few days short of his forty-first birthday, he had rejoined the army, crossing to France on 18 November 1915. As a yeomanry major in the Queen's Own Oxfordshire Hussars he had kept abreast of military matters, but realising he had a good deal to learn about trench warfare he attached himself to the 1st Battalion Grenadier Guards before taking over as commanding officer of the 6th Battalion Royal Scots Fusiliers on 5 January 1916. In the Royal Scots he was received with dismay, Captain Andrew Gibb recording the reaction to Churchill's impending arrival: 'When the news spread, a mutin-ous spirit grew.'

The battalion had sustained severe losses, and was resting near the town of Meteren, within five miles of the French–Belgian border and some ten miles from the front. Lieutenant Jock McDavid described the mood of the troops: '[Churchill] joined a conglomerated mess of young civilians and old reservists both of whom had experienced hell since they arrived in France in the spring of 1915. Morale was low, understandably so.' Churchill had two weeks to rally his battalion before it returned to the front line. McDavid recalled: 'After a very brief period he accelerated the morale of officers and men to an almost unbelievable degree. It was sheer personality. He let everyone under his command see that he was responsible, from the very moment he arrived, that they understood not only *what* they were supposed to do, but *why* they had to do it.'

The battalion went into the line at the Belgian village of Ploegsteert. Another officer, Lieutenant Hakewell-Smith, described Churchill's excursions into no man's land: 'It was a nerve-racking experience to go with him. He never fell when a shell went off; he never ducked when a bullet went past with its loud crack. He used to say, after watching me duck, "It's no damn use ducking: the bullet has gone a long way past you now."' His headquarters was at a place called Laurence Farm, in the courtyard of which he set up his easel, having, in the months since losing office, begun to paint as an antidote to frustration. Shells exploded round about, but he carried on. Hakewell-Smith recalled that as a particular painting neared completion Churchill became angry and difficult to talk to, then his mood changed abruptly for the better. Hakewell-Smith enquired what had happened, to which Churchill replied, 'I couldn't get the shell hole right in the painting. However I did it, it looked like a mountain, but yesterday I discovered that if I put a bit of white in it, it looked like a hole after all.'

Churchill was determined to return to the centre of policy-making, despite being deterred for a while by Clementine, who could see that 'People will always try to deny you power if they think you are looking for it.' However, the amalgamation of the 6th and 7th Royal Scots Fusiliers into a single battalion, which would be commanded by a more senior regular officer, provided Churchill with an ideal opportunity to return to politics.

Back in London in May 1916, he was still denied the responsibility he sought, and it was not until Asquith was replaced as Prime Minister by David Lloyd George in December that his fortunes began to change. In late May and early June he undertook, with the Prime Minister's approval, a visit to the French and British fronts. On 18 July he was back in the Cabinet as Minister of Munitions. This required him to go to France frequently, and he would save travelling time by flying to his destination, which in the early days of flight was a hazard in itself – twice, through engine failure, he was lucky not to finish up in the sea. His talents as a roving emissary were fully employed by Lloyd George, and he established an office at the Château Vechrocq, near St Omer, enabling him to stay in France for days at a time.

On the night of the armistice, 11 November 1918, Churchill and Clementine – who was expecting her fourth child that week* – dined with Lloyd George at 10 Downing Street. After four long years the Great War, 'the war that will end war', as it was hoped at the time, was finally over.

However, after an interval of just twenty-one years, on 4 September 1939, war again broke out with Germany, and Winston Churchill once more became First Lord of the Admiralty.

While nine months of 'phoney war' would pass before the German onslaught brought the rapid collapse of Holland, Belgium and France, the war at sea began immediately. Churchill was almost sixty-five, but his energy was undiminished. In spite of his onerous duties as First Lord he still made time to travel to France, not only to confer with the Commander-in-Chief of the French navy, Admiral Jean Darlan, but also, although it was not strictly within his remit, to visit the British Expeditionary Force and the massive French defences at the Maginot Line.

The German blitzkrieg began in the early hours of 10 May 1940, and with it came the demise of Neville Chamberlain's Cabinet, which had so far wrestled incompetently with the management of the war. A full-scale parliamentary debate on 8 and 9 May had left the Prime Minister convinced that he could no longer carry on. The Labour Party agreed to serve in

---

* Born on 15 November 1918, and christened Marigold Frances, she died of a sudden illness on 22 August 1921.

a coalition government under a Conservative Prime Minister other than Chamberlain. Churchill was by no means the guaranteed successor: Chamberlain attempted to pass the baton to the Foreign Secretary, Lord Halifax, who declined, ostensibly on the grounds that a Prime Minister could not operate effectively from the House of Lords; but not for nothing was he called 'the Holy Fox', and he probably saw political advantage in stepping aside at that juncture. Chamberlain resigned and advised the King to send for Churchill, who by the early evening of 10 May was Prime Minister.

With the Low Countries overrun, the British Expeditionary Force isolated and the French government in disarray, Churchill strove to keep France in the war, making four visits across the Channel within the month. Flying in a passenger plane, he was sometimes at considerable risk. He described one such flight, on 12 June: 'we started alone calling for an escort to meet us, if possible over the Channel . . . The skies cleared . . . Eight thousand feet below us was Le Havre, burning.' No escort had turned up when two German fighters appeared below and, oblivious of the prize above them, began strafing fishing boats. 'We were lucky the pilots did not look upwards.'

Within twenty-four hours Churchill was again crossing the Channel. The French government had abandoned Paris and was on the point of seeking an armistice. The weather was said to be too bad for flying, but Churchill's response was, 'To hell with that. I'm going, whatever happens. This is too serious a situation to bother about the weather.' He sent for his heavy pistol, saying, 'If we are attacked on the way I may be able to kill at least one German.' Accompanied by General Ismay, the head of his defence office, and Lord Halifax, the Foreign Secretary, he landed near Tours at an abandoned airfield cratered by bombs. There was no one to meet them, so, announcing himself in French as the Prime Minister of Great Britain, Churchill commandeered a taxi, declaring to his companions, 'Well, the journey does not promise well. Do you not think that a good luncheon is in order? The hotel in Tours used to have some admirable Vouvray in its cellars.' But lunch was not so easy to obtain, as Churchill later recalled: 'We found a café, which was closed, but after explanations we obtained a meal.'

He was upbeat when the French Prime Minister, Paul Reynaud, appeared in Tours, but the French government was too deeply demoralised for Churchill's advocacy to prevent its surrender. Reynaud was sure the Germans would go on to invade Britain. 'What will you do when they come?' he asked.

'If they swim we will drown them. If they land we will hit them on the head, *frappez* them *sur la tête*,' Churchill replied.

It would be four years before he returned to France. As they took off with an escort of twelve Hurricanes he was by no means downcast, and in good humour turned to Ismay and said, 'Do you realise we probably have a maximum of three months to live?' Then he slept: 'This was wise for there was a long way to go before bedtime.'

There would also be a long way to go before Churchill travelled abroad again. Britain now stood alone, and the threat of invasion would hang over it until the Battle of Britain was won. British industry had still to be fully geared to war production. The Battle of the Atlantic was only just beginning, and soon there would be the campaign in the North African desert to worry about; but for a time the demands of the home front were paramount.

If Britain lacked resources, America had them in plenty, and Churchill set out to court President Roosevelt, sending him a long letter on 8 December 1940. Covering all aspects of the conflict, he pointed out the mutual interdependence of

American security and British survival. From this sprang American Lend-Lease, by which America would lease Britain what it needed, the rental to be paid after the war when the leased items would be returned. Thus America was gradually becoming involved in the war, and when Hitler invaded Russia on 22 July 1941, the implications for Anglo–American strategy demanded a face-to-face conference between the leaders. On 4 August Churchill boarded the battleship the *Prince of Wales* in Scapa Flow, bound for Placentia Bay in Newfoundland and a meeting with President Roosevelt. He was again a travelling man.

Churchill was not one to rely on aides and speechwriters to put words in his mouth. His thoughts, conveyed in his own incomparable English, were personally dictated by him to a secretary. At Number Ten a relay of young women ensured that, day and night, someone was on hand to take dictation. At sea aboard the *Prince of Wales* there was no suitable accommodation for them, and a man had to be found at short notice.

Patrick Kinna, then twenty-seven, had been the Duke of Windsor's clerk in Paris. After the fall of France he hitched a lift home on a British warship and was then sent to Washington where, under Lord Halifax, the British Ambassador, he assisted in the setting up of a UK–US joint staff. That done, he returned to England to become a parliamentary recorder, a job which required accurate speed writing to record debates in the House of Commons. Instead he was summoned to Number Ten, where Sir John Martin, Churchill's Private Secretary, informed him that he was to accompany the Prime Minister on a 'secret and dangerous mission'.

During the first night at sea Kinna was summoned from his cabin by Churchill's valet, Frank Sawyers, to take dictation. It was his first encounter with Churchill and he was, he told me, terrified. He knocked on the door and entered to find Churchill lying on the bed in his dressing gown. 'Sit,' said the Prime Minister.

As Kinna waited for the next instruction, loud whistling could be heard from somewhere nearby. Kinna remembered with trepidation that he had been warned of Churchill's aversion to extraneous noise, tapping and whistling in particular.

The reaction was inevitable: 'Go and tell those matelots to stop whistling.'

This may seem a simple task, but Patrick Kinna is a small man whose considerable presence at the age of eighty-seven was not yet apparent in the twenty-seven-year-old sent off to find the offending sailors who, in their bare feet, would have towered over him.

'I said a Hail Mary and miraculously the whistling stopped,' he told me. 'It was not, however, divine intervention but the fortuitous arrival of an officer.'

The whistling silenced, a relieved Kinna returned to the Prime Minister's cabin and settled down to take his first dictation. As he sat, pencil in hand, Churchill said, 'This is a melancholy story.' Then, looking at Kinna, who thought he had merely been talking to him, he barked, 'Take it down! I am dictating. Don't be so stupid.' This inauspicious start was to be the beginning of a most successful and close wartime working relationship.

The *Prince of Wales* was ploughing through seas so heavy that a choice had to be made between slowing down or dispensing with the destroyer escort. The escort was dropped, and the battleship continued at high speed on a zigzag course to avoid presenting a straightforward target to any patrolling U-boats. Churchill was a notoriously bad sailor, but the *Prince of Wales* must have behaved itself in the rough sea, for he described the voyage as an agreeable interlude. With waves breaking over the ship the deck was unusable, but for Churchill the journey to the bridge four or five times a day, scaling the ladders between the many decks, was sufficient exercise.

For relaxing reading he had a copy of C.S. Forester's naval adventure *Captain Hornblower* which had been given to him by Oliver Lyttelton, the Minister of State in Cairo. When radio restrictions were briefly lifted he sent Lyttelton the message: '*Hornblower* admirable.' This caused consternation among the staff at Middle East Headquarters, who vainly searched their files for an operation code-named 'Hornblower', on which they thought they were being complimented. In the evenings there was a cinema where Churchill watched his favourite film, Alexander Korda's *Lady Hamilton*, for the fifth time. Featuring Nelson and his sea battles, it was an entirely appropriate film for the occasion, and Patrick Kinna recalled that when the final credits had rolled Churchill addressed the ship's officers, saying, 'Gentlemen, I thought this film would interest you, showing great events similar to those in which you have been taking part.'

The *Prince of Wales* arrived in Placentia Bay at 9 a.m. on 9 August. Later that morning Churchill went aboard the American heavy cruiser *Augusta* to meet the President, who, though usually confined to a wheelchair, was standing supported on the arm of his son Elliott. The Prime Minister was nautically dressed for the occasion in a blue peaked cap and short blue jacket, his uniform as a Brother of Trinity House, the association concerned with inshore maritime arrangements such as ships' pilots and lighthouses. Churchill and Roosevelt had met in 1918 when the latter, as Assistant Secretary for the Navy, represented the United States with a short speech at a dinner in London. The principal speakers had been Lord Curzon and Field Marshal

Jan Smuts, so it was hardly surprising that Churchill, already an international figure, had no recollection of the comparatively junior American politician, and assumed that at Placentia they were meeting for the first time. If the President was put out he showed no sign, and the two leaders established an instant rapport.

On Sunday the tenth, Roosevelt, his staff and several hundred personnel from all ranks of the United States Navy came aboard the British battleship and joined its company for Divine Service beneath the three huge guns of the after-turret. Once again Roosevelt, at the price of considerable pain, disdained the use of his wheelchair, but both he and Churchill sat through the service, which was conducted by American and British chaplains, the joint symbolism emphasised by the Union Jack and the Stars and Stripes draped either side of the pulpit. Churchill, who had chosen the hymns 'For Those in Peril on the Sea', 'Onward Christian Soldiers' and 'O God, our Help in Ages Past', later wrote, 'It was a great hour to live.' Fortunately for the morale of mortal beings, the future is unpredictable. Nearly half of those attending that service would die four months later when the *Prince of Wales* was sunk off the east coast of Malaya.

From this meeting between Churchill and Roosevelt came the Atlantic Charter, an explicit acknowledgement that Britain and America were pursuing the same ideals. Patrick Kinna told me that as a result of typing the successive drafts, he knew the Charter by heart. In it Britain and America pledged themselves to 'respect the right of all peoples to choose the form of government under which they will live', and 'to see sovereign rights restored to those who have been forcibly deprived of them'.

On this first wartime visit to Washington Churchill had caught the imagination of America, and tributes of all sorts arrived continually. A six-foot-high V sign composed of lilies, carnations and irises found its way into Churchill's bedroom in the White House. The Secret Service were kept busy opening hundreds of boxes of cigars, for no parcel was allowed into the White House without examination.

The homeward journey on the *Prince of Wales* was broken on 16 August in Iceland, where the battleship dropped anchor in Havals Fjord and the Prime Minister continued in a destroyer to Reykjavik. Here a huge and enthusiastic crowd turned out to welcome him. After meeting members of the Icelandic Cabinet, he reviewed a joint parade of British and American forces and visited airfields under construction before returning to Havals Fjord, where he visited the battleship *Ramilles* and addressed British and American sailors in the anchorage. As darkness fell the *Prince of Wales* weighed anchor. It had been a long day, and one during which it was unlikely that Churchill had been able to take his afternoon siesta, the routine hour's sleep which he said enabled him to cram a day and a half's work into every twenty-four hours. He reached Scapa Flow two days later, on 18 August.

Back in London, Patrick Kinna was again summoned by Sir John Martin to Number Ten, where he was told that Churchill wanted him to join his staff. Not wanting to spend the war in Whitehall, he refused, and was given two days to reconsider. His second refusal was met with consternation. 'This is the nearest thing you'll ever get to a royal command,' said Martin. 'This is a great honour. You have to do it.' Kinna relented, and became a temporary civil servant. He described the job, for which he received £400 per annum, as 'rather well paid because of the secrecy involved'.

At Placentia Bay Churchill and Roosevelt had discussed the growing threat from Japan. Four months after that meeting, at

8.25 in the morning of 7 December 1941, Japanese bombers struck the American Pacific Fleet at Pearl Harbor, on the Hawaiian island of Oahu. The assault continued for an hour and a half, at the end of which four battleships had been destroyed and the remainder severely damaged. Two thousand Americans were dead. Simultaneously the Japanese had struck at American bases in the Philippines and at the British colonies of Hong Kong and Malaya. Within three days two British battleships, the *Prince of Wales* and the *Repulse*, which had been sent to the Far East in anticipation of the Japanese threat, were at the bottom of the sea.

In a telephone conversation with Churchill immediately following the attack on Pearl Harbor, Roosevelt had said, 'We are all in the same boat now.' The following day Churchill made plans to leave for America. The crossing would again be by sea, as it was considered too risky to travel by air against the prevailing winter winds. On 12 December Churchill travelled by train to the Clyde and embarked on the *Duke of York*, the recently commissioned sister ship of the ill-fated *Prince of Wales*. He was accompanied by a large staff, and for the first time by his personal doctor Sir Charles Wilson – later Lord Moran.

Travel by sea may have been the lesser of two risks, but risky nevertheless it was. The *Duke of York* sailed down the Irish Sea into a storm-tossed Bay of Biscay, crossing the route taken by U-boats to and from their Atlantic hunting ground and passing within four hundred miles of German airfields in Brittany. The voyage was scheduled to take seven days sailing at twenty knots, but the destroyer escort could make no more than six knots in the heavy seas, and on the second night was dismissed. Thereafter the battleship plunged on alone, with no accompanying vessels to protect it from U-boat attack. Heavy clouds had grounded enemy aircraft and prevented all but an occasional air escort from circling above the ship, but the sudden appearance of blue skies signalled a possible danger. However, no enemy appeared, and the great ship continued unmolested into the wide reaches of the ocean. U-boats were frequently reported in the vicinity, and the German battleship *Tirpitz* was reported missing from her base, causing the Prime Minister to speak hopefully of taking part in a naval engagement.

Each day Churchill visited the bridge for a while but, not being a good sailor in heavy seas, he spent most of the day in bed holding court and working on his papers. Throughout the voyage he bent his energies to formulating a comprehensive strategy for the future prosecution of the war. It was a remarkable achievement. Thrashed out with his chiefs of staff it would shortly be put to the Americans and, with only minor amendments, be accepted as the Allied blueprint.

On 22 December the *Duke of York* anchored in Hampton Roads and Churchill, impatient to meet Roosevelt again, flew to Washington National Airport where his host was awaiting him. For three weeks, apart from a brief visit to Ottawa, Churchill was Roosevelt's guest at the White House, where the frenetic activity was interrupted only by festivities on Christmas Day.

On 26 December Churchill addressed Congress, reminding them of his American ancestry: 'If my father had been American and my mother British, instead of the other way around, I might have got here on my own.' That night the ceaseless work over many months, perhaps exacerbated by the particular excitement of a day with Congress, finally took its toll. Tackling a window which was reluctant to open, Churchill suffered a mild heart attack. Sir Charles Wilson decided to tell no one, not even the patient, for fear of precipitating public concern, and simply advised Churchill not to exert himself unnecessarily.

But business continued as usual and, after travelling to Ottawa by train, Churchill addressed the Canadian Parliament on 30 December. This was the occasion on which, recalling that the Vichy General Weygand had forecast that Britain would have her neck wrung like a chicken, Churchill remarked, 'Some chicken. Some neck!'

He returned by train to Washington on 1 January, having visited the carriage carrying the press to toast in the New Year: 'Here's to 1942. Here's to a year of toil – a year of struggle and peril, and a long step forward to victory. May we all come through safe and with honour.' Back in Washington, Churchill agreed to Roosevelt's draft declaration by the Allies and Associated Powers, who would be known, at Roosevelt's suggestion, as the 'United Nations'. The declaration pledged all signatories to employ their full resources against Germany, Japan and their allies. It would be signed by twenty-six nations, including several which were under Nazi rule.

In Churchill's absence in Canada the President had accepted an invitation for the two leaders to attend a service at Christ Church in Alexandria, Virginia. The historical associations of this lovely church would have made the visit irresistible to my grandfather. Not only had George Washington been a vestryman there in the 1760s, but it was also the place of worship and indeed confirmation of General Robert E. Lee, the Confederate commander in the American Civil War. The invitation from the rector, the Reverend Edward Randolph Welles II, asked the President 'to come to Christ Church on the National Day of Prayer bringing Mr Churchill so they could sit together in George Washington's pew'. It would have been hard to find a more evocative setting for the two leaders to join in worship just three and a half weeks after the attack on Pearl Harbor.

The rector announced 'The Battle Hymn of the Republic'

with the observation that 'it was time that the USA buried the hatchet of the War between the States as well as the British and the Americans burying the hatchet of the Revolutionary War of American Independence'. This had without doubt been long buried by the two men who had laid the foundations for the 'Special Relationship' between their two countries.

The congregation, a large part of which was made up of Secret Service agents, sang movingly, and according to the Reverend Welles' account, 'Winston Churchill was so deeply moved that in the middle he wept, with great tears running unashamedly down his cheeks.' 'The Battle Hymn of the Republic' was one of his favourites, and twenty-three years later would bring tears to the eyes of the congregation at his State Funeral in St Paul's Cathedral.

The service over, the rector introduced his wife and daughter Katrina, whose seventh birthday it was, to the President and the Prime Minister. Four hours later the little girl developed chickenpox, which caused much consternation lest she had passed it on to either leader.

On 5 January, after further discussions with Roosevelt, Churchill flew to Florida, largely to give the White House a rest and not to overtax the hospitality of the President. In Florida he stayed at Pompano near Miami, the beach estate of the American Secretary of State, Edward Stettinus. Catering was provided by Captain Theodore Knight, the proprietor of the nearby Club Unique, a supper club and casino known locally as Cap's Place. The visit, Churchill's first real break in nearly three years, was described as a rest, but throughout his stay in Florida Churchill wrestled at length with various intractable problems, and a good deal of work was done. There was also some swimming – Patrick Kinna recalled that, having no bathing costumes, they did without.

The President sent staff from the White House, and the cook, feeling he had been put on his mettle, produced an elaborately prepared clam chowder. This the Prime Minister declined, and surprised the staff by asking instead for a plate of double strength Bovril. He pronounced it 'Bove-ril', which caused further confusion in the kitchen. He also had supper in the Yellow Room at Cap's Place, whose present owner insists that Roosevelt and the Duke of Windsor were also present. This is an honestly believed myth which has become a local legend. Actually Roosevelt remained at the White House, while the Duke was serving as Governor of the Bahamas. There was lunch with Consuelo Balsan, the former Duchess of Marlborough who had been married to Churchill's cousin Sunny, the 9th Duke, at whose home in France Churchill had painted his last picture before the war.

On 11 January Churchill was back in the White House. As usual Sawyers summoned Patrick Kinna to take dictation. Churchill began while still lying in the bath, and continued as he clambered out to be wrapped by his valet in a huge bath towel. They moved to the adjacent bedroom, where Kinna sat on the bed while Churchill paced up and down with the towel intermittently in place. There came a rat-a-tat at the door. 'Come in,' called Churchill. His towel slipped to the floor, and the door opened to reveal a surprised Roosevelt in his wheelchair, leading Churchill to declare, 'As you can see Mr President, I have nothing to hide from you.'

On the fourteenth Churchill left Washington by the *Bristol*, a Boeing flying boat, for Bermuda, where he was to board the *Duke of York*. Thirty years before, when aircraft were little more than bits of wood, canvas and wire, Churchill had learned to fly. Now he took the controls of this thirty-ton aircraft and, after successfully trying a few gentle manoeuvres, decided it would be a good way to go home. He enquired of the pilot, Captain Kelly Rogers, if the flying boat could reach England from Bermuda, and, being assured that it could, put the suggestion to his service chiefs. They promptly vetoed the idea. Quite apart from the hazards of war, air travel in the 1940s brought its own perils. Aircraft did not have the performance to fly high above the weather; they had to go through or around it. Navigation aids were minimal, and after a long Atlantic crossing an accurate landfall was to be hoped for rather than expected. However, Churchill's persuasive powers won the day, and they took off after lunch on 15 January, expecting to land at Plymouth for breakfast the following morning.

At the end of the long flight the expected sight of the Scilly Isles through gaps in the clouds below failed to materialise. As the last ten hours had been through mist, with no possibility of a star-shot to aid navigation, it seemed likely that they had been blown off course. Captain Rogers turned north, and after another half-hour the coast of England was sighted below. Had they delayed their turn by only five minutes they would have arrived over Brest, and presented an easy target for German anti-aircraft guns or fighters. As it was they had only to avoid the barrage balloons at Plymouth before coming in to land at RAF Mount Batten, in sight of the bowling green on which in 1588 Sir Francis Drake had awaited the Armada. Soon afterwards, Captain Rogers was summoned to Number Ten, where Churchill presented him with an inscribed silver salver as a memento of the flight.

After five months at home, the agitation by Stalin to open a second front in Europe and the conflicting requirements of the many theatres of war led Churchill to cross the Atlantic for his third meeting with Roosevelt in ten months. Because of the urgency he decided to go by air once again, and asked that Captain Rogers should fly his party over. Before leaving London on 17 June 1942, the Prime Minister had written to the King suggesting the Foreign Secretary Anthony Eden as his successor 'in case of my death on this journey'.

It was not a contingency he dwelt on. Delighted at the prospect of the flight, he was in an effervescent mood as he and his entourage embarked at Stranraer, on the west coast of Scotland. Carrying a gold-topped malacca cane, he was dressed in his siren suit, a one-piece garment modelled on the overalls he had worn when bricklaying at Chartwell, zip-up shoes and a black Homburg hat. He began humming 'We're here because we're here because we're here because we're here.' General Sir Alan Brooke – later Lord Alanbrooke – noted in his diary that it was a very appropriate tune: 'It was at a time when the Atlantic had not been so very frequently flown . . . we were both somewhat doubtful whether we should get there . . . and whether we should ever get back.'

The Boeing took off after dark, in order to avoid a German aircraft which was apt to patrol the Western Approaches. Once they were airborne, Churchill sent for the steward in order to arrange meal timings: 'The clock is going to do some funny things while we are in the air but that is of little consequence, my stomach is my clock and I eat every four hours.' General Brooke noted: 'As I had to share every one of these meals with him and as they were all washed down with champagne and brandy, it became a little trying on the constitution.'

On these journeys Churchill's manservant, Sawyers, was an important element of his entourage. Once, arriving in Washington after a visit to American troops, Churchill donned his siren suit and a Panama hat. Sawyers would not let him disembark. 'What's wrong, Sawyers, why are you getting in my way?'

asked Churchill. Sawyers replied, 'The brim of your hat is turned up, does not look well, turn it down.' Churchill, looking rather cross, turned it down, whereupon Sawyers stood to one side, muttering, 'That's much, much better, much better.'

During this visit Churchill won the debate over the second front in Europe, which he believed should be delayed because of insufficient resources of men and materiel, and agreed the Anglo–American programme for the development of an atomic weapon. He landed back at Stranraer in the early hours of 27 June. Within five weeks he would be off once more on his travels.

Concerned that the war in North Africa was going badly and that changes in the high command were needed, Churchill decided to assess the situation personally, and make the necessary changes on the spot. He was also anxious about the reaction of Stalin to the news that the second front could not be launched until at least 1943, and felt that he should break the news himself, as 'it would be like carrying a lump of ice to the North Pole'. He telegraphed Stalin that he was going to Cairo, and proposed flying from there to Moscow. Stalin's agreement arrived within twenty-four hours. The only doubts about the Prime Minister's next journey came from within his own Cabinet, who feared for his health.

This time Churchill would not be travelling in the comfort of the Boeing Clipper, but in a draughty Liberator bomber, named 'Commando', from which the bomb racks had been removed and some rudimentary passenger accommodation installed – the most lavish of which were two shelves on which the Prime Minister and his doctor would sleep. The remainder of the party slept in the bomb bay. Patrick Kinna remembers one senior officer remarking, 'I hope the pilot remembers he is carrying people not bombs.' The aircraft was cold and unpressurised, so oxygen masks would be needed when flying over mountains. At the time Churchill's secretary Elizabeth Layton thought the journey a 'considerable risk' – not an unreasonable assessment as, quite apart from the hazards of flying and enemy action, Churchill was almost sixty-seven, and prone to pneumonia.

To test Churchill's likely reaction to flying at the unaccustomed altitude he spent fifteen minutes wearing an oxygen mask in a chamber with the atmosphere adjusted to fifteen thousand feet. He was passed fit for the flight, which took off a little after midnight on Sunday, 2 August 1942. At Churchill's request, his oxygen mask had been adapted so that he could enjoy both oxygen and a cigar.

After twenty-one hours in the air, and having stopped to refuel at Gibraltar and Malta, Churchill's party, flying in two Liberators, arrived in Cairo in time for breakfast on 3 August. In his diary General Brooke noted that Churchill 'turned up delighted with his trip and looking remarkably fresh. He has got his doctor with him who tells me he was a little worried about his pulse.' The same diary entry recorded an event nineteen hours later: 'PM again called me in and kept me up until 1.30am.' No doubt Churchill had managed his routine siesta, but even so he was setting a fast pace, making drastic and immediate changes in the high command of the British 8th Army in the Western Desert which, having wider repercussions, were by no means straightforward. Brooke's diary the following day noted a discussion with the Prime Minister at 1 a.m., followed by take-off for 8th Army headquarters at 4.45 a.m. Churchill remarked that breakfast at the headquarters was taken in 'a wire netted cube full of flies and important military personages'.

After a day with the 8th Army Churchill flew back to Cairo.

Some measure of the dangers of his travels is that two days later, flying exactly the same route, the man Churchill had just decided to appoint to command 8th Army, General Gott, was shot down and killed.

The entourage for Moscow filled three aircraft which took off at 2 a.m. on 10 August. Brooke remarked that 'Winston on these occasions loved to accumulate a large number of Generals, Admirals and Air Marshals.' By dawn the flight was approaching the mountains of Kurdistan. Churchill's young American pilot, Captain Vanderkloot, intended to fly between the peaks at nine thousand feet to avoid the passengers having to make use of oxygen. Churchill, poring over the map and seeing that the peaks ahead reached eleven thousand feet, asked to fly at twelve thousand, and everyone began 'sucking our oxygen tubes'.

Later, as they approached the runway at Tehran, where they would be making an overnight stop, he noticed the altimeter reading 4500 feet. Thinking it should be reading no more than a few hundred feet, he suggested that it needed adjustment before they trusted their lives to it among the mountains of Russia. 'Tehran is over four thousand feet above sea level,' replied Vanderkloot.

The main purpose of the stopover in Tehran was for Churchill to discuss American involvement in the Trans-Persian Railway, which, running from the Persian Gulf to the Caspian Sea, played an important part in supplying Russia with war materials. For these talks Averell Harriman, President Roosevelt's personal emissary, had joined the party. Lunch with the Shah of Iran in a palace amid great trees in the mountains, and a night in the summer residence of the British Legation a thousand feet above the busy city, provided a welcome contrast to the heat, dust and bustle of Cairo.

For Churchill, sitting beside Captain Vanderkloot, the flight into Russia provided a spectacle largely unknown to modern air travel, when aircraft fly so high that the land below, if seen at all, looks much the same whatever the route. He described it with his artist's eye. The Liberator

flew through the great valley which led to Tabriz and then turned northwards to Enzeli, on the Caspian. We passed this second range of mountains avoiding both clouds and peaks. In two hours the waters of the Caspian Sea shone ahead. On the western shore lay Baku and its oil fields. The German armies were now so near the Caspian that our course was set for Kibushev keeping us away from Stalingrad and the battle area. As far as the eye could reach spread vast expanses of Russia, brown and flat and with hardly a sign of human habitation. For a long way the mighty Volga gleamed in curves and stretches as it flowed between its wide, dark margins of marsh. Sometimes a road, straight as a ruler, ran from one wide horizon to the other.

After an hour of this Churchill clambered back along the bomb bay and slept. The spires and domes of Moscow came into view at five in the afternoon. Two hours later, having refreshed himself at State Villa No. 7, eight miles outside Moscow, he arrived at the Kremlin.

General Brooke's diary records the tense atmosphere in which the talks began. Stung by Stalin's abusive questions and his taunt, 'When are you going to start fighting?', Churchill 'crashed his fist on the table and began one of his wonderful spontaneous orations . . . and then went on to tell Stalin exactly what his feelings were about fighting'. Without waiting for a translation, Stalin replied, 'I do not understand what you are saying, but by God, I like your sentiment.'

On his return to State Villa No. 7 Churchill dictated a tele-gram to Clement Attlee, his Deputy Prime Minister, deprecat-ing Stalin's rudeness and lack of appreciation for all Britain's efforts. If Stalin's attitude did not change, Churchill declared, he would pack up and leave. The British Ambassador, Sir Archibald Clark Kerr, had been listening, and warned that as the room was certainly bugged, every word Churchill had said would be translated and sent to Stalin. This seemed only to increase the Prime Minister's irritation. It would appear that Stalin was told of Churchill's anger, as at their next meeting he turned on the charm and expressed gratitude for all that Britain was doing.

Their final discussion took place on 15 August, after which Stalin invited his guest for a farewell drink. This turned into a banquet which lasted for six hours. It was after three in the morning when Churchill got back to his villa, leaving only an hour before he needed to leave for the airport and his flight back to Cairo.

The next three days were spent in the Western Desert, where General Bernard Montgomery had been appointed to take com-mand of 8th Army after the death of General Gott. General Brooke's diary for 20 August records a day which had been 'a wonderful example of Winston's vitality . . . Called at 6am . . . a bathe in the sea . . . a very strenuous day touring the front . . . clouds of sand . . . long walks between troops . . . another bathe, contrary to his doctor's orders . . . rolled over by the wave and did a V-sign with his legs . . . a drive to the aerodrome and as soon as we emplaned he went to sleep and never woke up until we bumped down the [Cairo] runway . . . then followed a conference, dinner . . . he kept me up until 2am . . . at 7.30am I woke with my bed shaking.' It was the Prime Minister rousing him for breakfast.

Churchill landed back in England on the evening of 24 August, having been travelling for three weeks. It had been a momentous journey.

Such were the changing fortunes of war that by December Churchill saw the need for yet another meeting with Roosevelt and, if he could be persuaded, Stalin also. The Russian leader declined, simply asking to be kept informed of the others' deliberations. Thus the stage was set for the Casablanca conference. Elizabeth Layton was among those who saw Churchill off from Number Ten on 12 January 1943. She was holding Smoky, the Prime Minister's cat: 'Sure enough, when he emerged from his room, pink and beaming, ready to leave, he came and talked to Smoky, hugged him and told me to see he was not lonely.'

Once again Churchill was flying in 'Commando', which had recently had a heating device installed, run by a petrol engine in the bomb bay. He was woken during the night by one of the heating points burning his toes. As he thought it possible that the point would get so hot it would set the blankets alight, he woke up the Chief of the Air Staff, who had been sleeping rather less comfortably in a chair, and together they investigated the problem. Having decided it was distinctly dangerous, and that it would be better to freeze than burn, they ordered the petrol engine to be switched off, and the flight continued with the occupants shivering at eight thousand feet above the Atlantic.

On arrival at Casablanca the Prime Minister was meant, in the interests of security, to step straight into a car and drive away. However, he heard another aircraft approaching, and on being told that it was bringing General 'Pug' Ismay, the head of his Defence Office, he insisted on waiting to greet him. There was, he said, no danger, as he was in the uniform of an Air Force commodore. Dismayed at the breach of security, the

General commented that Churchill 'looked like an Air Force Commodore disguised as the Prime Minister'.

The conference was held in the Hôtel d'Anfa on the outskirts of Casablanca, and the participants were housed in adjacent villas, Churchill occupying the Villa Mirador, which is now the residence of the American Consul General. The Consul General being on leave, I had arranged to meet the American Vice-Consul, Paul Malik, at the villa. The Hôtel d'Anfa is now an empty shell standing in a quiet, affluent area, and the young girl caretaker had no understanding of its historic significance or the whereabouts of the Villa Mirador.

I could see nothing resembling the photograph, taken when my grandfather was staying there in 1943, which portrayed a couple of gateposts, the sign 'Villa No. 3', and two soldiers in tin hats on guard. However, as I approached a policeman who I thought might be able to help, I found that the imposing set of security gates he was standing beside marked the entrance to the Villa Mirador. The interior has been completely refurbished, but the 1943 map room, just inside the front door, has been retained as a small museum of the conference, and it is easy to imagine Churchill pacing the garden, the smoke from his cigar curling up towards the palm trees.

On 22 January Harry Hopkins, Roosevelt's trusted adviser, called early on Churchill. The following day he dictated a note for his diary. 'I found Churchill in bed in his customary pink robe and having, of all things, a bottle of red wine for breakfast. He told me he had, on the one hand, a profound distaste for skimmed milk and no deep rooted prejudice about wine and that he had reconciled the conflict in favour of the latter . . . He found the advice of doctors, throughout his life, was usually wrong. At any rate he had no intention of giving up alcoholic drink, mild or strong, now or later.'

The main business of the Casablanca Conference, of course, was the conduct of the war; but in its margins Roosevelt sought to intervene in French colonial politics – a subject to which Churchill, both through his knowledge of French politics and his visit to Morocco in 1936, was no stranger. During a dinner with the King of Morocco, Sultan Mohammed V, Roosevelt turned to the Sultan and asked, 'Why does Morocco, inhabited by Moroccans, belong to France? When we've won this war I will see to it that the United States is not wheedled into the position of accepting any plan that will further France's imperialistic ambitions.' Imperialism was a subject on which Churchill and Roosevelt would always be at odds, but which in their mutual wartime interests they would shelve. On this occasion Churchill was unable to remain silent, but rather than air any dissent he began to cough. When this interrupted the conversation he apologised, saying it was due to a new type of cigar. No doubt his temper had not been improved by Roosevelt's insistence that in deference to Islamic custom there should be no alcohol served during dinner.

Harry Hopkins' dictated note also mentions the dinner. 'Churchill looked glum at dinner and seemed real bored. A smart British marine walked in about the middle of dinner with a dispatch but I have a feeling Churchill cooked that up beforehand as I saw the dispatch later and it certainly wasn't one that required the PM's attention at the dinner.' Hopkins mentioned the absence of alcohol – 'No wonder WSC looked glum' – and described the Sultan's retinue: '. . . the Grand Protocol Officer, who was an old gent with white whiskers and bad teeth who talked incessantly and said nothing. There was a tough looking old bastard who was known as the Grand Vizier who didn't say a word and who, I learned later, runs the show.'

By 24 January the conference was over. Churchill decided to move on to Marrakech, persuading Roosevelt to accompany him for twenty-four hours.* The Prime Minister remained there for several days, corresponding with the War Cabinet and preparing to tackle the busy schedule which remained before his return to England: Cairo, a visit to the Turkish President at Adana, Cyprus, Cairo, Tripoli and Algiers.

General Brooke's diary records several amusing incidents. Arriving at the British Embassy in Cairo at breakfast time, Churchill was offered a cup of tea by Lady Killearn, the Ambassador's wife. He asked for a glass of white wine instead. Draining it in one go, he said, 'Ah! That is good, but do you know I have already had two whiskies and soda and two cigars this morning.' The military members of the entourage were not allowed to wear uniform when visiting Turkey, which was neutral in the war. The clothes they borrowed – Brooke's trousers eight inches too long, braced so that the waist appeared above the waistcoat – left them looking 'like a third-rate theatrical travelling company'. The Turkish President's dinner party 'was a screaming success. Winston was quite at his best ... In his astounding French, mixed with English words pronounced in French, he embarked on the most complicated stories which would have even been difficult to put across adequately in English.'

Churchill never seemed to weary of these travels. At the end of the longest day or in the most trying circumstances his wit would predominate. As they travelled home, Sawyers, while assisting him into bed in the cramped confines of the Liberator, was heard to say, 'You are sitting on your hot-water bottle. That isn't at all a good idea.' To which came the reply, 'Idea? It isn't an idea, it's a coincidence.'

---

* See Chapter 6.

On 7 February 1943 Churchill flew back to England. One of the Liberators taking the participants in the conference back had crashed, killing two of the British delegates. As he sat waiting for take-off at Algiers, Churchill remarked, 'It would be a pity to have to go out in the middle of such an interesting drama. But it wouldn't be a bad moment to leave. It is a straight run now, and even the Cabinet could manage it.' This would be 'Commando's last flight with Churchill aboard; later it also crashed, killing all on board. As so often there seemed to be some outside force protecting the man who, more than forty years before, as a cavalry subaltern under fire, had written to his mother, 'I have faith in my star that I am intended to do something in the world.'

CHAPTER 8

Wartime Journeys 1943–45

Stop pouring all that water out. It is too depressing a sight!
Winston Churchill to steward serving dinner aboard the
Queen Mary, 5 August 1943

A bout of pneumonia followed Churchill's return home. Confined to bed, he continued working: 'That is what does me good.' By May 1943, conscious of serious divergences in Allied strategy, he decided he needed to cross the Atlantic yet again. The Boeing flying boat could not be used because of late ice on the northern route, and Churchill's doctors did not want him to fly at the height required by a bomber. It was decided, therefore, to cross in the *Queen Mary*.

Elizabeth Layton had taken Churchill's dictation for two years, but had hitherto been excluded from the travelling entourage because of the unsuitability for women of the previous means of transport. Born in England and brought up on the western slopes of the Rocky Mountains, she had returned to London to work with the Red Cross. A trained shorthand typist, she had then been recruited through an employment agency by Number Ten. Having succeeded where others failed, she found herself the Assistant Personal Secretary to the Prime

Minister. Now, with an Atlantic crossing in prospect, she screwed up her courage and asked if she might go. The reply was immediate: 'Why didn't you ask sooner.' Twenty-four hours later she was aboard as the ship sailed from the Clyde on 5 May.

The luxury liner the *Queen Mary* had been converted to a troop ship capable of carrying fifteen thousand men. For this voyage the main deck, where the Prime Minister and his entourage, and the map and conference rooms were accommodated, had been restored in a very short time to almost pre-war standards. For reasons of security the main deck had been sealed off from the rest of the ship, a measure which it was hoped would keep out all unwelcome visitors, including the bugs which flourished in an overcrowded troop ship. But, as Elizabeth Layton recounted, a few did find their way in: 'alas, all the bugs had not been killed off' by fumigation.

At one point in the voyage British code-breakers reported that a U-boat was fifteen miles ahead of the *Queen Mary*. Churchill at once gave orders for a machine gun to be put in his lifeboat, saying, 'I won't be captured. The finest way to die is in the excitement of fighting the enemy.' However, no torpedoes or any of the hundred or so U-boats operating in the North Atlantic were seen, and the *Queen Mary* arrived in New York on 11 May. The conference, a series of separate meetings code-named 'Trident', lasted a fortnight. General Brooke described such events as 'the most exhausting entertainments ever . . . we age and get more and more weary'. For Elizabeth Layton, accommodated in the White House with the Prime Minister, the pace was even hotter and the hours longer than in London, but she had an hour or two off every other day to sample such shopping and food as had long since been unavailable at home.

On 14 May, it being a Saturday, Roosevelt invited Churchill to accompany him and Mrs Roosevelt to the presidential retreat, Shangri-La (now called Camp David), in the Allegheny Mountains, Maryland. With them was Harry Hopkins, the President's aide, who as they approached the battlefield of Gettysburg quoted from John Greenleaf Whittier's Civil War verse, 'Barbara Frietchie'.

> *'Shoot if you must this old grey head,*
> *But spare your country's flag,' she said.*

163

When no one else in the car offered to add to these lines, Churchill started from the beginning:

Up from the meadows rich with corn,
Clear in the cool September morn . . .

and demonstrated his prodigious memory by reciting the remaining fifty-eight lines of the complete poem. 'No one,' he later wrote, 'corrected my many misquotations.'

The poem came up again eight days later at a White House dinner. Jane Plakias, a family friend of the Roosevelts and then a young girl of twenty-three, was one of the guests, as she recounted in a letter to her grandmother the following morning:

The invitation came unexpectedly and informally by phone with no mention of who else was invited. This usually means a simple family evening . . . so I felt at ease and right at home as I was announced into the Red Room . . . The President was there, already seated as usual when his guests come, at a little table, happily mixing cocktails . . . I was delighted to see Richard [a personal friend] arrive and when he was served his drink we withdrew a bit to the doorway to chat . . . We were standing there when [the elevator] came down and the door opened and there stood Winston Churchill. We were both naturally dumbfounded . . . He smiled at our astonished faces and held out his hand, saying 'My name is Winston Churchill' as though we didn't know.

Then follows an account of the dinner, each of the principals 'obviously enjoying it best when they were in the limelight . . . I do think [Churchill] has greater depth, but there is great rapport in their interest and turn of mind. They seem to have become real personal friends.' Churchill wanted to know who had written 'Barbara Frietchie', and the President asked Jane Plakias, who could only remember 'the couplet we all know which the President recited in unison with me. Whereupon Mr Churchill almost rose in his seat in his great glee and proceeded to recite the entire poem . . . It was a tour de force and the table gave him a big hand . . . Another dissertation was on the subject of his recent pneumonia. He discussed at length the battle of the streptococci germs, how he had never had to fight anything that could become a grandmother in nine minutes, how he had been planning to outwit the germs with military strategy which would have put Montgomery to shame, until Sir Charles [Wilson] put him to bed and spoiled the fun.' It was clearly a convivial evening 'in spite of Mrs R's more serious nature'.

On 26 May, the conference over, Churchill and a reduced party flew to Algiers. They travelled in a Boeing flying boat as far as Gibraltar, and then in a Lancaster bomber converted for VIP travel. Churchill was accommodated in a villa adjacent to the chief of the Allied forces in North Africa, General Eisenhower, and his daily routine became a subject of much interest to the General's staff. Because only tinned milk was available he drank wine instead of tea at breakfast, and they seemed to think he rarely ate food at all. Churchill's naval aide, Commander Tommy Thompson, felt that:

So many odd stories circulated about the Prime Minister's alleged eccentricities in this direction that the truth deserves to be put on record. At home he usually drank a glass of white wine at lunch, champagne at dinner and then a glass of port or brandy afterwards. As a meal he disliked afternoon tea and if he had anything at that time he would ask for a whisky heavily diluted with ice and water. Cocktails he avoided altogether. He liked to provide champagne for his guests, but as the war went on champagne became more and more difficult to obtain. I therefore suggested that since champagne agreed with him and our stock was running low he might have half a bottle with his meals while his guests were given something more easily obtainable. This was brushed aside. 'What happens if we run out?' I asked. 'Get some more!' he said. He obviously found the question was slightly ridiculous.

On 5 June Churchill returned home in the converted Lancaster. The perils of his journeys were emphasised by the shooting down several days earlier of a scheduled civilian BOAC Dakota over the Bay of Biscay, across which his route took him.

Such was the tempo of the war that only two months later Churchill felt the need for yet another Anglo–American conference. On 5 August he embarked again on the *Queen Mary*, this time accompanied by Clementine and their daughter Mary, who as a subaltern in an anti-aircraft battery was travelling as her father's aide-de-camp. Churchill, on the move again, was in good humour. 'Stop pouring all that water out. It is too depressing a sight!' he said to a steward serving at dinner who was filling the water glasses before pouring the champagne.

Elizabeth Layton described the ship as a miniature Whitehall. Churchill remarked how quickly a voyage passes if there is enough to occupy every waking minute. He had been looking forward to a change from the 'perpetual clatter of war', but the holiday 'seemed to be over before it had begun'. In spite of the elaborate security precautions, crowds turned out when the *Queen Mary* docked at Halifax, Novia Scotia, on 9 August.

Painting at San Vigilio, Lake Garda, August 1949.

Painting at Camara de Lobos, Madeira, January 1950.

With Clementine at Reid's Hotel,
Madeira, January 1950.

Bathing at Venice, August 1951.

Aboard the *Christina* with Aristotle Onassis, 1956.

Golden wedding anniversary at Lord Beaverbrook's villa at Cap d'Ail, with son Randolph, Clementine and granddaughter Arabella, September 1958.

Boarding the *Christina*, 1958.

At La Pausa with Emery Reves and Sarah, 1958.

Reviewing a guard of honour, Marrakech, 1959.

With Wendy Reves at La Pausa.

Ashore at Rhodes, 1959. Left to right: Celia, Clementine, Maria Callas, Tina Onassis and Anthony Montague Brown.

Dining on the *Christina*, 1959.

Aboard the *Christina*, 1959.

At Tangier with Bryce Nairn and Hadj Mohamed
Erzini, 1959.

With Celia at the Hôtel de Paris,
Monte Carlo, 1960.

With Aristotle Onassis, 1960.

With Celia in the hills above Monte Carlo, 1962.

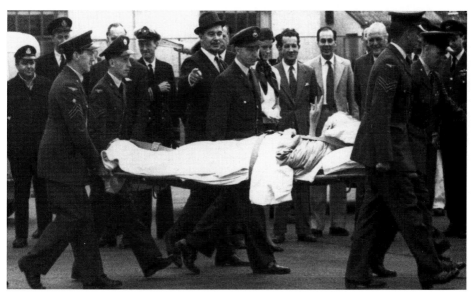

WSC returns from Monte Carlo after breaking his hip, 1962.

In the South of France, 1963.

State funeral, St Paul's Cathedral, 30 January 1965.

When the Prime Minister and his wife went to their train, people assembled around the saloon car, and Churchill asked them to sing 'The Maple Leaf' and 'O Canada'. Word of his arrival spread, and large gatherings turned out at each station *en route* to Quebec, where the conference, code-named 'Quadrant', was held.

During the conference Roosevelt and Churchill took some time off together. On the evening of 6 August, Churchill and Mary travelled by train across the border to Roosevelt's family estate at Hyde Park in upstate New York, viewing Niagara Falls on the way. When a journalist asked what he thought of them, Churchill replied, 'I saw them before you were born. I came here in 1900.' Asked if they looked the same, he said, 'Well, the principle seems to be the same. The water keeps falling over.'

While at Quebec Churchill and Roosevelt also spent a day at a log-cabin retreat on the Grand Lac d'Épaule, where while they fished they discussed the Far East. Elizabeth Layton was struck by the contrasting personal security arrangements of the two leaders. Roosevelt's car was 'smothered in Secret Service men', while his floor of the Citadel, the Governor General's summer residence in Quebec, was guarded by 'gorilla-like figures' whom she had to force her way past to deliver papers, 'inviting them to shoot me in the back if they wished'. Churchill, on the other hand, had two detectives, of whom only one was usually on duty at any time.

The conference ended on 24 August, and the Churchills and some of the chiefs of staff left for a holiday at La Cabane de Montmorcey, a fishing camp in the Laurentian Mountains where they were the guests of a Canadian industrialist, Colonel Frank Clarke. For Churchill there was no such thing as a real holiday, only a change of scenery and perhaps a little lowering of tempo. It was thus not surprising that a small filing cabinet of secret papers accompanied them. Normally this was looked after by security guards, but on this occasion the journey involved a lake crossing in a small boat in which there was no room for the security men, so Patrick Kinna was left to take sole charge of it. He told me, 'It was a rough crossing. I knew the cabinet contained papers concerning the atomic bomb and I thought to myself that if I drown I must hang on to the box.'

In the mountains the Prime Minister fished with Clementine, worked on a speech he was to make to the Canadian nation, and had meetings with various members of his delegation who were accommodated at other lakeside cabins.

Churchill travelled to Washington by train. In the next cabin was his bodyguard, Inspector Walter Thompson. At one point in the journey Patrick Kinna heard a shot and, dashing to see what had happened, discovered that Thompson had accidentally discharged his pistol while cleaning it. Churchill, who had narrowly avoided his first bullet in Cuba on his twenty-first birthday, was lucky once again. The shot went through Thompson's wall into the Prime Minister's cabin, but fortunately he was not there.

On 5 September Churchill travelled to Boston, and received an honorary degree at Harvard the following day. His acceptance speech was thought very good, even by those who were accustomed to his oratory. In an apparent slip of the tongue he made a reference to 'the infernal combustion engine', rapidly correcting it to 'the internal combustion engine'. This caused much amusement, and was quite deliberate – Elizabeth Layton had heard him rehearsing his speech while on the train journey from Washington. Churchill returned to Washington the same day. In his diary the Permanent Secretary at the Foreign Office Sir Alexander Cadogan wrote that 'Winston enjoyed himself hugely.' Wearing a flowered dressing gown, he rushed onto the rear platform of the train to talk to anyone he could find whenever they stopped.

On 10 September Roosevelt invited the vice president of the *Herald Tribune* newspaper, Mrs Ogden Mills, to lunch. Tending towards Anglophobia, she asked Churchill what he intended to do about those 'wretched Indians'. 'To which Indians do you refer?' came the reply. '[Those who under British rule have] multiplied and prospered exceedingly, or do you mean the unfortunate Indians of the North American continent which under your administration are practically extinct?' Churchill, through his mother, had distant American Indian ancestry, and even Roosevelt, himself a severe critic of British rule in India, laughed heartily at this riposte. After lunch Roosevelt left for Hyde Park, leaving Churchill the run of the White House. Thus, for twenty-four hours, 1600 Pennsylvania Avenue became the seat of British government.

At dinner on 12 September at Hyde Park, the President and company present toasted the Churchills' thirty-fifth wedding anniversary, after which Roosevelt drove with them to the station where they caught the train for Halifax to embark on the British battleship *Renown* for the voyage home. Some days before, Churchill had been anxious to lay his hands on a paper he had previously written which had started with the words that 'renown awaited' the commander who restored artillery to its predominant place on the battlefield, and Elizabeth Layton remembers that Tommy Thompson said to his master '*Renown* awaits' as they arrived in Halifax. The joke seemed lost on Churchill, who by now had other things on his mind. Elizabeth had noted that while his own effervescent wit and wisdom were ever ready to surface, he was often too preoccupied to notice it in others.

Embarking on the fourteenth, the Prime Minister worked

daily in the Admiral's sea cabin, to which Elizabeth Layton was summoned whenever there was dictation to take. Churchill's matches were always sliding about due to the rolling of the ship, and it became one of Elizabeth's tasks to provide a candle whenever his cigar needed relighting. Once the cigar was going again she would withdraw to the adjacent bathroom to blow the candle out, Churchill having said, 'We don't want that stink in here.' One alarming incident on the voyage was concealed from him at the time. Due to the bad weather, walking on the quarterdeck was forbidden. However, Churchill's daughter Mary accepted an invitation from a naval officer for a stroll. She was swept across the deck by a huge wave, and was left clutching the anchor cables, very lucky not to have been washed overboard.

When *Renown* reached the Clyde on Sunday, 19 September, Churchill sent for the chaplain, Henry Lloyd, who had won the Distinguished Service Order while serving in the Mediterranean aboard the aircraft carrier *Illustrious,* and said that the ship's company should be assembled for Divine Service, at which he would address them. When he proposed the hymn 'Onward Christian Soldiers' the chaplain protested, 'Surely not? After all, this is the Royal Navy.' 'You are quite right,' said Churchill ruefully. 'You had better choose the hymns after all.' So the company assembled beneath the huge guns of the *Renown* sang 'Eternal Father Strong to Save'. During the voyage Churchill had received some six thousand words a day on the progress of the war by wireless from London, and had been able to send replies through one of the *Renown's* escort vessels. As usual he had kept in touch the whole time.

Even as the ring began to close around the Axis powers there were strategic differences between the three major Allies, the arguments centring upon priorities between the various theatres of war. It was necessary for the Big Three – Churchill, Roosevelt and Stalin – to meet for the first time in person, and Tehran was chosen as the venue. Churchill wanted first a bilateral discussion with Roosevelt, and the two agreed to meet in Cairo before going on to Tehran. On 11 November 1943 Churchill sailed once more in the battleship *Renown*, his aide-de-camp on this occasion being his daughter Sarah, a section officer in the Women's Auxiliary Air Force. As they sailed, Captain Richard Pim, who ran the Prime Minister's travelling map room, calculated that Churchill had already travelled 111,000 miles on his wartime missions, spending 792 hours at sea and 339 hours in the air. During the voyage, being unwell with a heavy cold and the after-effects of inoculations, Churchill worked in his quarters, and received visitors on board when the ship called at Algiers and Malta. But he had recovered by the twenty-first when the *Renown* arrived at Alexandria, and flew immediately to Cairo.

The conference was to take place at the Mena House Hotel, in sight of the Pyramids and bristling with troops and anti-aircraft guns. Churchill and his personal staff were accommodated at Beit al Azrak, 'the Blue House', a mile from the Mena House. It was autumn and, the weather being pleasantly warm, the Prime Minister's favourite place for working was in the courtyard, sitting in the sun beside a central fountain. A Royal Marine orderly was always on hand, and on these occasions found his principal task was to operate the tap as Churchill, seeking a momentary distraction from his papers, or pausing in dictation to Elizabeth Layton while he sought the right words, ordered the fountain to be turned up and down. It is clear from Elizabeth's account of the three weeks spent in Cairo before and after Tehran that Churchill's personal staff worked as a well-oiled machine. Elizabeth, although hard-worked, had an exceptionally good time, being the only woman on the staff.

Roosevelt arrived a day after Churchill, who, having discovered that the President had never seen the Pyramids, reconnoitred the route in order that he could conduct his disabled friend around them. Thanksgiving Day, 25 November, was marked by a dinner with Roosevelt personally carving two huge turkeys. 'For a couple of hours we cast care aside,' Churchill later recalled. There was dancing to gramophone records, Sarah as the only woman present, having her work cut out. Churchill danced with 'Pa' Watson, Roosevelt's old and trusted aide. Two days later the two leaders flew in separate aircraft to Tehran.

The Tehran Conference lasted until 2 December, when Churchill flew back to Cairo. Agreement was reached on strategic matters, and in general the atmosphere was friendly. Stalin, however, was aware of Churchill's innate antipathy to the Soviet system, and his political and moral orientation was diametrically opposed to Churchill's. At the same time Roosevelt was cultivating Stalin, in the process somewhat reducing Churchill's influence. There were times when feathers were ruffled, such as the dinner when Stalin suggested that the fifty thousand or so members of the German General Staff should be liquidated after the war. Churchill, recognising that this was perhaps not entirely in jest, left the room, and Stalin had to pursue him and assure him it was not meant seriously before he would return to the table.

It was during the Tehran Conference that Churchill, on behalf of King George VI, presented Stalin with the Stalingrad Sword. Hugh Lunghi, one of Churchill's interpreters, told me what happened: 'Stalin received the sword and, visibly moved, kissed the hilt before passing it to his aide Marshal Voroshilov, who let it slide from the scabbard. As we left Voroshilov shuffled

up behind, stammered an apology and wished Churchill a
happy birthday, which in fact was the following day. The Prime
Minister growled at me, "A bit premature – must be angling
for an invitation – and he couldn't play a straight bat with the
sword."'

On 9 December Churchill was unwell, but carried on working. The following day he flew to Tunisia, an eight-hour flight
which ended at the wrong airfield. General Brooke described
a disconsolate Prime Minister sitting for an hour on his suitcase
on a windswept runway before flying on to Carthage, where
he went immediately to bed in General Eisenhower's quarters.
Walter Thompson kept vigil outside the bedroom door, not so
much for protection but as a trusted retainer whose presence
would not cause Churchill unnecessary concern.

Thompson had served Churchill for eleven years before the
war, beginning when he was Colonial Secretary in 1922. On
retirement from the police he had opened a grocery business,
but in 1939 he had received a telegram reading: 'Meet me at
Croydon Airport 4.30pm Wednesday. Churchill.' Churchill
had received warning while in France that he might be the
target of an assassination attempt, and at his own expense was
retaining Thompson in his former capacity. When war broke
out Thompson was recalled to the police force, and guarded
Churchill for the duration. It was not surprising that Churchill
felt able to confide in him when he awoke during the night in
Eisenhower's villa. Lying back on the pillows, he admitted to
being 'tired out in body, soul and spirit'.

'Not in spirit,' said Thompson.

'Yes, I am worn right out, but all is planned and ready.'
Then, suddenly sitting up, Churchill continued, 'In what better
place could I die than here – in the ruins of Carthage?' With
that he sank back and went to sleep.

He remained in bed on 11 December with pneumonia. Specialists and nurses arrived from Tripoli, but the protests of his doctor Sir Charles Wilson fell on deaf ears, and he continued to see visitors. On the fourteenth his heart gave cause for concern, and Wilson thought he would die. The patient remained philosophical. 'If I die, don't worry. The war is won,' he told Sarah.

Churchill continued to receive visitors, but only one at a time, and dealt with some telegrams. He defied the well-meaning efforts of General Eisenhower's personal dietician, and insisted on good plain food. Fortunately *Renown* was still at Gibraltar, and the naval cook who had been posted to the ship to look after the Prime Minister was dispatched to Carthage. Clementine arrived on 17 December. By Christmas Eve Churchill judged himself well enough to hold a conference with senior commanders, and on Christmas Day he entertained five commanders-in-chief to a conference and lunch. On the twenty-seventh, despite his doctor's worries about the need for an oxygen mask, Churchill flew to Marrakech, where he worked for the next eighteen days, taking time off for picnic lunches. On 14 January 1944 he flew to Gibraltar and boarded the battleship *King George V* for Plymouth. He reached London on the morning of the eighteenth, and was in the House of Commons two hours later for Prime Minister's questions. It was the conclusion of a remarkable demonstration of stamina – and more than that, of courage, echoing his words of advice when addressing the boys of Harrow School in 1941: 'Never, never give in.'

On D-Day, 6 June 1944, the Allied armies opened the second front. Churchill suggested that King George VI and he should observe the Normandy landings from one of the bombarding warships. The King thought that they should not run the risk, and Churchill, deferring very reluctantly to the monarch's wishes, waited until 12 June before visiting the army in the field. It was four years almost to the day since his hazardous departure from Tours in 1940. With Generals Brooke and Smuts he crossed the Channel in a destroyer, then transferred to Admiral Philip Vian's barge, in which he sang a song he had learned at Harrow: 'But snug in her hive, the Queen was alive/ And Buzz was the word on the Island.' He was disappointed that no one accompanying him knew the words.

From the barge Churchill boarded an American amphibious vehicle which ran him ashore at Courseulles. He then went by Jeep with General Montgomery, now the field commander of Allied ground forces in the Normandy campaign, to Montgomery's tactical headquarters within three miles of the front line. Emerging from the map caravan, Smuts sensed Germans close at hand, but was reassured by the aide-de-camp that this could not be so, as the area had been thoroughly searched. The Prime Minister and his party then re-embarked on Admiral Vian's barge and sailed along the coast observing troops, tanks and trucks going ashore, and the floating piers of an artificial harbour being towed into place. Back on board the destroyer Churchill had the gunners fire at shore targets, even though this meant sailing well within range of German artillery, before the voyage home.

Two days later, two demoralised and hungry young German soldiers emerged from the bushes about which Smuts had had his suspicions. They were armed, and had they not been scared witless might easily have shot the Prime Minister and his party at close range.

On 21 July Churchill again visited the Normandy front, spending two nights aboard a light cruiser before flying back to England. He took off again on 5 August for France, but his aircraft was recalled, much against his own inclinations, when the one preceding it crashed in fog on landing, killing all on board.

Five days later he flew to Algiers, en route to Italy. The next nineteen days were busy, even for Churchill. There were high-level conferences including not only the senior military commanders in the Mediterranean, but also Marshal Tito, the Communist partisan leader who the following year would become the leader of Yugoslavia. Churchill visited the front line in Italy, and from a destroyer watched the Allied landings in the south of France. He was not at all pleased when the destroyer's Captain explained that, on the orders of the Admiral, he was not to approach close inshore. Churchill retired to the Captain's bunk with a borrowed novel, the fly-leaf of which he inscribed: 'This is a lot more exciting than the invasion of Southern France.' Back in Italy, conferences and visits to the front continued. Describing the end of a conference on 21 August, Harold Macmillan, then Resident Minister at Allied Headquarters Mediterranean, wrote, 'all but Winston completely exhausted'. Churchill was perhaps more tired than he appeared, for, flying home on 29 August he was taken ill. It was pneumonia again, necessitating several days in bed.

Still feeling unwell, and suffering also from the course of malaria pills which had to be continued for a month after leaving Italy, Churchill boarded the *Queen Mary* on 5 September for Halifax, from where a twenty-hour train journey took him to Quebec for a second conference there with Roosevelt. In spite of his wide-ranging activities, few details escaped his attention. Churchill learned that American servicemen were about to lose a week's leave because their ship's sailing had been delayed to meet his programme. A message to Roosevelt rectified this situation.

Churchill and Roosevelt arrived in Quebec by separate trains, within ten minutes of each other, on 11 September. They and their wives then drove to the Citadel. The conference ended on 16 September, when the dignitaries of McGill University, Montreal, travelled to Quebec to present honorary degrees to both the Prime Minister and the President. In the course of the press conference which followed, Churchill remarked on the size of newspapers in America: 'I read some of the papers when I am over here, these great papers about an inch thick – (laughter) – very different from the little sheets we get in Great Britain.' He would return to the same theme the following day, when someone at the White House asked him for his thoughts on America. 'Toilet paper too thin, newspapers too fat!' was the reported reply.

Accompanied by Clementine, Churchill was Roosevelt's guest for two days at Hyde Park. Writing to Mary, Clementine noted how the President, 'with all his genius does not – indeed cannot (partly because of his health and partly because of his make up) function around the clock like your father'.

On 20 September the Prime Minister embarked at New York on the *Queen Mary*, and arrived at Greenock in Scotland on the twenty-sixth. Travelling overnight he reached London at ten in the morning, and an hour and a half later was in the House of Commons for Prime Minister's questions.

In October Churchill decided that various problems, largely concerned with Poland, required a face-to-face meeting with Stalin. Leaving by air on the seventh and flying via Naples, he landed in Moscow on the ninth. The next nine days were spent in conference, interspersed with banquets and ballet. After a marathon lunch which lasted until 6.30 p.m., Churchill was heard to say, 'I'm going back to the Embassy for my young lady.' This was Elizabeth Layton, to whom he said when collecting her, 'I think I'll dictate in the dark,' which caused some amusement among those present.

When working, Churchill could easily be annoyed by extraneous noises. A coughing sentry in Moscow caused him to break off dictation to Elizabeth with the sharp instruction, 'Go and fetch that secretary chap.' When the 'secretary chap', the man in charge of household arrangements, appeared in the bedroom door, the Prime Minister put on a kindly face, saying, 'There is a poor man at the door who has a very bad cough. I think he should be put on duty where there is less draught.'

The return flight from Moscow on 18 October was broken first at Simferopol, in the Crimea, where a lavish dinner flown from Moscow was provided. At this the Prime Minister proposed a toast to Elizabeth Layton, as the only woman present. Later she had to be rescued from a Russian general who had taken her aside, intent on a succession of personal toasts.

With stopovers in Cairo and Naples, Churchill was back home on 22 October. On 11 November, accompanied by Clementine and Mary, he was in liberated Paris at the invitation of General de Gaulle, and was moved to tears by the tremendous welcome from what seemed like the entire population lining the Champs Élysées. The suite set aside for him and his party at the Quai d'Orsay had a spectacular attraction, a gold bath which had been specially installed for Hermann Goering. Leaving Paris with de Gaulle, Churchill went overnight by train to Besançon, and then sixty miles by car through heavy snow to the French front, where in the icy cold with snowclouds massing his party began to fear for his well-being. Having reviewed a parade, he was about to be hustled away when a soldier jumped onto a farm cart and cried out, '*Attention! On va chanter.*' For a further twenty minutes in the dusk the Prime Minister was entertained by martial songs. The following day a further journey took him to the Supreme Allied Commander General Eisenhower's headquarters at Rheims.

Churchill was seventy on 30 November 1944, but there could be no let-up from the pressures of war. The threat of civil war in Greece and the growing power of Communist groups in the Balkans set him off on a further journey on Christmas Eve. When two of his secretaries, Elizabeth Layton and Marian Holmes, said they would toss up to see which of them would accompany him, he relented and took them both. Breaking the flight in Naples, Churchill landed at Kalamaki airport near Athens in the afternoon of Christmas Day. Fighting was in progress between Greek government forces and Communists as he drove to Phaleron Bay naval base, where he boarded HMS *Ajax*.

The following morning the ship was straddled by fire, and a shell burst close to the craft taking Churchill ashore where, his Colt revolver held across his knees, he was driven in an armoured car to the British Embassy. As he approached the Embassy two people were killed by machine-gun bullets, some of which struck a wall above his head.

Churchill left Greece on 28 December. At his press conference the previous day, which had been continuously interrupted by the noise of mortar fire, he had exhorted the Greeks to settle their differences democratically, rather than have a solution imposed upon them. Breaking the journey in Naples, he was back in London by 5 p.m. on the twenty-ninth. He finally went to bed at 4 a.m. on the thirtieth, having spent most of the night coercing the Greek King George II into accepting a provisional government under the regency of Archbishop Damaskinos of Athens.

With the war in Europe approaching its end, Churchill was now planning for the Yalta Conference with Roosevelt and

Stalin at which the outline of the post-war Continent would be discussed. Accompanied by Sarah, he left on 29 January 1945. His party travelled in three aircraft, one of which crashed, killing fourteen of the nineteen on board. After a three-day stopover in Malta for pre-Yalta talks which included Roosevelt, the Prime Minister and his party flew the 1400 miles to Saki in the Crimea, then endured a three-hour drive to Yalta.

Yalta was a frustrating conference for Churchill. Roosevelt felt he had the measure of Stalin, who throughout played on the President's inclination to conciliate whenever deadlock threatened. History has vindicated Churchill, who wanted a far more robust opposition to Stalin's ambitions for post-war Soviet domination of Eastern Europe, but at the time, with Britain's resources reduced almost to vanishing point, he could do no more than plead what he believed to be the right course. But eloquence was not enough in the face of his need not to fall out with Roosevelt.

Churchill had intended to remain for one more day after the conference ended on 11 February, leaving in the morning 'easily, orderly and quietly', as Sarah wrote to her mother. But late in the afternoon he suddenly said, 'I see no reason to stay here a minute longer – we're off!' Sarah recalled that 'Sawyers, surrounded by suitcases, laying out one suit after another, said, "They can't do this to me."' But after ninety minutes of hectic packing of suitcases and official papers, the party was on the road for the six-hour drive to Sevastopol and the SS *Franconia*, which, anchored offshore, was their home until the fourteenth. Having worked on board and visited nearby Balaclava, where the Light Brigade had charged during the Crimean War ninety years before, Churchill left by air for Athens and Alexandria.

Elizabeth Layton remembers sitting on her typewriter box as a stool beside Churchill's bunk in the tail of the converted bomber as he worked. There she was, 'with the greatest man in the world', taking dictation, passing him an ashtray just as she did at home, flying high over enemy territory while he carried on the work of the British government.

On Churchill's previous visit to Athens a civil war had been raging. Now, six weeks later, as he drove with the Regent, Archbishop Damaskinos, into Constitution Square, it was packed with cheering crowds. His speech was translated passage by passage, but the crowd cheered each before the interpreter had begun, seeming to understand the sense without any need for translation. He ended, 'Let there be unity. Let there be resolute comradeship. Greece for ever! Greece for all!' After dinner at the British Embassy, he took off for Egypt.

President Roosevelt had preceded him there, and the two men said farewell for the last time on 15 February 1945 on board the USS *Quincy*, in Alexandria harbour. Roosevelt, who had looked frail throughout the Yalta Conference, was ailing fast, and would die on 12 April.

Moving on to Cairo, Churchill was visited by Emperor Haile Selassie of Ethiopia and King Ibn Saud of Saudi Arabia. Any embarrassment which might have been caused by the King's lavish presents of diamond-hilted swords to the men in Churchill's party and diamonds and pearls for Sarah, which far outclassed Churchill's gift to him, was nimbly sidestepped. Churchill, having already presented the King with a gift bought locally for £100, said, 'What we bring are but tokens. His Majesty's government have decided to present you with the finest motor car in the world. Every comfort for peace, and every security against hostile action.' The subsequent secret sale of King Ibn Saud's gifts more than covered the cost to the British government of the Rolls-Royce later delivered to him.

★   ★   ★

Churchill was back in Britain on 19 February. On 2 March he lunched in Brussels with Mary, who was stationed nearby with her anti-aircraft battery. He then went on to meet General Eisenhower at Eindhoven in the Netherlands. Visiting the abandoned German fortifications along the Siegfried Line, he had to answer a call of nature. Turning his back on the phalanx of photographers who were present, he announced, 'This is one of the operations connected with this great war which must not be reproduced graphically.' They all obeyed.

Back in London on 6 March, Churchill decided to be with Montgomery when the Rhine was crossed by British troops. He flew out on 23 March and crossed the river two days later. Travelling along the bank by road, he was well within range of German artillery, and he came under shellfire while inspecting the wrecked railway bridge at Wesel. An American commander, General Simpson, had some difficulty in getting Churchill to leave. The Prime Minister put his arms around a twisted girder, his face, said Brooke, 'just like that of a small boy being called away from his sand castles'. He returned to London on the twenty-sixth.

Victory in Europe was celebrated on 9 May 1945, the instruments of surrender having been signed at midnight on the eighth. For Churchill the jubilation was overshadowed by events in Eastern Europe, where he anticipated a showdown with Stalin over the sovereignty of countries occupied by Russian troops. Russia had also to be persuaded to join in the war against Japan, which still needed to be pursued with vigour.

There had been no general election in Britain for ten years, but Churchill had hoped to maintain the coalition government and delay an election until after Japan was defeated. However, the Labour Party wished otherwise, and polling day was set for

5 July. Meanwhile, Churchill formed a caretaker government and prepared for the final Big Three conference scheduled for mid-July in Potsdam.

Badly needing a rest, he planned to spend a few days at Mimizan, near Bordeaux, where the Duke of Westminster had offered the use of his hunting lodge. Tommy Thompson was sent on reconnaissance. Together with Bryce Nairn, who had been transferred from Marrakech and was now the new British Consul in Bordeaux, he drove to Mimizan, where he discovered that the water supply was seriously damaged, with no hope of repairing it in time for Churchill's visit. Nairn then arranged that the nearby Château de Bordaberry, owned by a retired industrialist, Brigadier General Raymond Brutinel, would be made available. When the Brigadier, a naturalised Frenchman who had served with the Canadian Machine Gun Corps in World War I, explained that his family silver was still buried in various parts of the Pyrenees, and that with the prevailing shortage of food he would find it difficult to provide for an entire house-party, Nairn assured him that the British Consulate would supply whatever was needed.

On 7 July Churchill, together with Clementine and Mary, flew to Bordeaux. Churchill took an instant liking to his host, who had memories of Ploegsteert, or 'Plugstreet', where Churchill had commanded the 6th Battalion of the Royal Scots Fusiliers. It took a day or two for Churchill to put thoughts of the election out of his mind, but in the beautiful setting over-looking the Bay of Biscay painting soon took over, and in the days remaining he painted during every available hour of daylight. The local inhabitants respected his privacy, but insisted on staging a fête in his honour. At this the Churchill family were presented with Basque pottery, and Churchill himself with a sword stick the top of which bore the words '*Je suis le terreur de mes ennemis.'* On the last night of the holiday the Mayor of Hendaye gave a *vin d'honneur* at the casino, and for the first time in some years a traditional spectacle, the Toro del Fuego, was staged in the square. This entailed two men dressed in a bull's hide with fireworks sprouting from its horns and fire-crackers exploding from its tail as it ran among the crowds. The guest of honour was called upon to speak. Standing, he raised his hand and to loud cheers said just three words: '*Vive la France!'*

Voting in the general election had taken place in Britain on 5 July, but as there were many thousands of votes to come in from the forces abroad, the result was still unknown when Churchill, accompanied by Mary as his ADC, flew to Potsdam on 15 July for the conference which was to settle the outline of post-war Europe. Six days later he was standing on the saluting base for the British victory parade in Berlin. Mont-gomery thought the Prime Minister had 'put on ten years' since they had last met only three months before.

The Potsdam Conference was, like Yalta, both frustrating and disappointing for Churchill. By virtue of their countries' infinitely greater resources, Stalin, and Roosevelt's successor Harry Truman, had the major voices. Stalin went back on his word, and a horse and cart were driven through arrangements thought to have been agreed at Yalta. The conference broke halfway through for Churchill and Clement Attlee, his deputy and the leader of the Labour opposition, to return to London for the election results. Both Stalin and Truman expected Chur-chill to return, but the British people, despite their admiration for Churchill himself, had turned their back on the Conservative Party – just as the pre-war Conservatives had shunned Churchill until the going got too rough for them. It was therefore Attlee who represented Britain when the conference resumed on the twenty-seventh.

Clementine, recognising the strain under which her husband had laboured for six years, and the scale of the problems ahead, said of the election result, 'It may well be a blessing in disguise.' To which Churchill replied, 'At the moment it seems quite effectively disguised.'

His family decided he should have a painting holiday, and on 2 September, accompanied by Sarah, he left for Italy, where Field Marshal Alexander, the Supreme Allied Commander Mediterranean, had made a villa beside Lake Como available for him. Elizabeth Layton went as his secretary, and recalls the three weeks she spent there as among the happiest she can remember.

Marian Holmes remained at Number Ten to serve the new Prime Minister, Clement Attlee. Of him she wrote in her diary: 'Perfectly polite, and I'm sure he is a good Christian gentleman. But the difference is between champagne and water.'

There can be no doubt that during his wartime journeys Winston Churchill was at his most effervescent.

CHAPTER 9

Fulton and Beyond

---

*I am most grateful to the college authorities for their great
kindness in conferring upon me another of those degrees which I
value so highly. They have a double attraction for me in that they
do not require any preliminary examination.*
Winston Churchill at Westminster College, Fulton,
Missouri, 5 March 1946

A letter, dated 5 October 1945, to Churchill from Dr Franc
L. McCluer, the President of Westminster College, Fulton,
Missouri, begins: 'In 1936 an English-born woman, Mrs John
Findley Green, established at Westminster College a memorial
lecturership to be known as the John Findley Green Foundation
. . . This letter is to invite you to deliver the Green Lectures
in the winter of 1945–1946, or in the spring of 1946. We
should be glad to arrange the date or dates to suit your convenience.' Across the bottom of the page is a handwritten note:
'This is a wonderful school in my home state. Hope you can
do it. I'll introduce you. Harry Truman.'

When Churchill's acceptance became known, the *Kansas
City Times* could not resist taunting more prestigious educational establishments:

While learned educators are asking themselves and audiences what is to become of the small colleges, Westminster College prepares to entertain Winston Churchill (introduced by President Truman). The presidents of the great and powerful universities are still scratching their heads and talking to themselves . . . Small college presidents may shoot a sly grin at the big, famous universities with all their money and courses to solve every immediate problem of the modern world – except the problem of getting Winston Churchill the main event.

The President of a small college of only 212 students in heartland America had managed to achieve this coup through an old classmate, Major General Harry Vaughan, who at the time of the invitation was President Truman's military aide. What no one realised at the time was the international significance of what they had set in motion. Churchill's speech at Fulton would define the international politics of the next four decades.

Winston and Clementine embarked on the *Queen Elizabeth* on 9 January 1946. While at sea Churchill worked on his four-volume *History of the English Speaking Peoples*. On board were several hundred Canadians returning home after active service, and the day before they docked at New York Churchill spoke to the assembled troops. Having begun, 'My friends and shipmates,' and ranged over Canadian campaigns in Europe, his mind went back to a shared experience: 'We Englishmen always think of the days of 1940 when the Canadian Army corps stood almost alone in Kent and Sussex' – for the majority of the troops their first experience abroad. He concluded optimistically: 'the future will be fruitful for each and for all, and the reward of the warriors will not be unworthy of the deeds they have done'.

Waiting for him when he disembarked in New York at

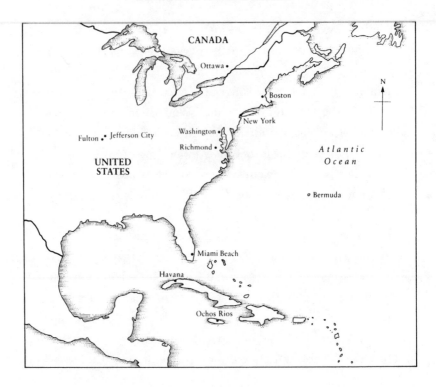

9.30 p.m. on 14 January was a huge contingent from the press and a large crowd of well-wishers. Churchill, making the V sign, thanked them for 'this very private reception' before being ushered into a press conference. There were some serious questions, but in the main he responded in a humorous vein. Asked about the programme of the new Labour government in Britain, he responded, 'I never criticise the government of my country abroad. I very rarely leave off criticising it at home.'

From New York the Churchills travelled to Miami Beach, where they were the guests of Colonel Frank Clarke, who had been their host at La Cabane de Montmorcey during a break from the Quebec Conference in 1943. On his first day in Florida Churchill gave a press conference on the patio of Clarke's house. One of the journalists present described him as a 'benevolent,

188

almost jolly gentleman without a vestige of a front'. He sat 'slumped, looking never an inch the statesman, this atomic bomb of an Englishman'.

The principal questions concerned the $4 billion loan Britain was seeking from America. Although no longer Prime Minister, Churchill was still the best-placed politician to explain. 'We suffered far more than any other country during the war. Some other countries were overrun, but they were not fighting. We were fighting and using up all our credit . . . If we're not given the opportunity to get back on our feet again we may never be able to take our place among other nations.' There were less serious questions. Had he brought a supply of cigars? 'That, with Havana so near, would be coals to Newcastle.' Once again the American journalists were eating out of his hand. The press conference over, 'the Gibraltar of his Britain turns to go . . . the man who fought at Omdurman almost fifty years ago and who has been fighting ever since must surely show somewhere the marks of his struggling years. As he turns his back – the back never shown to an enemy – we see in a sagging of the shoulders a sign of the burdens they have borne. Such, in the flesh, is the giant of the spirit whose deeds will echo through the centuries, a body needing the rest beneath the southern sun which so richly it has earned.'

It took a few days for Churchill to settle, but by the eighteenth he was painting and bathing in the tropical sunshine. He had brought his own secretary, Jo Sturdee, and another, Lorraine Bonar, was provided by Colonel Clarke. However, two were not enough to cope with Churchill's normal work, not to mention the three hundred letters which were arriving for him each day, so two additional secretaries were flown from the British Embassy in Washington to prevent the household becoming overwhelmed. Literary matters were never far from

Churchill's mind, and having virtually decided to write his wartime memoirs, he asked his pre-war European agent, Emery Reves, to come to Miami. Because of all that Reves had done in the twenties and thirties, he would handle what would become Churchill's most lucrative venture.

Following Churchill's footsteps through Florida I met Howard Kleinberg, who told me my grandfather was the perfect tourist. He attended the races at Hialeah with Colonel Clarke, and visited the Parrot Jungle at South Dade. Sometimes he would stand in front of the Colonel's house waving to passers-by and signing autographs. Kleinberg also told me how a photographer found Churchill painting beside the sea. He was at first reluctant to be photographed. Then, as the light began to fail, he asked if a picture could be taken of the scene so that he could continue the painting later in his studio.

While in Miami he also demonstrated his skill as a bricklayer, something he had not until then practised anywhere but Chartwell. At a cocktail party on DiLido Island he noticed a wall under construction. Telling his host he was a champion bricklayer, he seized a trowel and, to everyone's amazement and delight, laid a complete row of bricks.

Even before Churchill had arrived in America, the Cuban Foreign Office had been alerted to his visit by Mr H.C. Houghton of the Hotel Nacional, Havana, who suggested that 'an official invitation might be extended to Mr Churchill to revisit the scene of his youth as a guest of the Cuban government'. As a result the Churchills, joined by their daughter Sarah and accompanied by Colonel Clarke and Jo Sturdee, flew to Cuba on 1 February 1946 in an aircraft which President Truman had placed at their disposal.

They landed at Rancho Boyeros in the mid-afternoon. A

large crowd surrounded the aircraft, and it took some minutes for strong-armed police and troops to shepherd the party to the waiting presidential automobile. According to the Associated Press, 'detachments of Cuban soldiers guarded the twelve-mile right of way to the city'. Having briefly rested in the government suite at the Hotel Nacional, 'the indefatigable Churchill was off to the Presidential Palace and a fifteen-minute private conversation with President Ramon Grau San Martin. He caught the fancy of several hundred Cubans who gathered before the palace balcony . . . The crowd cheered lustily.'

The United Press release 'On Mr Churchill's Visit' stated simply: 'Wont be Cubas fault if Winnie seen at any time here without cigar stop Grau [Minister for Agriculture] presenting him magnificent humidor of Habanos on behalf government people stop.' Containing five hundred cigars, it would last my grandfather many months.

At a press conference in the Hotel Nacional ballroom, 'some 150 newspapermen and photographers gave the former Prime Minister a rough and tumble time . . . and got straight from the shoulder answers'. Relaxing on a large divan, Churchill leavened the serious discussion with his customary wit. He again declined to discuss the new government in Britain and when pressed to comment on the general election results which had put them there, he replied, 'In my country the people can do as they like, although it often happens that later they don't like what they have done.' When asked why he smoked so many Cuban cigars, he answered, 'I simply enjoy them. They greatly improve my temper.' Asked about current problems in the Cuban cigar trade with Britain, Churchill neatly sidestepped a contentious issue by saying that as an interested party he could express no impartial view, a reply which went down well.

The following day the Associated Press reported that

'Thousands of Havanans roared "Viva Churchill" as the ex-prime minister's motorcade wound through the city's narrow streets on a ten mile public tour. Churchill waved continuously, giving the famous V-sign, firmly clutching a big cigar in the other hand.' The tour culminated at the presidential palace for an official luncheon. Crowds again gathered beneath the balcony chanting, 'We want Churchill!', and once again he appeared with the President.

After a week in Cuba the Churchills and their party returned to Miami. Simultaneously, the cigars presented to Churchill by the Minister of Agriculture and a further nine hundred from the Chief of Police, various other individuals and cigar-makers were dispatched to London under Foreign Office arrangements. Her Majesty's Minister in Havana wrote to the Foreign Office to explain that 'These packages can rightly be described as "unsolicited gifts", and I hope that on these grounds it will be possible for you to have them sent to Mr. Churchill free of duty.' No doubt that was arranged, though it took some time, for a secretary's note to Churchill dated 8 April informed him: 'Your cigars from Cuba have not yet arrived in this country. As soon as they do the Foreign Office assure you they will let you know.'

A fleeting visit to Washington, where Churchill saw President Truman, raised speculation over the subject of his forthcoming speech at Fulton. Questioned by reporters, he was evasive, saying with a grin: 'I think "No comment" is a splendid expression. I got it from Sumner Welles [who had been the American Under-Secretary of State] during his tour of Europe.'

Back in Miami, Churchill was taken ill and confined to bed for three days, but this did not prevent him receiving the American Secretary of State James Byrne and Bernard Baruch, who flew from Washington to discuss the terms of the American loan to Britain. As the subject of their meeting remained secret, it served to increase the speculation about Fulton.

Before he left Miami there remained Churchill's first public appearance since arriving in America. This was an address on 26 February before a crowd of 17,500 in the Burdine Stadium, where he was to receive an honorary degree from the University of Miami. He thanked the university for the technical training it had given Royal Air Force cadets in the war years before America entered the conflict, and said of himself that 'one might almost say that no one ever passed so few examinations and received so many degrees. From this a superficial thinker might argue that the way to get the most degrees is to fail the most examinations. This would, however, be a conclusion unedifying in the academic atmosphere in which I now preen myself, and I therefore hasten to draw another moral with which I am sure we shall all be in accord: namely, no boy or girl should ever be disheartened by lack of success in their youth but should diligently and faithfully continue to persevere and make up for lost time.'

It was a speech full of humour, but the serious business was about to begin.

Churchill returned to Washington on 3 March and worked on his Fulton speech at the British Embassy, where he was staying. The following day he drove to the White House, where the President joined him for the drive to the railway station, and at midday they boarded the train for the twenty-four-hour journey to Jefferson City, Missouri. The two men had met at the Potsdam Conference in July 1945 when Truman, previously Vice President, had just inherited the presidency from the late Franklin D. Roosevelt. Having taken over from Churchill's personal friend, Truman had felt at a disadvantage, and now invited Churchill to travel on the presidential train in order that he could get to know better the man he called 'the first citizen of the world'. Drinks were served as the train pulled out of Union Station. Churchill ordered a weak whisky and water with no ice – to Americans an extraordinary mixture. Truman's naval aide, Clark Clifford, recalled Churchill's explanation: 'When I was in South Africa as a young man, the water was not fit to drink. I have felt that way ever since about water, but I have learned that it can be made palatable by the addition of some whisky.' The President roared with laughter. Within a few minutes, at Churchill's suggestion, the two agreed they should be on first-name terms.

Meanwhile at Westminster College there had been a scramble for seats; by mid-January some fifteen thousand requests for tickets had been received. The facts that Churchill was to be introduced by the President, that his speech on world affairs would be broadcast coast to coast, and that he did not 'contemplate any other public engagements' had fuelled expectations. The 2800 seats in the gymnasium and the nine hundred in the chapel had all been reserved, and the overflow would be catered for by public-address systems serving such places as the downtown churches and the courthouse square. The basement of the gymnasium was fitted out to cope with four hundred pressmen. While work went ahead at the college, the whole town of Fulton was mobilised under its chamber of commerce to cope with the unprecedented flood of visitors.

John David Marshall, now an Associate Professor at Middle Tennessee State University, described his quest for a ticket in a newspaper article on the thirty-fifth anniversary of what became known as the Iron Curtain speech. A junior student in 1946, 'interested in Churchill since about the sixth or seventh grade', he had first to 'try to find out just where Fulton was and how I might get there'. No doubt that was what many other hopeful people were also doing. His sheer persistence, which included letters to a Senator and to the White House, was rewarded by the arrival of ticket number 1476. There was no passenger-train service from his home in Carroll County, Maryland, to Fulton, so on the day his parents drove him there, a journey entailing an overnight stop in St Louis.

From the railway station at Jefferson City the presidential party transferred to a motorcade of thirty cars for the final twenty-five miles to Fulton. As his car entered the town, Churchill turned to Dr McCluer, the college President. 'Have them stop the car for a moment,' he said. 'I can't light my cigar in this wind and I know the people will be expecting it.' After lunch at the McCluer house, during which Churchill declared of the famous Calloway ham, 'The pig has reached the highest point of its evolution in this ham,' the academic processional began. It included Dr Sherman Scruggs of the then all-black Lincoln University, making it the United States's first desegregated academic procession.

This is not the place to discuss Churchill's speech, which is recognised as one of the most significant of the twentieth century, other than to describe, in the words of the seasoned American journalist David Brinkley, the atmosphere in the gymnasium. 'The audience sat still, quiet, entranced, eager to applaud but afraid to. The clapping of hands would somehow have seemed almost vulgar. Further, he was not talking to those of us in the hall. He was talking to the world.'

One of Churchill's last remarks to Dr McCluer as he left the Westminster campus was that he hoped he 'had started some thinking that would make history'. As we all now know, he had done just that: 'From Stettin in the Baltic to Trieste in the

Adriatic, an iron curtain has descended across the Continent.' The speech caused considerable waves throughout the world, and it would not be long before Churchill's warning of the growing threat posed by the Soviet Union was proved right. Only nine months later he would write to Governor Thomas Dewey of New York, 'If I made the Fulton speech today it would be criticised as consisting of platitudes.' But at the time it received an almost universally hostile press in the West for being unduly alarmist. In the Soviet Union, *Pravda*'s headline ran 'Churchill Rattles the Sabre'. There was, however, one favourable mention. In his home town the young John David Marshall became something of a celebrity when the *McKenzie Banner* of 8 March reported, 'Congress may have had some adverse reaction but the only McKenzie or Carroll County citizen who heard him was for him one hundred percent.'

Politically, President Truman was as yet unable to embrace Churchill's message, and went so far as to claim he had not read the speech in advance. But this did not inhibit the friendly relationship they had already established. The formalities over, it was a relaxed group who sat down to a game of poker as the President's train took them back to Washington. Churchill was not a good poker player, but on the President's instructions he was not allowed to lose heavily. The game over, most of the group went to bed, but Churchill, accustomed to working late, sat up with Clark Clifford and Truman's Press Secretary, Charlie Ross. Churchill, having said that he had just made the 'most important speech' of his career, felt like talking. This was the occasion when he said that if he could live again he would wish to be born in the United States. Having expounded on the subject he added, 'I say this despite the fact that you Americans have some barbaric customs.'

'Like what, Mr Churchill?' asked Ross.

'For one thing,' came the reply, 'you stop drinking with your meals.'

In March 1996 Margaret Thatcher spoke at Westminster College to mark the fiftieth anniversary of the Iron Curtain speech, and the organisers tried as far as possible to recreate the journey taken by Churchill and Truman half a century before. My brother and sister, Julian and Edwina, and I were invited. We were given a magnificent send-off from Saint Louis City, with a brass band and all the railway officials in formal dress. We travelled in a vintage train similar to the one that had been used by the President and his guest, but while they had had plenty of room to spread themselves, it seemed as though the whole world was going to Fulton with us. Everyone was in a high state of excitement and anticipation, particularly the journalists, of whom there were many. They all wanted us to speculate on the content of Lady Thatcher's speech, convinced that she would be using the occasion to make some earth-shattering pronouncement.

I had only heard of Fulton in connection with the famous speech, but I did not expect it to be such a small town. We drove through it in a motorcade of open cars to Westminster College past two remarkable and very different sights – a Christopher Wren church which had been transported from London and rebuilt brick by brick, and close by a sculpture by my sister Edwina carved from part of the Berlin Wall, complete with graffiti.

After Churchill's Fulton speech there was still a fortnight to go before he sailed home. In that time he spoke to the General Assembly of Virginia in Richmond and to a group of generals and admirals assembled in Washington by General Eisenhower.

Arriving in New York on 11 March, the Churchills again

took up residence in the Waldorf. Fourteen eventful years had elapsed since they were last there, and some of those years were marked by the tickertape reception the city gave Churchill four days later. The fifteenth was a wet day, but New Yorkers were not deterred, some four hundred thousand people turning out to wave and cheer his motorcade from the sidewalks, and thousands more from office windows, as it took a circuitous route to the City Hall. In spite of the downpour, Churchill insisted that the top of his convertible was lowered. 'I like to see the people,' he explained. That night he spoke at a dinner at the Waldorf to an audience of sixteen hundred which included eighteen ambassadors among the many VIPs. Broadcast coast to coast, he asked the rhetorical question of whether he regretted his Fulton speech, and gave a carefully enunciated answer: 'I do not wish to withdraw or modify a single word.' As at Fulton, he was addressing a far wider audience than those who were actually present to hear him.

On 20 March Winston and Clementine sailed from New York in the *Queen Mary*. Interviewed before sailing he jested, 'I am now going home to have a rest after the rest cure.' Two days into the voyage came the news that the Soviet Union had announced that its troops which had lingered in Persia, contrary to previous agreement, would be withdrawn. The *New York Times* attributed this change in Soviet tactics to Churchill's speeches at Fulton and New York.

The next three years saw the West enact the measures for which Churchill had argued at Fulton. The Marshall Plan had brought American aid to a war-ravaged Europe, and the North Atlantic Treaty Organisation had ensured collective security. Thus, when Churchill returned to America on 25 March 1949 he was able to thank the American people 'on behalf of Britain and on behalf of Western Europe, of free Europe, as I have some credentials to do, for all you have done and are doing'.

He had landed from the *Queen Elizabeth* two days before, accompanied by Clementine, their daughter Mary and her husband, Christopher Soames. Churchill had come at the invitation of the Massachusetts Institute of Technology to address their mid-century Convocation on the Social Implications of Science. The *New York Times* of the twenty-fourth reported that two hundred reporters and photographers stormed the ship as it docked, 'the largest press group that ever went out to meet an incoming vessel'. Bernard Baruch was there to whisk the visitors away to his apartment on East Sixty-sixth Street for a quiet evening before their train journey to Washington the following morning, where a large crowd turned up to meet Churchill at Union Station. At the British Embassy he halted his car at the gate on Massachusetts Avenue and walked between two lines of cheering British people to the Ambassador's residence. Into his stay of less than twenty-four hours were crammed a reception at the Embassy, a dinner hosted by President Truman, a discussion with General Marshall and a call to take leave of the President and present him with red Morocco-bound copies of Churchill's *Life of Marlborough*, published in 1933, and Volume II of his war memoirs, *Their Finest Hour,* which had just been published.

The days following his return to New York were filled with engagements, among which the most prominent were a large dinner in his honour at the Ritz-Carlton Hotel given by Henry Luce, the owner of *Life* magazine; dinner with Governor Dewey; a meeting with Eleanor Roosevelt, the widow of Franklin Roosevelt; dinner with the *New York Times*; lunch with the American Committee of a United Europe; and a discussion with American Zionist leaders. The first Arab–Israeli war had just ended with an armistice, and Churchill reassured the American Zionists of his support: 'I was all for a free and independent Israel all through the dark years when many of my distinguished countrymen took a different view. So do not imagine for a moment I have the slightest idea of deserting you now in your hour of glory.'

After travelling overnight, the Churchills arrived at Boston's South Station on the morning of Thursday, 31 March. The *New York Times* reported that Churchill was greeted by a throng of six thousand shouting 'Good old Winnie!' That evening fourteen thousand descended on the Boston Garden to hear him speak. Millions more were watching or listening on television and radio. 'Ladies and gentlemen,' he began, 'I frankly confess that I feel somewhat overawed in addressing this vast scientific and learned audience on the subjects which your panels are discussing. I have no technical and no university education and have just had to pick up a few things as I went along.' When the laughter subsided he surveyed the immense changes brought about by science in the first half of the twentieth century, and the failure of man to keep pace morally and intellectually: 'The scale of events around him assumed gigantic proportions while he remained about the same size. By comparison therefore he became much smaller.' Turning to the Cold War, as it had by now become known in America, he declared, 'We seek nothing from Russia but goodwill and fair play.' But if there was to be a war of nerves, 'let us make sure our nerves are strong and are fortified by the deepest convictions of our hearts'. He expressed his conviction that Europe would have fallen to Communism and 'London under bombardment but for the deterrent of the atomic bomb in the hands of the United States'. The headlines the following morning reflected the Cold War aspects of his speech. 'Churchill declares atom bomb alone deters Russia from war', splashed the *New York*

Herald Tribune, which followed with a second headline: 'Tells Boston crowd war can be avoided if West stays united and tough'.

President Truman had been unable to accompany Churchill to Boston as originally planned, and at first Churchill decided to return to New York as soon as his speech was over, rather than stay the night. Clementine could see that this would spoil the occasion, and wrote to him jointly with Randolph: 'Enormous pains have been taken about the banquet. The country has been combed for the finest food and wines, and we are both sure that it will not be as bad when it happens as it seems in advance . . . A great many of the faculty did not have dinner jackets, or their wives long dresses, and they have bought them specially because you are coming to the dinner.' Fortunately, not for the first or last time, Churchill took his wife's advice.

The following day, having received an honorary lecturership from the Institute, Churchill in his words of thanks noted, 'I carry away from this gathering sentiments which will enable me for the rest of my life to view with a totally different light the Boston Tea Party, of which I have heard in my early days.'

Catching the midnight train, the Churchills returned to New York and embarked immediately on the *Queen Mary*. There was a final press conference at which, wearing his siren suit, he told the reporters, 'I wore this once to the Kremlin. It didn't go down so well: pushing democracy too far.' The *New York Times* ended a warm farewell message, 'May he come again soon.'

He came again at the beginning of 1952. He was again the Prime Minister, the Conservative Party having been returned to power in the general election of October 1951. This was less a personal pilgrimage than an official visit, and he was accompanied by three cabinet ministers, the Chief of the Imperial General Staff and the First Sea Lord, as well as his Private Secretary Jock Colville, his doctor and numerous other staff. Having embarked on the *Queen Mary* on 31 December, the voyage was spent largely in preparing for the discussions ahead. The Prime Minister, now seventy-seven, no longer had the energy of previous years, and Colville found it difficult to get his master to read the necessary papers. Churchill had a ready excuse, saying he was going to America 'to re-establish relations, not to transact business'. There was no doubt that relations at government level needed re-establishing and that, according to the American press, his arrival was awaited with some apprehension. It did not help that he had chosen an awkward moment, when Truman was preoccupied with his annual State of the Union and budget speeches.

Churchill need not have worried, for the welcome was as effusive as ever it had been. A flotilla of fireboats sprayed streams of water into the air, and the presidential aircraft carried him to Washington, where to greet him on the tarmac was the full array of President, Cabinet, diplomatic corps and chiefs of staff. There was much press comment on Churchill's headgear that day. The British Embassy named it a 'billycock'. London hatters called it a 'Cambridge'. The *New York Times* consulted a local hatter, who declared, 'It's not a cut-down tall hat, it's a high-crowned low-crowned hat.' By the end of that day's discussions and dinner on the presidential yacht it was clear relations had been re-established. 'There never was a time when Winston Churchill could come to the United States and not find the red carpet rolled out for him,' wrote the *New York Times*.

Eight days of conference ensued, after which Churchill then left for New York and the hospitality of his friend Bernard Baruch before boarding the train for Ottawa. By comparison with Washington, the next five days as the guest of Field Marshal Alexander, the Governor-General of Canada, was a rest during which time Churchill prepared the speech he was to make to the United States Congress. It would be his third to that audience, and he had been showing some anxiety over its preparation.

He was due to address Congress at noon on 17 January 1952. At 11.20 a.m. he was still in bed in the British Embassy, discussing details of the speech with his Foreign Office official. With the assistance of a motorcycle escort he reached the Capitol on time, and as he began to speak he wasted no time in broaching the most sensitive of the issues between Britain and America. 'I did not come here to ask you for money . . .' he began, pausing to let the statement sink in. When it had, and laughter and applause followed, he resumed: '. . . to ask you for money to make life more comfortable and easier for us in Britain. Our standards of life are our own business.' During the war Britain had fought, for a while alone, to the utmost limits of her resources. Churchill had come 'not for gold but for steel: not favours but equipment'. His speech then ranged over the international scene – the wars in Korea and Indo-China, the tensions with Russia and China, and those in the Middle East. Britain and America spoke the same language. They must make sure that 'the supreme fact of the twentieth century is that they tread the same path'. Churchill need have had no qualms over his speech. It was a resounding success.

He returned to New York on the afternoon of 19 January with a bad cold, and was ordered to bed in the Baruch apartment. A City Hall reception had to be cancelled, but Mayor Impellitteri came to the apartment to present the city's Medal of Honour. On the twenty-second Churchill boarded the *Queen Mary* for home. To his doctor he gave his verdict on what had threatened to be a difficult conference: 'This visit to America has been a gamble. But it has come off, I think. It will do a lot of good.' *Newsweek* agreed: 'Not since the war had relations between Britain and the United States been put on such a friendly co-operative basis.'

On 6 February 1952, ten days after Churchill's return to Britain, King George VI died in his sleep. He was succeeded by his daughter, who as Queen Elizabeth II became the sixth monarch Churchill was to serve in Parliament. Not surprisingly, the years were beginning to tell. He had carried an immense burden during the war at an age when most men would have retired, and was now leading a government still grappling with post-war domestic and international problems. But he was not deterred from travelling, and the election of General Dwight D. Eisenhower as President of the United States in November 1952 meant that plans for a holiday in Jamaica were recast in order to re-establish relations with the President Elect. From Ten Downing Street came the announcement that Churchill would stop in the United States 'on the way'.

The *Queen Mary* docked at Pier 90 on New York's Fiftieth Street at 8 a.m. on 5 January 1953. Churchill was accompanied by Clementine, Mary and Christopher Soames, and Jock Colville, who noted, 'There was pandemonium as high dignitaries, low officials, Embassy people and pressmen swarmed aboard.' At the press conference in the ship's Verandah Grill Churchill reminded the reporters that it was only a year since he had met them last, and hoped they had 'had a good year'. Britain had, he said. When asked about the stalemate in the Korean War, he replied, 'Checkmate is worse, I believe.' The reporters departed delighted with their copy, and Bernard Baruch took Churchill and his travelling companions to East Sixty-Sixth Street. Eleanor

Roosevelt came for lunch, and Eisenhower arrived in the afternoon, returning for dinner and staying late to discuss the many world problems.

There were other discussions on subsequent days, notably with Secretary of State designate John Foster Dulles and Ambassador designate to England Winthrop Aldrich, as a result of which Churchill began to realise, in Colville's words, that 'he was welcomed and revered in America much more as Winston Churchill than as the Prime Minister of the United Kingdom'.

While in New York he visited the reputed birthplace of his mother Jennie Jerome (there was some doubt if she had actually been born there or at another address close by). Accompanied by Mayor and Mrs Impellitteri, his actress daughter Sarah who was working in New York, Borough President Cashmore and Baruch, Churchill went to 426 Henry Street in Brooklyn. Several hundred people, including the children from the nearby school, turned out to welcome him. 'Very nice house,' said Churchill to the current inhabitants, Mr and Mrs Joseph Romero and their four children. A reporter asked how it compared to Churchill's own birthplace, Blenheim Palace. 'I am equally proud of them both,' was the reply.

From New York Churchill flew in the President's aircraft on 8 January to Washington, where that evening he gave a dinner in President Truman's honour at the British Embassy. The following morning the presidential plane took Churchill to join Clementine in Jamaica. Here they stayed at a house near Ocho Rios which had been lent by a former Vice-Chairman of the Conservative Party, Sir Harold Mitchell. Churchill painted four pictures and worked on the final volume of his memoirs. There was also swimming and agreeable friends as neighbours, including Noël Coward. Churchill greatly enjoyed Coward's songs, and the composer was delighted to play them for him;

'Mad Dogs and Englishmen' and 'Don't Put Your Daughter on the Stage, Mrs Worthington' were Churchill's favourites. After a fortnight the Churchills flew to New York and embarked immediately on the *Queen Mary* for the voyage home.

The death of Stalin in March 1953 aroused in Churchill the hope of some relaxation in East–West tensions. However, America, which had been slow to understand the menace of the Soviet Union, had by now swung violently into an aggressive anti-Communist attitude. Liberals and anyone suspected of Communist sympathies were purged with zeal. Dulles, the sabre-rattling Secretary of State of whom Churchill would say 'He is the only bull who carries his own china closet around with him,' was bent on threatening use of the bomb. When Russia exploded its own hydrogen bomb in August, Churchill felt it was time for a further personal exchange of views with the American President. Eventually Eisenhower was persuaded to come to a meeting in Bermuda, but in order to play down suspicions of an unduly close relationship between Britain and the United States he was insistent that the French Prime Minister René Mayer, who had lobbied for an invitation, should come too.

In June Churchill suffered a major stroke, and arrangements for the conference had to be put on hold. He gave strict instructions to Jock Colville that the fact that he was temporarily incapacitated should not be made public, and that the administration should continue as if he was still in full control. The speed of Churchill's recovery and his ability to attend to the most pressing problems was remarkable. In this he was helped by the abilities and discretion of Colville and of his son-in-law Christopher Soames, and the co-operation of newspaper proprietors who, remarkably, suppressed what would have been a major story. In October he made a major speech at the Conservative Party conference, and in November his first parliamentary speech since his stroke. Both were masterpieces of presentation, delivered with his customary wit and style, *The Times* commenting on his 'complete authority over the Commons'. He was ready for the Bermuda Conference.

The conference in December brought some useful results, particularly on the exchange of nuclear information, but Churchill had been unable to persuade Dulles of the need for negotiations with the Soviet Union, the principal object of his transatlantic journey. Eisenhower seemed to leave foreign affairs entirely to Dulles, who remained resolutely against any talks with Russia. 'This fellow preaches like a Methodist minister,' said Churchill to his doctor. 'And his bloody text is always the same.'

In an endeavour to maintain co-ordinated policies, Churchill made one last effort while still Prime Minister. Six months after Bermuda he pressed for yet another meeting, and again he was invited to Washington. Accompanied by the Foreign Secretary Anthony Eden, Churchill landed in Washington by Strato-cruiser on the morning of 25 June 1954. That morning's *Manchester Guardian* had announced 'Bleak background for talks', but some useful things were achieved. Strenuous days of discussion ranging over many issues resulted in a joint Declaration of Principles, and agreement was reached that the German Federal Republic should take its place as an equal partner in the defence of the free world. The inevitable press conference, reported as 'the largest in the history of this capital', saw over a thousand reporters gathered in the Statler Hotel for what it was suspected would be Churchill's swansong with the American press. Although he suggested that the press should 'be generous, as you always are, and tender hearted to an aged guest', he produced a sparkling performance. 'Everybody greatly impressed,' was the personal diary entry by his Private Secretary.

On the afternoon of 29 June Churchill flew to Ottawa, where in a busy twenty-four hours he gave a dinner for the Canadian Prime Minister Louis St Laurent, attended a Cabinet meeting, gave a broadcast and a press conference and was the guest of honour at a dinner before flying to New York and boarding the *Queen Elizabeth* at one in the morning. The milling crowd who came to see him off when the ship sailed at noon was yet more proof that America could never resist Winston Churchill.

Despite the attitude of Americans towards him in person, the special relationship between Britain and the United States suffered when Churchill resigned as Prime Minister on 5 April 1955 and handed over to Eden. Then in October 1956, a week before a US presidential election, Britain, France and Israel invaded Egypt in response to the nationalisation of the Suez Canal by President Nasser of Egypt. Launched without the prior knowledge of Eisenhower and Dulles, the Suez operation caused an estrangement between Britain and America more serious than any since the War of Independence. Churchill, now almost eighty-two, issued a press statement supporting the British government's position, although privately he said he would never have invaded Egypt without first 'squaring the Americans'. Concerned over the harm done to Anglo–American relations, he wrote to Eisenhower on the theme that whatever the rights and wrongs of the matter, it would be folly to let these events come between Britain and America. Only Russia would gain. In reply the President expressed sadness that there was a problem over which the two countries did not see eye to eye, and said he would 'never be happy until our old-time closeness' had been restored. When Lord Moran said that a lot

of people were wishing Churchill was still in charge, he replied,
'I am not the man I was. I could not be Prime Minister now.'

Eisenhower, who had last seen Churchill in 1954, was surprised
and somewhat distressed at the visible deterioration in Churchill's condition when on 4 May 1959, against all medical advice
and travelling only with his Private Secretary Anthony Montague Browne and his valet/nurse, he arrived on another American visit. Installed once again in the White House, and suffering
from jetlag, Churchill joined the family at dinner. 'I only wish
you had known him in his prime,' Eisenhower said to his
daughter-in-law. Over the next three days Eisenhower devoted
himself almost entirely to his guest.

Mary Jean Eisenhower, the President's granddaughter, has a
clear recollection of Churchill's visit: 'The wonderful memory
of meeting him was that he was very kind and tolerant to us,
the grandchildren. I remember noting that, in the East Wing
living quarters, he sat in the seat my grandfather normally
occupied. On one occasion when my grandfather and Sir
Winston were talking my older sister, aged eight, plopped down
beside him and informed him that her doll's diaper had fallen
off and needed to be changed. Barely taking his eyes off my
grandfather, he replaced the diaper and handed the doll back
to my sister without a blip in the conversation. My sister was
quite enamoured and painted a picture for him. My grandfather
ensured that it was delivered and, to her delight, my sister
received a lovely letter thanking her. My father had the letter
encased in acrylic and it was in our family living area for years.
Some forty years on it is still very easy to understand my grandfather's devotion to Sir Winston.'

On the fifth, after Churchill had spent the morning
recovering from his journey, they visited the Walter Reed Army

Hospital, where John Foster Dulles and General Marshall were both seriously ill. That evening the mood lightened when a collection of generals and admirals who had worked under Churchill and Eisenhower during World War II dined at the White House. Writing that day, Churchill reassured Clementine, 'All goes well & the President is a real friend.'

The following day the pair flew by helicopter to visit Eisenhower's farm at Gettysburg, studying the Civil War battlefield from the air *en route*. At their destination Churchill, wearing a ten-gallon hat, was driven around the farm by his host in a golf cart, pursued by the press, from whom Eisenhower took care to protect his guest. To mark his visit Churchill presented Eisenhower with one of his Marrakech paintings, which was subsequently hung in the Oval Office in order that the President could 'display it proudly to each and every visitor'.

On 8 May Churchill left Washington for the last time, having the previous evening given a dinner at the British Embassy for the President. Flying into New York's La Guardia Airport he was met by Bernard Baruch, who warned reporters that 'He is not going to see a soul.' He did, however, have tea with Consuelo Balsan a few hours before being driven to Idlewild for his departure on the tenth. Several hundred people were there to see him off. 'I must now leave you and return to Britain,' he said. He paused and with a smile added, 'My other country.'

There would be one last brief visit. In 1961 Churchill was cruising in the West Indies with Aristotle Onassis on the *Christina*. She sailed slowly up the eastern seaboard of the United States, reaching New York on 12 April to be greeted by a salute of ships' sirens and cascades of water from fireboats. For the two nights that Churchill was there Bernard Baruch dined on board. A telephone call on the first night came from President Kennedy, asking if Churchill would like to fly down to Washington in the presidential aircraft and 'spend a couple of days with me'. His health unfortunately precluded such a journey, as his Private Secretary personally explained to the President.

On 14 April 1961, with the Union Jack and Stars and Stripes flying from the wings of their car, Churchill and Baruch were driven to Idlewild. At the Pan American terminal, supported by a stick on one side and Baruch on the other, Churchill made his way to the aircraft. As he was about to board he turned towards the waving crowd and raised his hat. He was leaving his 'other country' after his sixteenth and final visit.

In 1963, when Congress voted to make Churchill an honorary citizen of the United States, it became his other country in fact as well as in mind.

CHAPTER 10

Madeira: Warm, Paintable, Bathable

I have been greeted by many people in the world for whom
I have done something, but never in my whole life been
greeted with such enthusiasm by people for whom I have
never done anything.
Winston Churchill, Madeira, 1 January 1950

Winston Churchill first visited Madeira in October 1899. It was the only port of call for the *Dunottar Castle*, on which the young war correspondent was travelling to South Africa. Disenchanted by sea travel, impatient lest the fighting should be over before he arrived, and finding no news from the front when he went ashore, he took no pleasure in the visit. On his return voyage nine months later he was equally anxious to reach his journey's end. He had made his name, and was in a hurry to capitalise on all the favourable publicity which had turned him into an international hero.

Fifty years later, now the most revered man in the world, he wanted sun, warmth and somewhere to paint. Bryce Nairn, who had first met the Churchills when he was British Consul in Marrakech, was now serving in Madeira. His wife Margaret, an artist herself who had accompanied Churchill on painting

212

expeditions in Morocco and in the south of France in 1945, was probably an added reason for the telegram Churchill sent to her husband in November: 'query warm, paintable, bathable, comfortable, flowery, hotels etc. We are revolving plans. Keep all secret. Should so much like to see you both again.'

The idea for this visit had been conceived in August 1949, when plans were being made for Reid's Hotel in Funchal to reopen after being closed for nine years because of the war. It was owned by a British family, the Blandys, who had discussed with the Nairns the difficulty of attracting sufficient custom in the face of post-war exchange regulations and restricted travel. However, should some famous person come to stay others would be likely to follow, and the Nairns agreed to recommend Madeira, with Reid's as a base, as a suitable spot for the Churchills to spend a holiday.

With Churchill booked in, Reid's made special arrangements to furnish his suite, the same one which Lloyd George had occupied during a visit in 1925. Various residents of Madeira lent special pieces of furniture, silver and linen for the suite, and pictures were provided by Madame Monier Vinard. There were no double beds in the hotel, and, alerted to the fact that their impending visitor would want one, John Blandy provided his own.

The Churchill party was made up of Colonel Bill Deakin, two secretaries, a manservant, Churchill's bodyguard Evan Davies, and Diana, who, having married Duncan Sandys in 1935, was revisiting the place where she had spent her first honeymoon with John Bailey in 1932. They embarked on the *Durban Castle* on 29 December 1950. The ship was late in sailing as, having just left Chartwell, Churchill remembered he had not fed his black swans, and turned the cars around in order that he could do so.

★   ★   ★

My grandfather's official biography by Martin Gilbert covers his time in Madeira in half a dozen lines. To discover more I followed him there in 1999, and was welcomed by Reid's Hotel, now part of the Orient Express Group. The first people I met were Adam and Christina Blandy, who from their family archives showed me a letter by Adam's mother, Mildred Blandy, describing Churchill's arrival on the evening of 1 January 1950: '. . . a wonderful night, the whole island brilliantly illuminated with millions of lights, and huge set pieces on the hillside. As the *Durban Castle* came round the Brazen Head people started letting off fireworks. Blandy's office had a huge V in triple lights which could be seen miles out to sea. Thousands of people in the streets and on the pier, and the local guard of honour all lined up.' As Churchill went ashore the crowd at first remained silent, which is the Portuguese way of showing respect, until someone shouted '*Viva Mr Churchill!*', at which the cheering began.

Alec Zino, who had been a spectator that night, described to me an amusing incident on the quayside. 'The crowd all made the V sign. One man made it wrong. Mr Churchill went up to him and firmly turned his hand the right way round.'

The Blandys' Buick took the Churchills to Reid's, with Churchill sitting on the folded-down roof acknowledging the cheers of the crowd. 'I have been greeted by many people in the world for whom I have done something,' he remarked, 'but never in my whole life been greeted with such enthusiasm by people for whom I have never done anything.'

That evening Winston and Clementine received a standing ovation when they entered Reid's dining room. The manager, John Paqot, made a brief speech of welcome, and asked the other guests to respect the Churchills' desire for a quiet holiday. Graham and Mildred Blandy and the Nairns were included in the dinner party. Mildred's letter described Churchill as being 'in amazing form. Astonishing as you would have expected him to be exhausted after a four day voyage of bad weather, all the fuss of landing, etc . . . He got onto ancient British history and we listened enthralled.' Graham's account describes the arrival of the port. 'He asked me what was the best Madeira on the list, to which I replied that I believed it was the Blandy 1792 Solera. When it came he said, "I must do honour to this," and got up, put his napkin over his elbow, and poured out the wine for each of us. Then he sat down and talked about the time when the 1792 was born – three years after the French Revolution – and when Louis XVI and Marie Antoinette were still living.' The bottle had originally formed part of a pipe (105 gallons) delivered to HMS *Northumberland*, which was taking Napoleon into exile on St Helena in 1815, but he was unable to drink it for medical reasons, and as it had not been paid for it was returned to Madeira when he died.

The weather was cold and wet. When a maid put up mosquito netting Churchill remarked, 'I would have thought the devils would have died of the cold.' In spite of the bad weather, he did manage some painting. Mildred Blandy's letter reported: 'He goes to Camara de Lobos, the very beautiful but smelly little fishing village on the west, and he is painting the harbour there. He is also painting a view of the town from George Dalziel's garden.' The place where he set up his easel in the fishing village is now marked by a plaque and a restaurant named after him. For transport on these expeditions, one of Madeira's prominent families, the Leacocks, provided their Rolls-Royce, which for the occasion had its boot equipped as a bar. Because of the weather his war memoirs occupied a good deal of Churchill's time. Bill Deakin had come out specifically to help with these, while General Sir Henry Pownall, who was also assisting, had arrived in advance. Those unused to Churchill's methods were surprised that the dictation went on well past midnight.

It was a very informal holiday, Mildred Blandy having Clementine sprung on her with scant warning for lunch: 'This gave me horribly little notice, however I dashed around in circles and up they [Clementine and Margaret Nairn] came at one. Graham came too as I phoned him telling him he had got to come ... Tomorrow I am having a lunch party for Mr Churchill's two secretaries, Miss Sturdee and Miss Gilliat. They are both charming girls and very keen to get around and see something of the island. Mr C uses them in the early morning hours and very late at night.'

Looking after the Churchill suite was Joseph, who later became well known as Reid's hall porter. He performed so well that Churchill asked him if he would come to London and work for him. On seeking the advice of the manservant who had accompanied Churchill, Joseph was told, 'I'm leaving as soon as we go back to London because of all the work. I'm on my feet all day, and I can't stand it any more.' Joseph fully understood: 'Looking after the Churchill suite, I was starting at six in the morning and often did not leave the hotel until midnight.' When he declined the offer, Churchill said, 'I thought that would be your answer. It's a pity, as I should have liked you to come.'

It had been intended that the holiday would last several weeks, but Churchill decided to cut it short when the Labour Prime Minister Clement Attlee announced that a general election would be held on 23 February 1950. At 6.30 on the morning of 12 January, dressed in his Trinity House jacket and cap, he boarded the Aquila Airways Sunderland flying boat which had been standing by for him. The First Officer, Christopher Blackburn, recalled: 'We looked at the angry sea. Chur-chill was dead keen, we heard. We must have a go at least. He came aboard with a party of four, with plenty of champagne and cigars. We headed out into the swell. It must have been a good four feet and [the flying boat] was taking a real pasting. In the end we made it and turned for home.' The following day Churchill telegraphed Clementine, 'We were lucky yester-day with fog which obligingly lifted [on their arrival at South-ampton] for half an hour.' The nine-hour flight had been most comfortable, but he recommended she return by sea.

CHAPTER 11

The Old World

Many remedies are suggested for the avoidance of worry and
mental strain . . . But the element which is constant and common
in all of them is Change. Change is the master key.
Winston Churchill, *Thoughts and Adventures* (1932)

For Churchill, change came through the variety of his pursuits, of which politics, writing and painting were only the foremost. But his restless nature demanded also a variety of surroundings, and from early on the Continent, close at hand, fulfilled that need. For short excursions there were friends to provide accommodation. For extended periods, running into months, there were agreeable hotels and, on one occasion in 1922, a rented villa near Cannes paid for by letting Churchill's London house. Late in life there were generous friends to welcome the entourage essential to his lifestyle and the mammoth war memoirs he was writing.

Of all the European countries through which my grandfather travelled and in which he spent holidays, France was unquestionably his favourite. His love of the country grew through politics, two world wars, the agreeable climate and the wonderful light by which to paint on the Côte d'Azur. Towards the

218

end of his long life he would spend many months of each year there.

Although the empathy with France which Churchill had shown during his first visit in 1883* would be demonstrated throughout his life, the young Winston bridled at a suggestion by the headmaster of Harrow, Dr Welldon, that he spend part of the summer holidays of 1891 in France. 'I beg and pray that you will not send me to a Vile, nasty, fusty, beastly, French Family,' he pleaded in a letter to his mother. He successfully fought off the idea, but Dr Welldon returned to the charge, and by Christmas Winston was forced to capitulate. However, he negotiated a compromise. He did not have to stay with 'a horrid French family', but was accommodated at the home in Versailles of one of the Harrow French masters, with whom he travelled to France.

In a letter to Lady Randolph from Versailles the seventeen-year-old Churchill described the rigours of a standard of travel hitherto unknown to him. 'We travelled 2nd classe but notwithstanding the horrible smell of Brandy and beer on the boat, I was not sick. Fatigue, the passage, The strange food, The cold, home sickness, the thoughts of what was behind & what before nearly caused me to write a letter which would have been very painful to you. The food is very queer. There is wine and beer to drink.' However, something was apparently being achieved, for he added, 'I have already made great progress in French. I already begin to think in it.'

I never heard my grandfather utter a word of French. Many years later Jock Colville recalled a hilarious lunch party where he launched into French, frequently throwing in English words when the French did not come to mind. My father told of a

---

* See pp. xxii–xxiii.

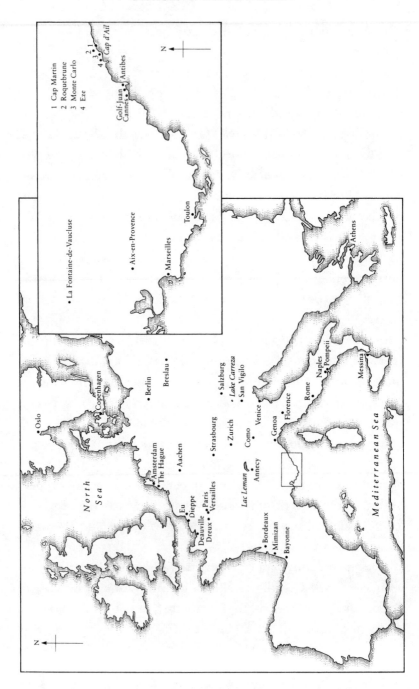

1 Cap Martin
2 Roquebrune
3 Monte Carlo
4 Eze

conversation with General de Gaulle during which my grand-father declared, '*Si vous m'opposerez, je vous get-ridderai!*' But one can imagine him speaking French with enthusiasm in 1891, and eighteen months later, on a walking tour in Switzerland, his tutor described his French as 'voluble'.

In the event he enjoyed his Christmas visit in 1891, being invited out by various friends of his parents. One of these, Baron Hirsch, found an unusual way of entertaining his school-boy guest, who wrote to Lady Randolph, 'He took me to the morgue . . . I was much interested. Only 3 Macabres – not a good bag.'

Fifteen years later, gambling for a few nights in the casino at Deauville, Churchill, then Under-Secretary of State for the Colonies, came away the richer by £12,000 at today's value. He was staying on the yacht of a friend, Baron de Forest, at the start of a holiday which would include the 1906 German army manoeuvres. After spending some of his winnings in Paris on 'beautiful French editions', he travelled by train to Switzer-land to stay for a fortnight at the mountain villa of his friend and financial adviser Sir Ernest Cassel. Together they climbed to the summit, at 9625 feet, of the Eggishorn. Cassel, the older by twenty-two years, managed the round trip on foot, while Churchill needed the assistance of a mule on the way back.

From Switzerland Churchill moved on to Berlin, and then to Breslau as guest of the Kaiser, King Edward VII's nephew, for the manoeuvres. In spite of his busy life he maintained a keen interest in military matters. Between 1906 and 1910 he attended manoeuvres – British, French or German – each year, and as he had seen more active service than many professional soldiers his opinion on military matters was listened to with respect. As a yeomanry major he commanded a squadron in the Queen's Own Oxfordshire Hussars, and had the King's

permission to wear uniform at foreign manoeuvres. He therefore asked his brother Jack, who had also been in the Oxfordshire Hussars, for the loan of his Hussar plume and leopardskin
for ceremonial purposes. Jack replied that the plume was lost,
and the leopardskin had long been in use as a hearthrug, whereupon Churchill's cousin, the Duke of Marlborough, provided
both items of uniform.

The following year, immediately before a tour of the African
colonies, Churchill attended the French army manoeuvres,
which impressed him more than the 'theatrical display' he had
seen in Germany. However, in 1909, having again watched the
German army, he described it as 'a terrible machine', going on
to say, 'Much as war attracts me I feel more deeply every year
what a vile & wicked folly & barbarism it all is.' Those who,
throughout more than half a century, attached to Churchill
the label of warmonger, ignored or were unaware of his true
feelings.

Work and pleasure were inextricably mixed in all these
excursions. Churchill's ministerial boxes followed him everywhere, and at every stop along the way he could not wait to
get his hands on the latest newspapers.

In 1908, between his African journey and the German
manoeuvres, Churchill had married Clementine Hozier. Their
honeymoon had begun at Blenheim Palace, from where Churchill wrote to his mother that they longed for 'warm Italian
sun'. Accordingly they went first to Baveno, on Lake Maggiore,
and then to Venice. From Venice Churchill took Clementine
to stay at Eichorn in Austria with his friends Baron de Forest
and his wife.

Rising very quickly through the political ranks, Churchill in
1911 became First Lord of the Admiralty. With the Admiralty
yacht, the *Enchantress*, at his disposal he could now travel far

and wide without even the inconvenience of shifting bedrooms. He described her as 'largely my office, almost my home', and spent so much time afloat – a total of eight months in the three years leading up to the outbreak of war in 1914 while visiting the fleet at home and in the Mediterranean – that Lloyd George, then the Chancellor, chided him: 'You have become a water creature. You think we all live in the sea, and all your thoughts are devoted to sea life, fishes and other aquatic creatures. You forget that most of us live on land.' Occasionally Clementine accompanied him, but these were working voyages, and not the sort of cruises she enjoyed.

Violet Asquith, a companion on the *Enchantress* when Churchill was visiting the Mediterranean with her father the Prime Minister, Herbert Asquith, recorded in her diary: 'W. in glorious form', but noted that he was 'incapable of lotus-eating even for a few hours'. Not so the Prime Minister, who was absorbed in classical history as they cruised the Mediterranean coasts, leading Churchill to protest, 'Those Greeks and Romans, they are so overrated. They only said everything *first*. I've said just as good things myself. But they got in before me.' And when, leaning over the rail watching the beautiful sun-bathed Adriatic coastline glide past, Violet remarked, 'How perfect,' she was startled by his reply: 'Yes – range perfect – visibility perfect – If we had some six-inch guns on board . . .'

By the early 1920s Churchill had become a competent painter. In Paris in 1921 as Secretary of State for War, he took time off from his official visit to see an exhibition at the Galerie Druet of paintings by a hitherto unknown artist, Charles Morin. He was accompanied by the head of the British Military Mission, who reported that the Secretary of State was most interested in the works on show, discussing them at length with an accompanying art critic. The Secretary of State would indeed have been interested: the paintings were his own, and 'Charles Morin' no more than a pseudonym. The exhibition had been arranged by an artist and art critic, Charles Montag, whom Churchill had met during the war.

In retrospect it is fitting that Churchill's paintings, which would later be exhibited all around the world, should first have hung publicly in France, for that was the country whose landscape, in the 1920s and thirties, inspired him above all else. 'Chance led me one autumn,' he wrote, 'to a secluded nook in the Cote d'Azur, between Marseilles and Toulon, and there I fell in with one or two painters who revelled in the methods of the modern French school . . . We owe a debt to those who have so wonderfully vivified, brightened, and illuminated modern landscape painting. They have brought back to the pictorial art a new draught of *joie de vivre*; and the beauty of their work is instinct with gaiety, and floats in a sparkling air. I do not expect these masters would particularly appreciate my defence, but I must avow an increasing attraction to their work.'

His first extended visit to France to allow much painting began in December 1922 when, having been defeated at the general election, he was without a seat in Parliament. General Louis Spears, a friend who had just been elected for the first time, offered up his seat, but Churchill in thanking him wrote, 'I want you to enjoy yr seat in Parliament . . . What I want now is a rest.' He and Clementine rented out their London house and spent the winter months at Villa Rêve d'Or near Cannes. The rest entailed continuous work on his history of the First World War, *The World Crisis*, which was not interrupted by two visits to London, during the second of which he informed Clementine, 'I am so busy that I hardly ever leave the Ritz except for meals.'

After 1924, when Churchill was back in Parliament, France

continued to beckon him, and there was no shortage of hospitality. His most frequent hostess in these years was Maxine Elliott,
a beautiful, talented American actress, then in her mid-sixties,
who owned the Château de l'Horizon at Golf-Juan. Lord
Rothermere, at La Dragonniere at Cap Martin, and the Duke
of Westminster, at Les Landes in Mimizan, or in the Forêt
d'Eu in Normandy, were also frequent welcoming hosts. Daisy
Fellowes, the daughter of the Duc de Decazes, who had married
a cousin of Churchill's, provided another agreeable holiday
home. Churchill spent his days writing – he was invariably
accompanied by a secretary – and painting. He made time to
swim, and in the evenings enjoyed being in the company of
the visitors who congregated along France's southern coast.
There was also the attraction of the casinos. Mary Soames, in
her book *Winston Churchill: His Life as a Painter*, describes how
his hosts and hostesses allowed him to lead his own life, excusing
him the behaviour normally expected of guests. Maxine Elliott's
niece, Diana Forbes-Robertson, wrote, 'He towered above the
other familiars of the Chateau. He was the only one I saw
permitted to be late for meals, and the only one who could
leave the Chateau to paint all day without being scolded.'

Mary Soames also records that while her father enjoyed the
Riviera, her mother came to dislike it. 'God,' wrote Clementine
to her daughter Sarah, 'the Riviera is a ghastly place. I expect
it's alright if you keep a flower shop or if you're a waiter.'
She seldom stayed long, in spite of her husband's persuasive
arguments, but confined her appearances to brief visits lest his
hosts should be offended by her absence.

One of the very few exceptions she made was the home of
Consuelo and Jacques Balsan, Lou Sueil, perched high on a
cliff at Eze in the Alpes Maritimes. Consuelo had remained a
close friend of the Churchills after her divorce from the 9th

Duke of Marlborough and her remarriage to Balsan. Clementine found life at Lou Sueil and the people she met there more interesting than she did Churchill's other haunts in the south of France.

The Balsans also owned Château St Georges-Môtel, at Dreux, fifty miles west of Paris. In her memoirs Consuelo describes Churchill's routine:

> He used to spend his mornings dictating to his secretary and his afternoons painting . . . His departure on these occasions was invariably accompanied by a general upheaval of the household. The painting paraphernalia with its easel, parasol and stool had to be assembled; the brushes, freshly cleaned, to be found; the canvases chosen, the right hat sorted out, the cigar box replenished. At last, driven by our chauffeur, he would depart with the genial wave and rubicund smile we have learned to associate with his robust optimism.

Florence in 1925 and Venice two years later were also exceptions to Winston and Clementine's general rule of taking their holidays separately, both cities providing what each like best: painting for him, sightseeing and art for her. Churchill's five years as Chancellor of the Exchequer from 1924 to 1929 did not impede agreeable holiday times. There were other joint expeditions, such as the tour of Marlborough's battlefields in the summer of 1932. On this they were accompanied by Sarah, Professor Lindemann and Colonel Pakenham-Walsh, who was assisting Churchill with his life of Marlborough. The battlefield tour was to be followed by a family holiday in Venice, but Churchill contracted paratyphoid and found himself instead confined for a fortnight in a clinic in Salzburg.

Although he could no longer cruise at will as he did when

the Admiralty yacht was at his disposal, friends were still able to provide Churchill with holidays afloat. In 1923 he wrote to Clementine from the Duke of Westminster's yacht at Bayonne: 'It is absolute quiet and peace. One need not do anything or see anyone.' However, as he was still at work on *The World Crisis*, it is unlikely that he was idle. A later holiday constructed around Admiral Sir Roger Keys' invitation to join him at Messina for ten days' cruising is more typical of Churchill's holiday routine. It came at the end of 1926, after a gruelling year during which he had been the leading member of the Cabinet wrestling with the General Strike. 'I greatly look forward to such a complete change from my daily grind here,' he wrote.

Accompanied by Randolph, Churchill travelled across France, reaching Genoa on 5 January 1927. Here, he told Clementine, he 'worked on the proofs of the final chapter of the World Crisis 'till 2.30 this morning and from 8 till now'. He added, 'I hope it will secure us two easy years and by that time I will think of something else.' Three days later, having reached Naples by boat from Genoa, he and Randolph watched an eruption of Vesuvius and visited Pompeii. In Malta Churchill played what he had already decided would be his last game of polo, and wrote a long letter to the Prime Minister, Stanley Baldwin, in which, after commenting on his 'interesting trip', he went on to argue the need to protect the rights of individual members of trades unions in the forthcoming Trades Union Bill. These were nettles 'best grasped firmly'. On 13 January he was in Athens, expressing his pleasure, as reported in *The Times*, at the restoration of parliamentary government. The following day he reached Rome, where, having met the Italian leader Mussolini, he stressed in a press statement the traditional friendship between Britain and Italy, and extolled the way

Mussolini had successfully grappled with Communism – causing an uproar in the Labour and Liberal press at home. Then came an audience with the Pope which required, in Randolph's words, 'a lot of careful protocol'. The early part of the conversation was sticky, 'then my father and the Pope got to the subject of the Bolsheviks and had a jolly half hour saying what they thought of them'.

From Rome Churchill travelled by train to meet Clementine at Consuelo Balsan's villa at Eze. Here he painted and, learning that British troops were being sent to China to protect British subjects from Chinese warlords, fired off a letter to the Secretary of State for War, Sir Laming Worthington Evans: 'My motive in writing to you is to urge you to send out plenty of Tanks to Shanghai.' In Paris on 26 January Churchill lunched with Ministers and Members of Parliament representing all parties. Then followed three days hunting wild boar with the Duke of Westminster at Eu, wreath-laying on the graves of Clementine's mother and brother at Dieppe (where Lady Blanche Hozier had settled in 1911) and a visit to the British military cemetery there. The three-week holiday ended when Churchill crossed by night ferry from Dieppe to Newhaven, where his car and a box of ministerial papers were waiting for him.

Churchill often painted in the company of the French artist Paul Maze, whom he had met during World War I. Maze had later asked Churchill to write a foreword to his war memoirs. He had been a sergeant in the French army, and had been highly decorated by both his own country and the British. Gallantry in action was invariably a passport into Churchill's affections, and the two men had much in common.

Consuelo Balsan describes in her memoirs what happened when she invited Maze and three other artists to lunch. Churchill was painting on the lawn. The artists gathered around, whereupon Churchill handed out four brushes and directed each man to paint a part of the picture – one the trees, another the sky, the third the water and the fourth the foreground. Churchill supervised, offering directions. Each signed the finished canvas.

In 1939, in what would be the last month of peace, though few believed war was quite that close, Churchill and Maze were painting together at Château St Georges-Môtel. In his diary for 20 August Maze recorded: 'I worked alongside him. He suddenly turned to me and said "This is the last picture we shall paint in peace for a very long time."' With the brief exception of Marrakech, it was indeed the last time Churchill would paint for six years.

After the end of the war in Europe, during the three-week interval between polling day in the British general election and the declaration of the result, Churchill took a short holiday at the Château de Bordaberry, south of Bordeaux, where he painted daily. While there he drove one afternoon to nearby St Jean de Luz, and was the guest of the British Consul at Bordeaux, Bryce Nairn, and his wife Margaret, whom he had first met at Marrakech during the war.

Meanwhile, Britain had voted for a change in government. With hindsight it was, as Clementine suggested at the time, a blessing in disguise. Churchill was now seventy, and had been under tremendous strain for the past six years. He had suffered a serious bout of pneumonia, and had resumed work against medical advice. The void in his life created by the loss of office would soon be filled. He would start his volumes on the Second World War. He would also finish his *History of the English Speaking Peoples*, which he had started before the war. For the present the family prescribed a painting holiday.

World affairs could not be banished entirely from Churchill's holiday at Como. His successor as Prime Minister, Clement Attlee, consulted him about atomic weapons and the means of their regulation. There were other official communications, but when Elizabeth Layton presented him with some twenty letters and telegrams of a more personal though routine nature, she was told, 'Oh, you write and thank them and I'll sign.' Churchill's holiday mood was something she had never encountered before, and gave her more time to enjoy the change of air. When Field Marshal Alexander came for two days he and Churchill painted side by side, crossing the lake by speedboat to find suitable places. Besides painting with Churchill, the Field Marshal joined in criticism of some of the pictures which hung in the villa. Sarah Churchill, who had accompanied her father, described them wandering around the building suggesting to one another how the pictures could be improved. She reported her father saying, 'Now come here, Alex, come here, now really look at this, we really paint better than the bastard who painted this one.' When Alexander had gone to bed, Churchill, despite the protests of his daughter and two young officers present, got out his paints and turned the dismal canvas into what Sarah described as 'a bird of paradise'. The household was heartbroken the following morning when the new paint was cleaned off and the picture restored 'stagnant and gloomy as before'.

After seventeen days Churchill left Lake Como and motored west to the Villa Pirelli, on the coast east of Genoa. When he set up his easel to paint some bomb-damaged houses in the nearby village of Recco, the inhabitants began to boo and shake their fists. He immediately packed up his equipment, admitting to the local British commander, Colonel Wathen, that 'it was a tactless thing to do. I would have been damned annoyed if Hitler had started to paint the bomb damage in London.'

Ploegsteert – called 'Plug Street' by the British Army. 6th Battalion Royal Scots Fusiliers, which Churchill commanded in 1916, held the front line just forward of this Belgian village. 1916, 20 x 24 in.

Jerusalem. Painted after the Cairo Conference. 1921, 20 x 24 in.

Clementine and Diana in a gondola in Venice. 1927, 18 x 22 in.

Lake Louise, Canada. Painted during a North American tour. 1929, 14 x 20 in.

Château St Georges-Môtel, fifty miles east of Paris. Churchill often stayed and painted here. It was owned by Consuelo Balsan, who had previously been married to Churchill's cousin the Duke of Marlborough. c.1930, 18 x 22 in.

Sunset at Cannes. c.1933, 20 x 30 in.

The pyramids. Painted during a month's holiday touring the eastern
Mediterranean. 1934, 25 x 30 in.

La Montagne St Victoire. c.1935, 25 x 30 in.

Sunset over the Atlas Mountains, painted during Churchill's first visit to Marrakech.
1935–36, 20 x 24 in.

Tower of Katoubia Mosque, Marrakech. This was the only picture Churchill
painted during the Second World War. 1943, 20 x 24 in.

The Surf Club, Miami. Painted while in Miami before travelling to Fulton, Missouri, to deliver the 'iron curtain' speech. 1946, 25 x 30 in.

La Fontaine-de-Vaucluse, near Avignon, painted while Churchill was on holiday at Aix-en-Provence. 1948, 18 x 24 in.

San Vigilio, Lake Garda. Painted from the balcony of the Locando di San
Vigilio. 1949, 25 x 30 in.

Lake Carezza. Glimpsed through the trees, it became the subject of a painting completed in
twenty minutes after Churchill called his entourage to a halt and demanded his easel and
paints. It was subsequently hung in the Royal Academy. 1949, 20 x 24 in.

Cap d'Ail, Alpes Maritimes. Churchill often stayed here with Lord Beaverbrook. This painting
was his diploma work for the Royal Academy. 1950s, 25 x 30 in.

The fishing port of Camara de Lobos. Bad weather marred Churchill's twelve days in Madeira,
but he managed some painting. 1950, 22 x 27 in.

Continuing westwards to Monte Carlo, Churchill stayed for two days at the Hôtel de Paris before moving on to Antibes and a villa provided by General Eisenhower. From there, after twenty-five days in the sun and having painted fifteen canvases, he returned home, where awaiting him was the invitation to speak at Fulton, Missouri.

In the post-war years cities and universities all over Europe conferred a profusion of honours on Churchill. He was to comment more than once how many degrees he had received without passing a single relevant examination. In Copenhagen in 1950, when receiving an honorary degree in philosophy, he remarked that he was now treated as 'quite a learned man'. A three-day visit to Paris in 1947 to receive the Médaille Militaire was particularly memorable, Susan Mary Alsop, an American diplomat's wife, recalling that she 'had never felt Paris so alive and enthusiastic'. She reported that Churchill looked 'smashing' in the uniform of Colonel of the 4th Hussars. He had apparently intended to wear his Air Commodore's uniform, because he liked the colour, but Clementine had said, 'Winston, if you must wear a showy uniform please wear something that you really have a right to.' He had the right to both, but most of all to his own regiment's, and he gave in with bad grace.

Freed from the daily responsibilities of the war years, Churchill could turn his mind more readily to international relations. At Fulton he had spoken of future threats. He had also been thinking deeply about the shape of Europe, and it was at the University of Zürich, on 19 September 1946, that he outlined his vision of 'a kind of United States of Europe'. This was during a family holiday when a group of Swiss individuals offered him a delightful house, the Villa Chosi, on the shores of Lac Leman. Clementine, Diana and Duncan, and Mary, recently demobilised, accompanied him, while other visitors came from time to time, including Field Marshal Smuts and Charles Montag, who had arranged Churchill's 'Charles Morin' exhibition in 1921. Nothing proved too much trouble for Churchill's Swiss hosts. General Guisan, the Swiss Commander-in-Chief, lent his campaign tent in order that Churchill could paint in spite of the indifferent weather. In addition to painting he was now contemplating his war memoirs, a project which would become a dominating feature in his life and would absorb an enormous amount of time and energy.

The vision Churchill outlined at Zürich was shared by his son-in-law Duncan Sandys who, playing a leading part beside him in the movement for a united Europe, described it in a letter to his father-in-law as 'our movement'. Churchill proposed, in the first instance, a partnership which would 'astonish' people: 'The first step in the re-creation of the European family must be a partnership between France and Germany.' The process required 'friends and sponsors' – Britain and the Common- wealth and 'mighty America' – and he suggested Russia, not as a permanent adversary but as a partner, 'for then all would be well'. Whereas Fulton had predicted the perils ahead and the means of avoiding them, Zürich sketched a happier picture. Like Fulton, this speech took many by surprise, but half a century later the imaginative sketch has become a reality.

In December 1947 Churchill, *en route* to a holiday in Mar- rakech, had stopped overnight in Paris to attend the farewell ball of the British Ambassador, Duff Cooper. Crowds gathered in the rue du Faubourg St Honoré, and he went out to speak to them. The ball was a glittering occasion. Susan Mary Alsop described Churchill 'wearing orders and decorations, with Odette in a superb red satin dress on his arm'. His companion was Odette Pol-Roger, then aged forty-eight, and one of the most beautiful French women of her generation. The charming *grande dame* of the Pol-Roger family, makers of Churchill's favourite champagne, had served as a courier for the French Resistance during the war. Churchill had been introduced to her by Duff Cooper, and they began a harmless flirtation, indulged by Clementine. On his birthday each year she sent him a case of the finest vintage. He sent her a copy of his memoirs inscribed '*Churchill cuvée de réserve/Mise en bouteille en Chartwell*', and gave instructions that whenever he was in Paris she was to be invited to dinner. He described Odette's home, 44 avenue de Champagne, Epernay, as 'the world's most drinkable address'. 'Invite me to Epernay,' he said, 'and I will press the grapes with my feet.' However, he never did visit the home of his favourite champagne. But he did name one of his favourite racehorses after the sparkling nectar, and invited Odette to Brighton to see it run.

A conference to advance the movement for a united Europe took place at The Hague in May 1948. Speaking before a large assembly which included the leading politicians of Europe, academics and others, Churchill, at seventy-three, demonstrated that he had lost none of his characteristic vigour and breadth of view. Two days later, addressing an open-air meeting in Amsterdam, he declared it was not against any nation 'that we range ourselves. It is against tyranny, in all its forms.' Before returning to Britain, Churchill and Clementine were invited to Oslo as the guests of the King of Norway. Here he received yet another doctorate, and made four speeches – without, as he noted to Clementine, 'repeating myself'.

Visits to smaller places excited local interest which persists to this day, as I discovered when, in 1998, I first followed my grandfather's footsteps to a well known beauty spot in the South of France, La Fontaine-de-Vaucluse. In 1948 he had painted there during a family holiday based at the Hôtel du Roy René in Aix-en-Provence. At the time I was writing my book on his adventures during the Anglo–Boer War, and I had decided that my next one would be about his travels. An overnight detour to Vaucluse seemed worthwhile because Evan Davies, Churchill's detective, had told me how Britain's wartime leader had been fêted in the town, which during the Second World War was a centre of the Resistance, whose fighters had been inspired by his call to 'set Europe alight', and enabled to do this by his provision of the necessary weapons.

The local tourist office was more than helpful, and suggested I stay at the Park Hotel which, being owned by Aladino Panza, an ex-Resistance man, would be the best place to start my search for information about Churchill's visit fifty years before. Otherwise there was Philip Pomères at Philip's Restaurant, from the terrace of which Churchill painted, and Jean Garçin, who had been the head of the local Resistance and Mayor of Vaucluse.

Unfortunately it was the height of the season, and the Park Hotel was full. Moreover, its owner was away. We found rooms only with difficulty, but thought the trail was getting warm when we met a local man who had been present during Churchill's visit. However, he seemed strangely reticent – for reasons I would later discover – and in the early evening we moved on to Philip's Restaurant.

Sitting, sipping drinks, watching the River Sorge gush from beneath the towering limestone cliffs opposite the terrace and stream foaming past our feet, it was obvious why the painter in Churchill had been drawn to this spot. Pomères treated us to an enthusiastic account of his visit, took us through his photographic album of the occasion and gave us a table for dinner under the tree where my grandfather had painted half a century before. He suggested we should walk up the path to the Source, the cavern in the base of the cliffs with its deep, dark pool whose water, from time immemorial, has percolated through the limestone strata to feed the fast-flowing river.

Now the way to the Source is paved to provide an easy walk for the thousands of tourists who come each year, and there are steps to enable them to negotiate the steeper places. In 1948 it was no more than a rough track, which Evan Davies thought would be too taxing for my grandfather. The only transport available was a donkey which normally pulled the local refuse cart. Now, with Churchill astride, it was prodded up the path to the Source. A photographer recorded the scene, but Davies, thinking that the once-accomplished horseman did not look his best slumped astride a donkey, confiscated the film.

The morning after our evening at Philip's Restaurant we drove into the country to call on the man who had been the head of the local Resistance. My eleven-year-old son Alexander was fascinated by the collection of sten guns and other assorted weaponry, all still in working order, which in the early 1940s had been parachuted into France and which now lay scattered around the large house. But Churchill's visit had been too long ago for Jean Garçin to provide me with much information, and as we left I knew I would need to return again to the Fontaine-de-Vaucluse.

Two years later I booked into the Park Hotel, and was met by Aladino Panza. An Italian by birth, he had joined the Resistance to avoid being conscripted into the German army when France was occupied. Together we laughed over my grandfather's donkey ride. It had been the secretary to the Mayor, Armand Boudin, who had suggested the means of transport, and on his instructions the animal was promptly unharnessed from the refuse cart and paraded at Philip's Restaurant.

I learned in passing about the man who on my previous

visit had been so reticent about Churchill's visit. 'He was a collaborator, worked for the Germans, and when liberation came he was lucky to get away with only a prison sentence,' I was told. 'He was to have been shot but the Mayor interceded on his behalf. He doesn't say much about those days!'

By the time of my second visit Philip's Restaurant was in the hands of his son, Hervé Pomères, who, alerted in advance, had photographs of Churchill's time in Vaucluse awaiting me at dinner. They included a picture of the donkey ride. At least one photographer had eluded Evan Davies!

The River Sorge, which springs from beneath the cliffs opposite Philip's Restaurant and rushes through Vaucluse, grows into a broad, shimmering stream below the town. Having first painted near the Source, Churchill wished to capture the water lower down, and Aladino Panza took me to the spot where my grandfather set up his easel on a large, flat rock where a woman had been washing clothes. She was Panza's mother. And the rock was recognised locally as her site for washing.

'You have not the right to do this,' said Mme Panza.

'Do you realise this is Winston Churchill?' replied one of his French bodyguards.

'I don't care who it is,' she said. 'Even Winston Churchill must ask my permission.'

The cause of the altercation understood the conversation perfectly, and asked politely in French, 'Madame, may I please put my easel here.'

'Yes,' said Mme Panza. 'But you could at least have asked first.' Her grandson Édouard Baffoni, who was ten at the time, remembers collecting several coins which Churchill had dropped on the ground.

Aladino Panza had not been to the large rock for many years, and when he took me there after breakfast it could be seen no more, having been built over by the boundary wall of a riverside property. However, the owners, Félix and Valerie Capaldo, welcomed us in. Looking up the river as it flowed serenely between tall trees, we were able to compare the scene today with my grandfather's rendering of it in his day. Not much seemed to have changed – a tribute to both his painting and the timeless quality of much of provincial France.

As usual during Churchill's post-war journeys there were visitors to Aix-en-Provence who came in connection with his war memoirs, which occupied a good deal of his time. One was Walter Graebner of his publishers Time-Life, who recalled an incident after Churchill had been painting the imposing Mont St Victoire, which had been made famous by Cézanne. At dinner Churchill, deep in thought, suddenly broke into the conversation. 'I have had a wonderful life, full of many achievements. Every ambition I've ever had has been fulfilled – save one.'

'Oh, dear me, what is that?' asked Clementine.

'I am not a great painter,' he said, slowly looking around the table. For a few seconds the embarrassment was so great that nothing was said, and then the party talked of other things.*

From Aix Churchill moved to Lord Beaverbrook's villa, La Capponcina, at Cap d'Ail. Clementine, who never quite approved of her husband's close association with Beaverbrook and mistrusted his influence, returned home. This was the first of many visits to La Capponcina, which would become a favourite place for my grandfather, with or without Beaverbrook in residence. Here he could work in secluded luxury,

---

* In fact Churchill was a very good painter, and thanks to the far-reaching research done by my aunt Mary Soames for her book *Winston Churchill: His Life as a Painter*, we now know a lot about this important side of his life.

the usual procession of visitors could come and go and he could paint highly coloured coastal scenes from the rocks above the Mediterranean.

The New Year of 1949 was spent in France. On New Year's Eve Churchill gave a dinner in Paris for the Duke and Duchess of Windsor before taking the night train for Monte Carlo and the Hôtel de Paris, where he was the guest of Time-Life. A visit to America followed in March, and it was July before the Continent saw him again. Holiday plans revolved around the inaugural meeting at Strasbourg of the Council of Europe, and were to include Lake Garda and a visit to La Capponcina. On Lake Garda the Locando di San Vigilio could barely accommodate Churchill's entire party, but, refurbished for his visit and on a promontory with the water lapping the dining terrace, it seemed an ideal place to write and paint. It has been in the Guariente family since the sixteenth century, but the present owner, Conte Agostino Guariente, told me that at the time of Churchill's visit it had been rented to an Irishman who on leaving 'took all the papers with him'. I was thus unable to verify the legend that the visitors' book contained the signatures of Churchill, Hitler and Mussolini; the two dictators apparently met there during the war.

In the summer of 1949 Churchill found the temperature and humidity at the Locando di San Vigilio unbearable, and after a week was on the verge of abandoning the holiday. It was feared, however, that this would cause offence to the Italians. Before the war Evan Davies as a boy had stayed at the Grand Hotel Carezza, high in the Dolomites. Here the climate would surely be acceptable. Unsure how well the hotel had weathered the intervening years, he nevertheless took the risk of recommending it. Telephone calls were made, rooms were hurriedly cleared and the local dignitaries at Carezza made aware of the impending visit. The motorcade set off from the lakeside, and late in the afternoon was approaching its destination when Churchill called a halt and demanded his painting equipment. He had seen Lake Carezza shimmering through the trees and, in spite of the waiting crowds a few miles ahead, was determined to paint it. The result became known as the twenty-minute sketch. Some sketch – it measured two by two and a half feet. The following day Churchill wanted to continue with it but Clementine, fearful that any tinkering would spoil it, told Davies to say it had been temporarily misplaced. He hid it under his bed and denied all knowledge of it when asked by Churchill. It was subsequently exhibited at the Royal Academy. The lake today looks just as it was captured on canvas, although the Churchill suite in the hotel, which is now a tourist dormitory, can have little resemblance to the one my grandfather occupied.

The working holiday was broken in mid-August when Churchill travelled to Strasbourg to address the Council of Europe. His dramatic outburst as he looked around the hall during his speech, 'Where are the Germans?', resulted in Germany becoming a member with full voting rights. For his promotion of the European Movement, and in particular of the reconciliation of France and Germany, Churchill would be awarded the Charlemagne Prize, which he received in Aachen in 1956. From the personal hand of President de Gaulle in 1958 would come the extraordinary honour of the French Croix de la Libération, the highest award to those who had served with the Free French forces or the Resistance. Over the years following his Zürich speech in 1946, Churchill's views on a united Europe may have undergone subtle shifts, as those on both sides of the federal argument today find Churchillian quotations to support their case. Four years after Strasbourg he said that he 'had never meant that Europe should be a federal state, no matter what people pretended he meant'. On another occasion he saw Britain occupying a place in three separate circles: 'the Empire and Commonwealth, the English-speaking world, and a united Europe'. At another time he declared, 'If I had to choose between Europe and the deep blue sea, I would choose the sea.'

From Strasbourg in August 1949 Churchill went on to Cap d'Ail, where he intended to continue work on his war memoirs with Denis Kelly, his assistant. Also at La Capponcina was the film star Merle Oberon, whom Churchill amused one afternoon by turning somersaults while swimming. As the three sat in their towels afterwards, two with dry martinis and one with his usual weak whisky and soda, Churchill turned to Kelly and, surveying his slim body, said, 'Denis, you're a disgrace to the British Empire.' That evening Churchill suffered a mild stroke. Lord Moran was summoned from London, and arrived with his golf clubs so as to avoid press speculation. Churchill's return to Strasbourg was cancelled, but after three days he felt able to continue his dictation.

The incident was concealed from all but a few. It was announced that Churchill had caught a chill. He remained in France until the end of August, and while there he invited Denis Kelly to dinner at a restaurant in Monte Carlo. Kelly recounts how 'a French lady in full evening dress passed by, stopped, gasped and curtsied. Churchill bowed from his chair while I stood up.' Kelly realised that Churchill had chosen this outing to show the world that he was fit and well.

Accustomed during the war to having an aircraft for his exclusive use, it must have been quite a change for Churchill to share his transport with other travellers. Anne Andersen, a stewardess with BOAC during the early fifties, told me: 'Sir

Winston handed me a pair of velvet-monogrammed slippers and asked me to warm them up. I passed them to the head steward who put them in the oven. Other duties intervened and twenty minutes later he returned the slippers, cracked and curling up at the toes, on a silver tray to Sir Winston. Churchill looked up with a wry smile and said, "That was rather a silly idea."'

In early 1950 Churchill came back in a hurry from Madeira for a general election which returned the Labour Party to power, though with an overall majority reduced to only six. Churchill was determined to carry on as leader of the opposition, foreseeing that this Parliament would not last long and that he might well be Prime Minister again in the near future. Work on his war memoirs, which he was determined to finish before then, Parliament and Chartwell kept him at home for the rest of the year, apart from another brief visit to Strasbourg where he spoke at the opening session of the Consultative Assembly of the Council of Europe.

After a month in Marrakech over Christmas 1950 and the New Year, the rigours of Parliament and his memoirs again kept Churchill at home until the following August, when he set off to join Clementine and Mary in Paris, from where they all set off for Annecy in the Haute Savoie. As so often in the post-war years when currency restrictions limited travel and holidays abroad, this holiday was financed by an advance from Churchill's American publishers on the final volume of his memoirs, at which, in the words of one of his two secretaries, Lettice Marston, they were now 'just slogging away'.

The weather at Annecy was bad, and the party moved on to Venice. When Jane Portal, Churchill's other secretary, told him that the train did not stop at Annecy and they would have to drive to Geneva, he replied, 'Kindly remember I am Winston

Churchill. Tell the stationmaster to stop the train.' It stopped as directed. Anxious to see Venice as the train approached it, Churchill leaned well out of the window. His detective, Edmund Murray, pulled him back sharply as a concrete pylon carrying the overhead electric lines flashed past. 'Anthony Eden nearly got a new job then, didn't he?' was Churchill's unconcerned comment.

In Venice he swam at the Lido, where the press waited patiently each morning for him to appear. There were expeditions to outer islands, and the grandees of Venetian society arranged dinner parties. But work on the memoirs never stopped. A secretary accompanied the painting expeditions so that Churchill could dictate on the launch or, if it got too hot, during a break from painting. He would work at the book after dinner, sometimes into the early hours. The holiday ended after a fortnight in Venice, and a week later a general election was called for 25 October 1951. On 26 October Churchill was again Prime Minister.

It was almost a year before he again had time to escape to the Continent. There was first a need to visit America to confer with President Truman in early 1952, and shortly after that the death of King George VI and the ascension of Elizabeth II caused a pause in domestic politics. Thereafter the pace picked up, and the immense amount of governmental work covering affairs at home and abroad, and the anxieties of the Cold War, were a heavy load for a man of seventy-seven.

Holidays to far-flung places were out of the question unless tacked on to a journey for state business. However, La Capponcina was within easy reach, and in September 1952 Churchill spent a fortnight there, bringing back several canvases including *Cap d'Ail, Alpes Maritimes from La Capponcina*, his diploma work as an Honorary RA, now in the collection of the Royal

Academy. A year later he was there again, having only three months before suffered a severe stroke. Many doubted his ability to wrestle again with public life, although Walter Graebner, recalling an afternoon going over proofs of the memoirs with him, wrote that 'his mind was never sharper than on that grey August afternoon in 1953'. In the event Churchill made a remarkable recovery, and continued in office until resigning as Prime Minister on 5 April 1955. Six days later he set off with Clementine and his easel for a fortnight in Sicily. The weather was indifferent, and he only painted two dull canvases. However, he had already begun to revise the 1939 proofs of *A History of the English Speaking Peoples*.

Epilogue

LAST JOURNEYS

When I get to heaven I mean to spend a considerable portion
of my first million years in painting, and so get to the bottom
of the subject.
Winston Churchill, *Thoughts and Adventures* (1932)

The Mediterranean warmth and light, particularly that of the south of France, which illuminated so many of his paintings, appeared to become more and more important to my grandfather in his later years.

He made several visits to Lord Beaverbrook's house, La Capponcina at Cap d'Ail, enjoyed eight cruises on Aristotle Onassis's magnificent yacht, the *Christina*, made numerous visits to the Hôtel de Paris in Monte Carlo and, between January 1956 and April 1959, spent a total of more than twelve months at La Pausa, the home of his old friends Emery and Wendy Reves at Roquebrune, a few miles from Monaco.

In January 1956 I was with my mother at a house she had been lent in La Turbie, in the hills above Monte Carlo. During our holiday my grandfather arrived at La Pausa, and shortly afterwards we were invited to lunch there. Emery Reves, a Hungarian Jew, had known Churchill during the thirties, when he had placed his articles warning of the menace of Nazi Germany in publications on both sides of the Atlantic, thus giving him a wider platform from which to air the views that many people in Britain and America did not want to hear.

I had never before seen anything quite like La Pausa, or indeed met anyone like Wendy Reves. The house, the former home of Coco Chanel, built for her by Bendor, Duke of Westminster, was filled with a wonderful collection of priceless furniture, sculptures and Impressionist paintings. Despite being surrounded by objects of the kind usually found in museums or art galleries, the visitor's overwhelming impression was one of immense comfort, luxury and an atmosphere of warmth and fun.

Wendy was a very beautiful and captivating young woman who exuded charm and glamour. She was horror-struck when at nine o'clock one morning, just a few months after she and Emery had moved into La Pausa, he told her that Winston Churchill was coming to lunch that very day. This would have been a nerve-racking experience for anyone, but for a perfectionist such as Wendy, combined with the fact that the house was not finished and she had no staff, it was the last thing she wanted. However, not just beautiful but resourceful as well, she was ready four hours later to entertain her guest.

Emery was clearly not so relaxed, as Wendy, still a beautiful and charming hostess, told me when I visited her at La Pausa forty years after Churchill's first visit. 'There was a crunching of tyres on gravel as your grandfather's car and his police escort drew up in front of the house. It was a terrific noise that became one of the noises of my life for the next few years. Emery told me that I must not talk too much and not touch Sir Winston.'

These instructions to a woman who is as talkative as she is tactile were not long adhered to. From the minute Wendy decided to 'be herself' the lunch was a huge success, so much so that before he left the guest of honour had invited himself to come back and stay.

Three weeks and a lot of preparations later, the crunching of the gravel announced Churchill's return to La Pausa. In the meantime Wendy had finished the house, and with the help of the local Mayor had engaged an army of staff. Determined that everything would be perfect, she had managed to get the chef from the Château de Madrid, the best restaurant for miles around, to agree to cook one meal a day.

Wendy and Emery did everything in their power to make their guest happy. They succeeded to such an extent that he would spend twelve out of the next thirty-nine months at La Pausa. Of course he did not go alone: he always took Anthony Montague Browne, sometimes a woman secretary, his body-guard Sergeant Murray and his valet. The Reves gave him *carte blanche* to invite whoever he wanted to stay or for meals, so there was a constant stream of family and friends who came to stay, and many others who were invited for lunch or dinner. My grandmother did not go very often; she did not like the south of France, was in fragile health and welcomed some time to rest, relax and enjoy the theatre and art galleries for which there was never time when her husband was at home.

After he had been at La Pausa for three weeks that first time, Churchill announced that he must leave, and told Wendy that he felt bad that Emery had given up his room for him. Realising that he wanted to return, she told him that she would prepare a room specially for his use. This she did, and from then on he occupied a large room with a magnificent view of the sea. She ordered a special bed with armrests so that he could work comfortably in bed, and even had the carpenter make a template of his girth so that a bed table could be made that fitted him perfectly!

My grandfather was old-fashioned in some respects, and was uneasy about the fact that Wendy and Emery were not married. He raised the subject with Wendy on more than one occasion, and she told me that he mentioned that it had given rise to comment that his host and hostess were not married. It was not this which preoccupied him most, but Wendy's situation. He asked her, 'Why does he not marry you?' She replied that she had been married twice before without success, and did not want to risk losing Emery by formalising a very happy relationship. Churchill, however, found it hard to accept that any woman would not want marriage. The subject was dropped, but some time later Churchill suggested a ceremony in the library at La Pausa, with him as best man. Eventually, Wendy and Emery married in 1964.

We sat on the terrace where my grandfather had spent so many happy hours, and I asked Wendy what they had talked about. 'The Boer War and the Dardanelles, but never the Second World War,' she answered. We wandered in the garden and she described how her guest's large white Stetson attracted swarms of white butterflies as he strolled around.

Back in the library, Wendy told me how one wet afternoon, when everyone else had gone out, my grandfather asked for his budgerigar Toby to be brought to him. Looking at the roaring log fire, he said how nice it would be for Toby to have a bath right there. Wendy jumped to her feet and returned a few minutes later with a silver bowl filled with warm water and rose petals, and put it on a small rug in front of the fire. Toby was released from his cage, and to the delight of his owner and his hostess splashed around, then did a few circuits of the room, spraying all the works of art with water before returning for another dip. Suddenly they heard the sound of cars on the gravel. Realising how ridiculous the scene must have looked, Churchill quickly restored Toby to his cage and removed all evidence of his bath. Simple, innocent and happy moments like these were what brought him back to La Pausa again and again.

It was during his first visit to 'Pausaland', as my grandfather called his Mediterranean haven, that Churchill met Ari Onassis. Randolph, who was staying on the *Christina*, asked Anthony Montague Browne to get Wendy to invite Onassis to La Pausa to meet his father. The dinner was not a success, and Ari felt he had thrown away his one opportunity to get to know the man he admired so much. If Wendy had not taken pity on him and suggested that he invite everyone on board the *Christina* later in the week, it is quite possible that they would never have met again, and that the cruises which Churchill so enjoyed would not have taken place. Also, a lot of unhappiness might have been avoided.

That evening Emery Reves told Wendy, 'Inviting Ari here was the biggest mistake of your life.' Wendy voiced her surprise at this reaction, to be told, 'You will see. You will see.' And see she did, but not until some time later.

In September 1958, shortly after they had celebrated their golden wedding anniversary at La Capponcina, Winston and Clementine went on their first cruise on the *Christina*. In itself this was a successful holiday, and one which would be repeated seven more times in less than five years, all except two of them in the Mediterranean or the Adriatic. It did however lead to a more or less permanent rift between the Reves and the Chur-chills, caused Emery and Wendy great hurt and unhappiness, and deprived Winston of his favourite south of France retreat.

Onassis was anxious to please his guest, and asked Anthony Montague Browne for help. Since Anthony is the sole witness of this sorry tale, he is the only person who knows what happened. He recounted the facts with tact and sympathy in his book *Long Sunset*, from which he has given me permission to quote:

> The selection of fellow guests caused unhappiness. To Ari's initial request for suggestions, I replied, after consultation with WSC and CSC, that our host should choose whomever he thought appropriate. To our consternation the Duke and Duchess of Windsor were included in his list. WSC then said that in that case he would not go. It wasn't that he disliked the Windsors, but he was a formalist and envisaged constant jumping up and down to suit their whims. Moreover, since 1940 he had never felt the same about the Duke and thought that it would be wrong for him to associate with him so closely.
>
> I telephoned Ari and conveyed the news. He had already invited the Windsors but immediately put them off, adding in his telegram that he would thereafter lend them the yacht and that they could take it out and sink it if they felt so inclined.
>
> Next came even worse embarrassment. CSC approached me in a somewhat agitated frame of mind. She loved the sea, she thought that the cruise would be a wonderful opportunity for her to be with WSC, but she did not want any association with the south of France background and would not come if those with this connection were invited. This included Wendy and Emery Reves. She knew that it was not my responsibility, but would I please, please see to it? And to prevent any further gaffes such as the Windsor invitation, would I telephone at once to Ari and if I could not get him, then telegraph him?
>
> Here was sadness. WSC owed the Reves debts of hospitality

and kindness, and indeed he had met Ari at their table. They might be bitterly hurt. The least that could be done was a letter of explanation, however delicate and difficult to frame, or even a telephone call. I prepared a draft letter and broached it over lunch alone with WSC and CSC. CSC was emphatic. No explanation was called for; Winston could go where he liked and with whom he liked, and he was under no obligation to give explanations. WSC was undecided but he desperately wanted his wife to accompany him and was rightly convinced that a cruise would benefit her nervous tension and exhaustion. It would be best, he said, to treat the cruise as just a different social engagement. I was making a mountain out of a molehill. His friendship for Emery and affection for Wendy would be undiminished and he would return to stay at La Pausa as before.

As I feared, much hurt was done. Ari, pressed by the Reves for an explanation of their omission from the guest list, told them of my telegram. It was couched in Foreign Office style, where the word 'not' is rendered as 'not repeat not' for clarity, and this did not help. I was cast in the role of the serpent responsible for the expulsion from the Garden of Eden, which distressed me, for I shared King Lear's feelings on ingratitude. The full results were not evident until quite some time later, when WSC stayed in the penthouse of the Hôtel de Paris in Monte Carlo instead of going to La Pausa, and the wound never fully healed, in spite of resumption of social relations after an interval.

To some extent everyone was a loser as a result of this incident. The Reves lost their honoured and treasured guest, Clementine was deprived of the long periods of rest which she so badly needed, and Winston in the future stayed in the penthouse of the Hôtel de Paris. This may seem not too bad an option, but however luxurious, it was a very sterile alternative to La Pausa. One visit there in 1960 was particularly sad when Toby, my grandfather's beloved budgerigar, flew out of the window never to return. That same year he wrote to Wendy Reves, 'The months I spent at your charming house were among the brightest in my life, and I shall always think of them as such.'

Although his visits to the south of France were now less agreeable than before, Winston did join Onassis for seven more cruises on the *Christina* between 1958 and 1963. Clementine, who loved sea travel, accompanied him until Tina left Ari following the memorable cruise of 1959. Thereafter he went alone apart from his usual entourage, thus giving Clementine the time she needed to herself. These cruises gave him enormous pleasure, and since age was taking its toll were probably the ideal holidays for him at that stage.

I had three holidays with my grandfather at the Hôtel de Paris during the early sixties. I just happened to be an available grandchild of an appropriate age. My brother Julian and my sister Edwina were busy embarking on their adult lives; my cousin Winston, probably the closest to my grandfather, was at Oxford; and younger cousins were still at school.

In the summer of 1961 Winston was invited by my grandfather to spend a few days with him at the Hôtel de Paris. In his book *Memories and Adventures*, he recalls an evening dining with Aristotle Onassis. Seated next to Churchill was Greta Garbo, who suddenly announced that she had a problem. Not hearing her clearly, he turned to Ari, asking, 'What did Miss Garbo say?' Ari replied in a loud voice, laced with a heavy Greek accent, 'Miss Garbo, she say, she is too hot in her long English lambswool underpants, so she proposes to take them off.' This announcement caused a considerable stir among the diners at adjacent tables. Not sure that he had heard correctly, my grandfather repeated his question, '*What* did Miss Garbo say?' Ari repeated what he had said, even more deliberately so that it should be understood. By now all eyes in the restaurant were on Miss Garbo as she executed a discreet striptease beneath the table. 'Poor lamb, poor lamb,' said my grandfather, patting her on the knee as the offending garment was removed.

My cousin also describes accompanying my grandfather to the Casino at Monte Carlo, which was thronged with the 'glamorous, glittering if shallow *demi-monde* with which it amused Grandpapa on occasion to mingle. Clementine strongly disapproved of gambling but had given up telling my grandfather what a folly it was. Fortunately he was in no way a serious gambler although he had his moments.' Young Winston recalls Clementine's account of one such successful outing: 'I rolled over in bed and heard a strange noise. Reaching out in the darkness, I sensed the bed was covered in pieces of paper. I turned on the light and to my amazement saw that it had been transformed into a patchwork quilt of 10,000 Franc notes!'

My holidays with my grandfather were more sedate, but they were a great treat, as I had the opportunity to spend time with him in a relaxed manner, without other people competing for his attention. These were my first experiences of staying in grand hotels, or indeed in any sort of hotel. Apart from the extreme luxury, the degree of service was exceptional, and I imagined that the treatment we were given was standard in this class of hotel. I have never had my bath run or my clothes unpacked for me since.

As I grew up, my grandfather was ageing. Therefore these interludes consisted largely of slow-paced, companionable days spent sitting on the balcony or driving up into the hills above Monte Carlo. All his life, but particularly in his youth, Churchill had lived beyond his means, and he was still preoccupied by a shortage of funds. Before I left he would invariably ask, 'Are you all right for money?', and without waiting for an answer would thrust a wad of notes into my hand, possibly the result of an expedition along the underground passage from the hotel to the casino.

One day in late June 1962 I went down to the hotel lobby and was immediately struck by the heavy atmosphere of doom and gloom. My cheerful *bonjours* were received with astonished glances, prompting me to ask what had happened. I was told that my grandfather had had an accident, and was in hospital.

Anthony Montague Browne returned from the hospital and told me that Grandpapa's hip was broken. He also told me of his request: 'Remember, I want to die in England. Promise me that you will see to it.' As Anthony recalled in *Long Sunset*: 'I gave the required promise unhesitatingly, but privately wondered if I would be able to carry it out, for he seemed mortally stricken. I rang Number Ten, and within a very short time Harold Macmillan had ordered an RAF Comet ambulance to stand by to fly to Nice to bring WSC home.'

The hordes of reporters outside the hospital were a clear indication of the anxiety that had been engendered by the news. I had been struck by how vulnerable my grandfather looked in his hospital bed with his leg newly plastered, but strapped into the stretcher bed in the body of the Comet, he looked even more fragile. I sat and held his hand, and could only hope and pray that he would make it home. In fact, as he was carried off the plane he spotted the crowd that had gathered to see him, and with characteristic spirit and typical determination raised his hand and gave a V sign. It was worth the effort. Hugely relieved, they clapped and clapped, and he smiled as he was gently lifted into the waiting ambulance.

★　　★　　★

He did recover, but this incident aged him considerably. Life took on an even slower pace, and apart from one more visit to Monte Carlo his travels were largely confined to the road between Chartwell and his London house in Hyde Park Gate.

During the long days of his last illness and decline towards what we all knew was the inevitable, my Aunt Sarah was staying with me in my little Chelsea flat. We went each day to sit by his bed as he slumbered on, his faithful marmalade cat by his side. Early in the morning of 24 January 1965 we were called to Hyde Park Gate. Seventy years to the day, and almost to the minute, since Lord Randolph's death, we gathered round as Winston Churchill slipped imperceptibly away to meet his Maker. Of course we were sad, extremely sad – but for ourselves, not for him. He had for some time been tired of living, and was more than ready to go.

The reaction of the country was incredible, and deeply moving. As arrangements for the State Funeral – some of which had been long planned, code-named 'Operation Hope Not' – swung into place, people descended on London from all over Britain and beyond to pay their last respects. It was a remarkable sight to see the thousands of mourners of all ages queuing for hours in the freezing cold to file silently past the catafalque in Westminster Hall.

On the morning of 30 January we all gathered at Westminster Hall for the final journey along the streets of London, packed with silent crowds, to St Paul's Cathedral. The men of the family together with Anthony Montague Browne walked behind the gun carriage. The women rode in carriages from the Royal Mews. My grandmother travelled with her two surviving daughters, Sarah and Mary, in the Queen's Town Carriage. My sister Edwina and I were in the one behind. It was an unforgettable experience. Every so often we made eye contact with someone in the crowd as we passed. They were so close that we could have touched them.

After the service we proceeded to Tower Pier, where the launch the *Havengore* was waiting to take Churchill up the Thames to Waterloo station. It seemed that everyone wanted to say farewell to the man who meant so much to Londoners, his fellow countrymen and the world beyond. As the *Havengore* started to move, all the cranes on the other side of the river bowed their heads. Suddenly the silence was broken by an almighty roar from the skies as Royal Air Force fighter planes in perfect formation swooped low overhead. At Waterloo the coffin was placed on the train behind the Battle of Britain class locomotive which had been named *Winston Churchill* by my brother Julian in the early days of the war.

It may seem strange that, after these hours of pride and sadness, we should have sat down to lunch and champagne as the train chugged its way towards Oxfordshire. One thing is sure: Grandpapa would have understood. All along the railway line were people who had come to salute the man who was now on the last lap of his final journey.

We buried him at Bladon, within sight of Blenheim Palace, where his long journey had begun ninety years and so many adventures before.

Acknowledgements

I wish to express my gratitude to all those, in many parts of the world, who have helped me learn so much about my grandfather's travels during his long life.

First I want to thank my aunt, Mary Soames, for her support, for reading the manuscript and for all her invaluable suggestions and comments, for agreeing to write the Foreword and for permission to quote from her books, *Winston Churchill: His Life as a Painter* (copyright © Mary Soames 1990) and *Speaking for Themselves*, also for allowing me to quote from the books of Sarah Churchill, *Keep on Dancing* and *A Thread in the Tapestry* (reproduced with permission of Curtis Brown Ltd, London on behalf of Lady Soames. Copyright © Mary Soames).

Once again I am most grateful to my cousin Winston S. Churchill for his kindness in allowing me to quote from the works of Sir Winston Churchill (reproduced with permission of Curtis Brown Ltd, London on behalf of The Estate of Winston S. Churchill. Copyright © Winston S. Churchill) and from his own book, *Thoughts and Memories* (reproduced with permission of Curtis Brown Ltd, London on behalf of Winston S. Churchill. Copyright © Winston S. Churchill 1989), and to reproduce certain documents and photographs.

My thanks go to Sir John Boyd, Master of Churchill College,

and Lady Boyd for their kind hospitality on my visits to Cambridge.

I am enormously grateful to Allen Packwood, Keeper of the Archives and his staff at the Churchill Archives Centre for the help they have given me throughout the researching and writing of this book.

I want to thank Trevor Jones, who while introducing me at a dinner in Cleveland, Ohio, said, 'Celia has been chasing Churchill round the world,' thus instantly giving me the title for this book.

Over the last five years I have spoken to so many people in so many places and received such a fund of information. My thanks go to every single person who gave me a story, a photograph or a recollection of any sort.

My particular thanks go to the following, who have shared their memories and photographs of the time they worked with my grandfather: Evan Davies, the late Grace Hamblin, Patrick Kinna, Hugh Lunghi, Sir Anthony Montague Browne, Elizabeth Nel and Jo, Countess of Onslow. I am especially grateful to Sir Anthony Montague Browne for allowing me to quote from his book, *Long Sunset*, and to Elizabeth Nel (*née* Layton) for her extraordinary generosity in allowing me the use of her personal diary.

I am extremely grateful to Wendy Reves for her hospitality at La Pausa and for allowing me to tape her memories of my grandfather's time there.

I also want to thank: President Fidel Castro; Vice President Ramon Jose Fernandez; His Excellency Rodney Lopez, former Cuban Ambassador to London; His Excellency Mohamed Belmahi, Moroccan Ambassador to London; Major Colin Gedge, British Honorary Consul, Madeira; Paul Malik, American Vice Consul, Casablanca; and Mohamed Skhiri, British

Honorary Consul, Marrakech. David Aikman, Anne Andersen, Annie Austin, Juliet Barclay, Perry Belmont Frank, Christopher Blackburn, Adam and Christina Blandy, Carrie Bobolitz, Senator Harry Byrd Jr, Randolph S. Churchill, Gianni Clerici, Gerard Dumont, Mary Jean Eisenhower, Ali El Kasmi, Patricia and the late Abdulkader Erzini, Nicholas Gage, Sir Martin Gilbert, Taffy Gould, Simon Hazlerigg, Craig Horn, Kenneth Houston Paterson, Pippa Isbell, Madeleine Kingsley, Howard Klemberg, Tom Kunniholm, Scott Lambert, Richard Langworth, Dr Ian MacFarlane, the Duke of Marlborough, John David Marshall, Antonio Martinez, Mercedes Mosteiro, Aladino Panza, John Papanicolaou, Jane Plakias, Christian and Danielle Pol Roger, Hervé and Phillippe Pomares, Julia Randle, Jim Roberts, Lady Sargant, Hank Slack, Mary Slack, Robin Stafford, Fergus Torrance, Helen Walch, Kathryn Wilson, Alec and Yvonne Zino.

I am grateful to the following organisations and companies for their assistance: Air Cubana; American Legation, Tangier; Cuban Tourist Board; El Minzah Hotel, Tangier; Es Saadi Hotel, Marrakech; Hôtel de Paris, Monte Carlo; Hotel Nacional, Havana; La Mamounia, Marrakech; Leading Hotels of the World; Locando di San Vigilio, Lake Garda; Moroccan National Tourist Office; Morocco Made to Measure; Mount Nelson Hotel, Cape Town; Orient Express Hotels; Parrot Jungle, Miami; Reid's Hotel, Madeira; Royal Air Maroc; Winston Churchill Memorial Library, Westminster College, Fulton, Missouri.

My thanks to my publisher Richard Johnson and my editor Robert Lacey for their enthusiasm, encouragement, advice, patience and friendship, and to Juliet Davis for finding so many wonderful photographs. Also to Anthea Morton-Saner of Curtis Brown for her help and advice with copyright permissions.

The greatest thanks must go to my husband, Ken Perkins, who has given me unlimited help and support during the research and writing of this book.

Celia Sandys
November 2002

Source Notes

Abbreviations

AJ: Winston S. Churchill, *My African Journey*
AL: Martin Gilbert, *Churchill: A Life*
CAC: Churchill Archives Centre, Churchill College, Cambridge
DMP: Dispatches to *Morning Post*. Dated as printed in *London to Ladysmith* and *Ian Hamilton's March*
EL: Winston S. Churchill, *My Early Life*
TT: Arthur Bryant, *The Turn of the Tide*
WSC I–II: Randolph S. Churchill, *Winston S. Churchill*, Vols I, II
WSC III–VIII: Martin Gilbert, *Winston S. Churchill*, Vols III–VIII
WWII I–VI: Winston S. Churchill, *The Second World War* (6 vols)

Prologue: The Gifts of Travel

p. xxii 'all my dreams . . .' EL, 71
p. xxiii 'I remember quite . . .' AL, 5
p. xxiii 'There is only . . .' *Smithsonian Magazine*, April 2001, 81–90
p. xxiv 'I never take holidays.' Jenkins, *Churchill*, 442
p. xxiv 'Many remedies . . .' WSC, *Thoughts and Adventures*, 216
p. xxiv 'restless energy . . . vivid description . . .' WSC II, 228
p. xxv 'Fortune's favoured . . .' WSC, *Thoughts and Adventures*, 218

Chapter 1: The *Christina*

p. 13 'It will always . . .' Hansard, House of Commons, 20 March 1917

Chapter 2: A New World

p. 16 'There are no . . .' CAC
p. 17 'The swift road . . .' EL, 83
p. 19 'What an extraordinary . . .' CAC
p. 20 'good citizens . . .' ibid.
p. 20 'the monopoly . . .' ibid.
p. 20 'We have . . .' ibid.
p. 21 'irreconcilable . . .' ibid.
p. 21 'Picture yourself . . .' ibid.
p. 22 'presented a spectacle . . .' ibid.
p. 22 'kindness and courtesy' ibid.
p. 22 'He was my model . . .' WSC I, 283
p. 24 'Tomorrow we start . . .' CAC
p. 24 'more homely . . .' *Daily Graphic*, 17 December 1895
p. 24 'filthy, crowded . . .' EL, 88

p. 25 'The long Spanish column . . .' ibid., 89

p. 26 'the sympathy . . .' *Daily Graphic*, 13 December 1895

p. 27 'So at any rate' EL, 93

p. 28 'The General . . .' CAC

p. 32 'a national and justifiable . . .' *Daily Graphic*, 13 January 1896

p. 33 'within five minutes . . .' *New York Herald*, 15 December 1895

p. 33 'I read in the papers . . .' CAC

p. 34 'I pursue profit . . .' ibid.

p. 35 'You are quite right . . .' *Springfield Republican*, 16 December 1900

p. 35 'kin in sin' *New York Tribune*, 13 December 1900

p. 36 'a success . . .' *Evening Register*, 14 December 1900

p. 36 'made a pleasant . . .' *Baltimore Sun*, 17 December 1900

p. 37 'commend itself . . .' CAC

p. 38 'a most unpleasant . . .' ibid.

Chapter 3: Warrior and Writer

p. 40 'to scenes of . . .' CAC

p. 40 'the desire for . . .' ibid.

p. 41 'She is the . . .' ibid.

p. 43 'When the retirement . . .' ibid.

p. 43 'Bullets are not . . .' ibid.

p. 43 'When I think . . .' ibid.

p. 44 'Young Winston Churchill . . .' WSC I, 361

p. 44 'After all they . . .' EL, 177

p. 45 'no charge of . . .' CAC

p. 45 'I saw the Union . . .' EL, 188

p. 45 'many bottles of . . .' ibid., 190

p. 45 'ten or twelve . . .' ibid., 202

p. 45 'I saw the gleam . . .' ibid., 203

p. 47 'A fierce and . . .' CAC

p. 48 'He wanted to . . .' *Estcourt Gazette*, 14 December 1940

p. 50 'Had I not . . .' Haldane, *A Soldier's Saga*, 142

p. 50 'No man is . . .' EL, 260

p. 51 'I can't leave . . .' *Estcourt Gazette*, 14 December 1940

p. 51 'tall figures . . .' EL, 264

p. 53 'a far seeing . . .' DMP, 3 December 1899

p. 55 'shot into the . . .' EL, 298

p. 56 'every resource of . . .' ibid., 331

p. 56 'We shall carry . . .' *Natal Mercury*, 25 December 1899

p. 57 'lived from day . . .' EL, 320

p. 58 'My mother . . .' Mrs Lette Bennet to author

p. 58 'self-appointed . . .' Pakenham, *The Boer War*, 303

p. 59 'acre of massacre' Atkins, *The Relief of Ladysmith*, 237

p. 59 'Men were . . .' DMP, 25 January 1900

p. 60 'I put my hand . . .' EL, 329

p. 60 'He wore . . .' Martin, 'Diary of the Siege of Ladysmith'

p. 61 'more colonels . . .' DMP, 13 April 1900

p. 61 'Come on . . .' ibid., 22 April 1900

p. 62 'the best tinned . . .' EL, 360

p. 63 'resumed his full . . .' ibid., 367

p. 63 'This expectation . . .' ibid., 368

p. 64 'It is my . . .' National Archives Repository, Pretoria

Chapter 4: Jungle, Bush and Thankless Deserts

p. 66 'mind his health . . .' WSC II, 221

p. 66 'The aspect of . . .' AJ, 7

p. 68 'To appreciate these . . .' ibid.

p. 68 'reserved his points . . .' WSC II, 228

p. 68 'a vivid description' ibid.

p. 68 'rolls along as . . .' AJ, 9

p. 69 'secure British predominance . . .' ibid., 10

p. 69 'full accounts of . . .' ibid., 229

p. 69 'dining & sleeping . . .' ibid., 231

p. 69 'a grim . . .' ibid.

p. 69 'with a heavy . . .' ibid., 232

p. 70 'All the time . . .' ibid.

p. 70 'great Durbar . . .' ibid.

p. 70 'also made . . .' ibid.

p. 70 'So we chucked . . .' ibid., 233

p. 70 'the Governor . . .' ibid., 234
p. 71 'We mean . . .' AJ, 32
p. 71 'political instability . . .' ibid., 35
p. 71 'Rich in . . .' ibid., 41
p. 71 'I am clearly . . .' ibid., 42
p. 71 'disciplined soldiers . . .' ibid.
p. 71 'the smart . . .' ibid.
p. 71 'the population . . .' ibid.
p. 71 'will have . . .' ibid., 43
p. 72 'it would . . .' ibid., 49
p. 72 'floating population . . .' ibid., 50
p. 72 'choppers more . . .' ibid.
p. 72 'no good . . .' ibid.
p. 72 'Uganda is defended . . .' ibid., 60
p. 72 'order and science . . .' ibid., 65
p. 72 'master in . . .' ibid.
p. 73 'three separate influences . . .' ibid., 56
p. 73 'secular, scientific . . .' ibid.
p. 73 'a native Government . . .' ibid.
p. 73 'missionary enterprise . . .' ibid., 57
p. 73 'island of . . .' ibid., 71
p. 73 'Dear Mr Winston Churchill . . .' WSC II, 235
p. 74 'Your vision . . .' ibid.
p. 74 'system of . . .' AJ, 85
p. 74 'a perfectly frightful . . .' ibid., 86
p. 75 'throb with . . .' ibid., 101
p. 75 'could not . . .' ibid., 117
p. 75 'Uganda is . . .' ibid., 118
p. 76 'nowhere presented . . .' ibid., 123
p. 76 'taking away . . .' ibid.
p. 77 'It is absolutely . . .' CAC
p. 78 'The *Sphinx* . . .' ibid.
p. 79 'When things . . .' WSC IV, 557
p. 79 'Cheers for . . .' *et seq.*, ibid., 558
p. 80 'I believe . . .' ibid., 570
p. 80 'if they are . . .' WSC VII, 689

Chapter 5: Coast to Coast
p. 83 'I want . . .' Baruch papers
p. 83 'I do not . . .' ibid.
p. 83 'We must discuss . . .' WSC V, 334
p. 83 'What fun . . .' ibid., 338
p. 85 'thought it would . . .' ibid., 335

p. 85 'I have been . . .' CAC
p. 85 'The Heights . . .' *et seq.*, John Spencer Churchill, *A Crowded Canvas*, 65
p. 86 'twenty members . . .' CAC
p. 86 'Fancy cutting . . .' WSC, *His Father's Son*, 57
p. 86 'a wonderful . . .' CAC
p. 87 'He was in . . .' ibid.
p. 87 'I think I now . . .' John Spencer Churchill, *A Crowded Canvas*, 66
p. 87 'Cultured people . . .' WSC, *His Father's Son*, 58
p. 88 'Darling, I am greatly . . .' CAC
p. 89 'clear out of . . .' ibid.
p. 89 'We are now . . .' WSC, *His Father's Son*, 58
p. 89 'What are you . . .' *et seq.*, John Spencer Churchill, *A Crowded Canvas*, 68
p. 90 'We realise . . .' *New York Times*, 8 September 1929
p. 90 'The Constitution . . .' *Daily Telegraph*, 30 December 1929
p. 91 'the garden . . .' ibid., 23 December 1929
p. 91 'The Jews have . . .' *San Francisco Chronicle*, 8 September 1929
p. 91 'one worries . . .' CAC
p. 93 'if patter & wit . . .' ibid.
p. 93 'I met all . . .' ibid.
p. 93 'wonderful and . . .' ibid.
p. 94 'What you are . . .' *et seq.*, John Spencer Churchill, *A Crowded Canvas*, 75
p. 95 'Nudity was not . . .' *et seq.*, letter from Perry Belmont Frank to author
p. 95 'the South had . . .' WSC, *History of the English Speaking Peoples*, Vol IV, 190
p. 96 'No one can . . .' CAC
p. 98 'Friends and *former* . . .' ibid.
p. 98 'this financial disaster . . .' ibid.
p. 98 'My lecture tour . . .' Baruch papers, 12
p. 99 'swore and banged . . .' Thompson, *Assignment Churchill*, 103

p. 100 'I do not know . . .' *Daily Mail*, 5 January 1932

p. 101 'Buried in . . .' Moir, *I was Winston Churchill's Private Secretary*, 30

p. 102 'the most lovely . . .' WSC V, 424

p. 102 'I expect . . .' ibid.

p. 103 'the immensely dignified . . .' Moir, *I was Winston Churchill's Private Secretary*, 82

p. 103 'I have not . . .' WSC V, 426

p. 103 'I thought it . . .' *Evening Transcript*, 10 March 1932

Chapter 6: The Paris of the Sahara

p. 104 'the Paris of the Sahara . . .' WWII IV, 622

p. 105 'You cannot . . .' ibid., 621

p. 106 'I feel . . .' *Realities*, September 1954

p. 106 'We stood . . .' Moran, *Churchill: The Struggle for Survival*, 82

p. 109 'a definite declaration . . .' CAC

p. 109 'your wandering . . .' WSC V, 694

p. 109 'We are getting . . .' ibid., 695

p. 110 'I refused . . .' ibid.

p. 111 'It is vy nice . . .' Soames, *Churchill: His Life as a Painter*, 104–5

p. 111 'my last . . .' WSC V, 698

p. 112 'I was Astonished . . .' *Daily Mail*, 6 February 1936

p. 114 'We've really had . . .' Elizabeth Nel papers

p. 115 'Some fifteen . . .' CAC

p. 115 'Mr Churchill desires . . .' ibid.

p. 117 'I worked . . .' WSC VIII, 379

p. 117 'Wake about . . .' ibid., 380

p. 117 'I have . . .' Sarah Churchill, *Keep on Dancing*, 101

p. 118 'if you and . . .' CAC

p. 118 'Thank you . . .' ibid.

p. 118 'six pictures . . .' ibid.

p. 119 'the money . . .' ibid.

p. 119 'Crazy French colonel . . .' WSC VIII, 385

p. 119 'When midnight . . .' Sarah Churchill, *Keep on Dancing*, 104

p. 120 'You will never . . .' ibid., 105

p. 120 'So keep . . .' ibid.

p. 120 'I shall be . . .' *et seq.*, CAC

p. 121 'Don't listen . . .' ibid.

p. 121 'if necessary . . .' ibid.

p. 122 'turned themselves . . .' Graebner, *My Dear Mr Churchill*, 72

p. 122 'It is six . . .' WSC VIII, 577

p. 122 'We are . . .' ibid., 580

p. 123 'I never saw . . .' ibid.

p. 123 'painting for . . .' ibid., 579

p. 123 'the one thing . . .' ibid., 580

p. 123 'We have . . .' CAC

p. 123 'Returned safely . . .' ibid.

p. 124 'Departure time . . .' Graebner, *My Dear Mr Churchill*, 76

p. 125 'Now we can . . .' ibid., 81

p. 127 'spent a very . . .' letter to M. Christian Pol-Roger

p. 127 'Go and put . . .' Montague Browne, *Long Sunset*, 250

p. 128 'Oh dear . . .' Herbert, *Engaging Eccentric*, 73

p. 129 'The establishment . . .' WWII VI, 607

Chapter 7: Wartime Journeys 1914–18 and 1939–43

p. 130 'To hell . . .' AL, 659

p. 131 'If disposal . . .' ibid., 730

p. 131 'A man who . . .' WWII V, 551

p. 133 'Travelling seemed . . .' Elizabeth Nel to author

p. 133 'an adventurous soul . . .' Grace Hamblin to author

p. 133 'It will always be . . .' CAC

p. 134 'When the news . . .' WSC III, 630

p. 134 '[Churchill] joined . . .' ibid., 633

p. 134 'After a very . . .' ibid., 635

p. 135 'It was a . . .' ibid., 658

p. 135 'I couldn't get . . .' ibid.

p. 135 'people will always . . .' ibid., 753

p. 137 'we started . . .' WWII II, 141

p. 137 'To hell with that . . .' AL, 659

p. 138 'Well, the journey . . .' Alsop, *To Marietta from Paris*, 108

p. 138 'We found . . .' WWII II, 159

p. 138 Conversations Churchill–Reynaud and Churchill–Ismay, Alsop, *To Marietta from Paris*, 108

p. 138 'This was wise . . .' ibid., 162

p. 140 'Go and tell . . .' *et seq.*, Patrick Kinna to author

p. 141 '*Hornblower* admirable' Brendon, *Winston Churchill: A Brief Life*, 161

p. 141 'Gentlemen . . .' Lord Cadogan, quoted in WWII III, 382

p. 143 'This is the . . .' Patrick Kinna to author

p. 144 'We are all . . .' WWII III, 538

p. 145 'If my father . . .' CAC

p. 146 'Here's to 1942 . . .' *New York Times*, 3 December 1941

p. 146 'to come to . . .' *et seq.*, Welles, *The Happy Disciple*, 66

p. 148 'Come in . . .' Patrick Kinna to author

p. 150 'in case of . . .' CAC

p. 150 'We're here . . .' TT, 399

p. 150 'It was at . . .' ibid., 12

p. 150 'The clock . . .' ibid., 400

p. 150 'As I had . . .' ibid.

p. 150 'What's wrong . . .' ibid., 411

p. 151 'it would be . . .' WWII IV, 428

p. 152 'turned up . . .' TT, 438

p. 153 'Winston on these . . .' ibid., 453

p. 153 'sucking our . . .' WWII IV, 426

p. 154 'When are you . . .' TT, 461

p. 155 'a wonderful . . .' ibid., 479

p. 156 'Sure enough . . .' Nel, *Mr Churchill's Secretary*, 95

p. 157 'looked like . . .' Pawle, *The War and Colonel Walden*, 3

p. 157 'I found . . .' Franklin D. Roosevelt Library

p. 158 'Why does Morocco . . .' Elliott Roosevelt, *As He Saw it*, 115

p. 159 'Ah! That is . . .' TT, 566

p. 159 'like a third-rate . . .' ibid., 570

p. 159 'was a screaming . . .' ibid., 572

p. 160 'It would be . . .' AL, 740

p. 160 'I have faith . . .' CAC

Chapter 8: Wartime Journeys 1943–45

p. 161 'Stop pouring . . .' TT, 693

p. 162 'Why didn't you . . .' Nel, *Mr Churchill's Secretary*, 98

p. 162 'alas, all the . . .' ibid., 101

p. 162 'I won't be . . .' AL, 744

p. 162 'the most exhausting . . .' TT, 628

p. 164 'No one . . .' WWII IV, 712

p. 164 'The invitation . . .' Mrs Jane Plakias to author

p. 165 'So many . . .' Pawle, *The War and Colonel Walden*, 239

p. 166 'Stop pouring . . .' TT, 693

p. 166 'perpetual clatter . . .' WWII V, 71

p. 167 'smothered in . . .' Nel, *Mr Churchill's Secretary*, 113

p. 168 'the infernal combustion . . .' Elizabeth Nel to author

p. 169 'wretched Indians . . .' Speech by Earl Mountbatten, 4 March 1970

p. 170 'We don't want . . .' Elizabeth Nel to author

p. 170 'Surely not? . . .' Pawle, *The War and Colonel Walden*, 253

p. 172 'For a couple . . .' WWII V, 301

p. 173 'Meet me at . . .' Thompson, *I was Churchill's Shadow*, 11

p. 173 'tired out . . .' ibid., 129

p. 174 'If I die . . .' WSC VII, 606

p. 176 'This is a. . . .' CAC

p. 177 'I read . . .' WSC VII, 967

p. 177 'Toilet paper . . .' Halle, *The Irrepressible Churchill*, 204

p. 177 'with all his . . .' WSC VII, 969

p. 177 'I'm going back . . .' ibid., 997

p. 178 'Go and fetch . . .' Elizabeth Layton to author

p. 180 'easily, orderly . . .' Sarah Churchill, *Keep on Dancing*, 77

p. 181 'Let there . . .' Pawle, *The War and Colonel Walden*, 359

p. 181 'What we bring . . .' WSC VII, 1226

p. 182 'This is one . . .' AL, 829

p. 184 '*Vive la France*' Pawle, *The War and Colonel Walden*, 390

p. 184 'put on ten years . . .' AL, 850

p. 185 'It may well . . .' ibid., 855

p. 185 'Perfectly polite . . .' ibid., 856

Chapter 9: Fulton and Beyond

p. 186 'In 1936 . . .' CAC

p. 187 'While learned . . .' *Kansas City Times*, 22 December 1945

p. 187 'My friends . . .' *Daily Express*, 21 September 1961

p. 188 'this very private . . .' *New Yorker*, 26 January 1946

p. 188 'I never . . .' *New York Times*, 15 January 1946

p. 188 'benevolent, almost . . .' Walter Locke, 'Churchill in Miami', Lorraine Bonar collection of press cuttings

p. 189 'We suffered . . .' *Miami Daily News*, 16 January 1946

p. 189 'the Gibraltar . . .' Walter Locke, Lorraine Bonar collection

p. 190 'an official . . .' CAC

p. 191 'detachments . . .' ibid.

p. 191 'some 150 . . .' *Daily Press*, Havana, 2 February 1946

p. 192 'These packages . . .' CAC

p. 192 'Your cigars . . .' ibid.

p. 192 'I think . . .' *New York Times*, 30 January 1946

p. 193 'one might . . .' ibid.

p. 194 'When I was . . .' Clifford, *Counsel to the President*, 100

p. 194 'interested in Churchill . . .' *Kingdom Daily News*, 8 March 1946

p. 195 'Have them . . .' *Westminster College: An Informal History*, 206

p. 195 'The pig . . .' ibid.

p. 195 'The audience sat . . .' Brinkley, *A Memoir*, 74

p. 195 'had started . . .' ibid., 211

p. 196 'If I made . . .' Clifford, *Counsel to the President*, 108

p. 196 'most important . . .' ibid., 106

p. 196 'I say this . . .' ibid., 107

p. 198 'I like to see . . .' Pilpel, *Churchill in America*, 227

p. 198 'I do not . . .' ibid., 228

p. 198 'I am now . . .' *New York Times*, 22 March 1946

p. 198 'on behalf . . .' WSC VIII, 463

p. 200 'I was all . . .' Halle, *Irrepressible Churchill*, 90

p. 200 'Ladies and . . .' Pilpel, *Churchill in America*, 237

p. 200 'The scale . . .' et seq., WSC VIII, 466

p. 201 'Enormous pains . . .' ibid., 465

p. 201 'I carry away . . .' *New York Times*, 2 April 1949

p. 201 'I wore this . . .' ibid.

p. 202 'to re-establish . . .' Colville, *The Fringes of Power*, 636–7

p. 202 'It's not a . . .' *New York Times*, 6 January 1952

p. 202 'There never was . . .' ibid.

p. 203 'I did not . . .' et seq., WSC VIII, 688

p. 204 'This visit . . .' Pilpel, *Churchill in America*, 250

p. 204 'Not since . . .' *Newsweek*, 21 January 1952

p. 204 'There was . . .' WSC III, 789

p. 204 'Checkmate . . .' *New York Times*, 5 January 1953

p. 205 'Very nice . . .' et seq., *New Yorker*, 17 January 1953

p. 207 'This fellow . . .' WSC VIII, 936

p. 207 'the largest . . .' *New York Times*, 29 June 1954

p. 207 'be generous . . .' ibid.

p. 208 'squaring the Americans' WSC VIII, 1222n

p. 208 'never be . . .' ibid., 1223

p. 209 'I only . . .' Pilpel, *Churchill in America*, 267

p. 210 'All goes . . .' WSC VIII, 1293

p. 210 'He is not . . .' *New York Times*, 8 May 1959

p. 210 'I must now leave . . .' ibid., 11 May 1959

p. 211 'spend a couple . . .' WSC VIII, 1322

Chapter 10: Madeira

p. 213 'query warm . . .' WSC VIII, 498

p. 214 'a wonderful . . .' Blandy papers, Reid's Hotel, Funchal

p. 214 '*Viva Mr Churchill*' Jorge Figueira de Sousa to author

p. 215 'He asked . . .' Blandy papers

p. 215 'I would have . . .' Cecil Miles to author

p. 215 'He goes to . . .' Blandy papers

p. 216 'This gave me . . .' ibid.

p. 216 'I'm leaving . . .' et seq., Weaver, *Reid's Hotel*, 68

p. 217 'We looked . . .' Christopher Blackburn to author

p. 217 'We were . . .' WSC VIII, 500

Chapter 11: The Old World

p. 219 'I beg and pray . . .' CAC

p. 219 'We travelled . . .' ibid.

p. 221 'He took . . .' ibid.

p. 221 'beautiful French . . .' ibid.

p. 222 'Much as . . .' ibid.

p. 223 'largely my . . .' WSC, *The World Crisis*, Chapter 5

p. 223 'You have become . . .' WSC II, 576

p. 223 'W. in glorious . . .' Bonham Carter, *Winston Churchill as I Knew Him*, 274

p. 223 'Those Greeks . . .' ibid., 262

p. 223 'How perfect . . .' ibid.

p. 224 'Chance led . . .' WSC, *Painting as a Pastime*, 25

p. 224 'I want you . . .' WSC V, 3

p. 224 'I am so busy . . .' ibid., 4

p. 225 'He towered . . .' Soames, *Winston Churchill: His Life as a Painter*, 97

p. 225 'the Riviera is . . .' Balsan, *The Glitter and the Gold*, 217

p. 226 'He used to . . .' ibid., 88

p. 227 'It is absolute . . .' WSC V, 11

p. 227 'I greatly . . .' ibid., 222

p. 227 'worked on the . . .' ibid., 224

p. 228 'a lot of . . .' ibid., 226n

p. 228 'My motive . . .' ibid., 227

p. 229 'I worked . . .' ibid., 1103

p. 230 'Oh, you . . .' Elizabeth Layton to author

p. 230 'Now come . . .' Sarah Churchill, *A Thread in the Tapestry*, 95

p. 230 'stagnant and gloomy', ibid., 98

p. 230 'it was a . . .' WSC VIII, 152

p. 231 'Winston, if you . . .' Alsop, *To Marietta from Paris*, 103

p. 231 'a kind of . . .' WSC VIII, 265

p. 232 'The first . . .' ibid.

p. 232 'wearing orders . . .' Alsop, *To Marietta from Paris*, 121

p. 233 'the world's . . .' *Daily Telegraph*, 30 December 2000

p. 233 'Invite me . . .' ibid.

p. 233 'that we range . . .' WSC VIII, 409

p. 236 'He was . . .' and subsequent conversations, Aladino Panza to author

p. 237 'I have . . .' Graebner, *My Dear Mr Churchill*, 92

p. 239 'Where are . . .' WSC VIII, 483

p. 239 'had never meant . . .' Alsop, *To Marietta from Paris*, 228

p. 240 'the Empire and . . .' Best, *Churchill: A Study in Greatness*, 286

p. 240 'Denis, you're . . .' WSC VIII, 485

p. 240 'a French lady . . .' ibid., 487

p. 241 'just slogging away' ibid., 631

p. 241 'kindly remember . . .' ibid.

p. 242 'Anthony Eden . . .' ibid., 632

p. 243 'his mind . . .' Graebner, *My Dear Mr Churchill*, 70

Epilogue: Last Journeys
p. 249 'The selection . . .' Montague
  Browne, *Long Sunset*, 242
p. 251 'What did . . .' *et seq.*, WSC,
  Memories and Adventures, 116

p. 252 'I rolled . . .' ibid., 117
p. 253 'Remember, I want . . .' *et seq.*,
  Montague Browne, *Long Sunset*,
  312

Bibliography

Alsop, Susan Mary, *To Marietta from Paris 1945–1960*, Doubleday, 1975

Atkins, J.B., *The Relief of Ladysmith*, Methuen, 1900

Atkins, J.B., *Incidents and Reflections*, Christophers, 1947

Balsan, Conseulo Vanderbilt, *The Glitter and the Gold*, Heinemann, 1953

Best, Geoffrey, *Churchill: A Study in Greatness*, Hambledon & London, 2001

Bonham Carter, Violet, *Winston Churchill as I Knew Him*, Eyre & Spottiswoode, 1965

Brendon, Piers, *Winston Churchill: A Brief Life*, Secker & Warburg, 1984

Brinkley, David, *A Memoir*, Knopf, 1955

Bryant, Arthur, *The Turn of the Tide*, Collins, 1957

Chaplin, E.D.W., *Winston Churchill and Harrow*, Harrow School Bookshop, 1941

Churchill, John Spencer, *A Crowded Canvas*, Odhams, 1961

Churchill, Randolph S., *Twenty-One Years*, Weidenfeld & Nicolson, 1964

Churchill, Randolph S., *Winston S. Churchill*, Vols I, II, Heinemann, 1966–67

Churchill, Randolph S., *Winston S. Churchill: Companion*, Vols I, II, Heinemann, 1967

Churchill, Sarah, *A Thread in the Tapestry*, André Deutsch, 1967

Churchill, Sarah, *Keep on Dancing*, Weidenfeld & Nicolson, 1981

Churchill, Winston S., *The World Crisis*, Thornton Butterworth, 1923

Churchill, Winston S., *My Early Life*, Macmillan, 1930

Churchill, Winston S., *Thoughts and Adventures*, Thornton Butterworth, 1932

Churchill, Winston S., *Painting as a Pastime*, Odhams, 1948

Churchill, Winston S., *The Second World War*, Vols I–VI, Cassell, 1948–54

Churchill, Winston S., *A History of the English Speaking Peoples*, Vol IV, Cassell, 1958

Churchill, Winston S., *My African Journey*, Octopus, 1989
Churchill, Winston S., *Memories and Adventures*, Weidenfeld & Nicolson, 1989
Churchill, Winston S., *His Father's Son*, Weidenfeld & Nicolson, 1996
Clifford, Clark, *Counsel to the President*, Random House, New York, 1991
Cohen, Mark and Hahn, *Morocco: Old Land New Nation*, Fredrick A. Praeger, 1966
Colville, John, *The Fringes of Power*, Hodder & Stoughton, 1985
Gilbert, Martin, *Winston S. Churchill*, Vols III–VIII, Heinemann, 1971–88
Gilbert, Martin, *Churchill: A Life*, Heinemann, 1991
Graebner, Walter, *My Dear Mr Churchill*, Michael Joseph, 1965
Haldane, Aylmer, *A Soldier's Saga*, Blackwood, 1948
Halle, Kay, *Irrepressible Churchill*, Cleveland World Publishing Company, 1966
Hamilton, Ian, *Listening for the Drums*
Hardwick, Joan, *Clementine Churchill*, John Murray, 1997
Herbert, David, *Second Son*, Peter Owen, 1972
Herbert, David, *Engaging Eccentrics*, Peter Owen, 1990
Humes, James C. (ed.), *The Wit and Wisdom of Winston Churchill*, Harper Perennial, 1995
Jenkins, Roy, *Churchill*, Macmillan, 2001
Martin, B.W., *Diary of the Siege of Ladysmith*, Ladysmith Historical Society, 1970
Menpes, Mortimer, *War Impressions*, A. & C. Black, 1901
Moir, Phyllis, *I was Winston Churchill's Private Secretary*, W. Funk, 1961
Montague Browne, Anthony, *Long Sunset*, Cassell, 1995
Moran, Lord, *Churchill: The Struggle for Survival*, Constable, 1966
Nel, Elizabeth, *Mr Churchill's Secretary*, Hodder & Stoughton, 1958
Pakenham, Thomas, *The Boer War*, Weidenfeld & Nicolson, 1979
Pawle, Gerald, *The War and Colonel Walden*, Harrap, 1963
Pilpel, Robert H., *Churchill in America*, Harcourt Brace Jovanovich, 1976
Roosevelt, Elliott, *As He Saw it*, New York, 1946
Soames, Mary, *Clementine Churchill*, Cassell, 1979
Soames, Mary, *Winston Churchill: His Life as a Painter*, Collins, 1990
Soames, Mary, *Speaking for Themselves*, Doubleday, 1998
Thompson, W.H., *I was Churchill's Shadow*, Christopher Johnson, 1951
Vaidon, Lawdon, *Tangier: A Different Way*, Scarecrow Press, 1977
Weaver, H.J., *Reid's Hotel*, Souvenir Press, 1991
Welles, Edward Randolph II, *The Happy Disciple*, Learning Incorporated, Maine, 1975

BIBLIOGRAPHY

Journals

Atlanta Constitution
Baltimore Sun
Boston Evening Transcript
Chicago Tribune
Daily Express, London
Daily Mail, London
Daily Telegraph, London
Estcourt Gazette
Kansas City Times
Kingdom Daily News, Fulton
Miami Daily News
Natal Mercury
New Haven Evening Register
New York Herald
New York Tribune
New York Times
New Yorker
Newsweek
Smithsonian Magazine
Springfield Republican
The Times, London
Vancouver Colonist
Vancouver Sun

Unpublished Sources

Blandy papers, Reid's Hotel, Funchal
'Churchill in Miami': Lorraine Bonar collection of press cuttings
Churchill Archives Centre, Churchill College, Cambridge
de Souza C.W.L., de Souza papers, National Archives Repository, Pretoria
de Souza, Marie, Diary, de Souza papers, National Archives Repository, Pretoria
Elizabeth Nel papers

Index

The Churchill Centre and Societies
(www.winstonchurchill.org)

The author is pleased to be a Trustee of The Churchill Centre and strongly recommends membership to anyone interested in Winston Churchill.

Headquartered in Washington, D.C. and active internationally, The Churchill Centre was founded in 1968 to inspire leadership, statesmanship, vision and boldness among democratic and freedom-loving peoples through the thoughts, words, works and deeds of Winston Spencer Churchill. Membership numbers over three thousand with an average age of forty-eight, including the affiliated Churchill Societies of the UK and Canada.

The Churchill Centre publishes a quarterly magazine, *Finest Hour*; a newsletter, the *Chartwell Bulletin*; and periodic collections of papers and speeches, the *Churchill Proceedings*. It sponsors international and national conferences, and Churchill tours which have visited Britain, Australia, France, South Africa and Morocco. Its expansive website www.winstonchurchill.org now includes a 'classroom' component to help educate young people on Churchill's life and leadership.

The Churchill Centre has helped bring about republication

of over twenty of Winston Churchill's long-out-of-print books. In 1992 it launched a campaign for completion of the remaining document volumes to the official biography, three of which have been published to date. More recently, it sponsored academic symposia in America and Britain; seminars where students and scholars discuss Churchill's books; scholarships for Churchill Studies at the Universities of Edinburgh and Dallas; and important reference works. In 1998 it launched the Churchill Lecture Series, in which prominent world figures apply Churchill's experience to the world today.

In 2003 The Churchill Centre opened its first official headquarters in Washington, which houses its administrative staff, library, and computer facilities linked to the major Churchill archives. Future programmes include video aids for schoolchildren; college and graduate-level courses on aspects of Churchill's career; fellowships to assist students; and visiting professorships. The overall aim is to impress Churchill's qualities of leadership firmly on the leaders of the twenty-first century.

Membership in The Churchill Centre and Societies is available for a modest subscription, with special rates for students. For further information please contact:

The Churchill Centre
Suite 307
1150 17th Street, N.W.
Washington DC
USA 20036
telephone: (888) WSC-1874
website: www.winstonchurchill.org

International Churchill Society
PO Box 1257

Melksham
Wilts SN12 6GQ
telephone: (01380) 828609

International Churchill Society
3256 Rymal Road
Mississauga
Ontario
Canada L4Y 3C1
telephone: (905) 279-5169